Telecommunications and Politics

For Arthur Barnicott

Telecommunications and Politics

The Decentralised Alternative

Andrew Davies

Pinter Publishers
London & New York

Distributed in the United States and Canada by St. Martin's Press

Pinter Publishers Ltd
25 Floral Street, Covent Garden, London WC2E 9DS, United Kingdom

First published in 1994

Distributed exclusively in the USA and Canada by St. Martin's Press Inc., Room 400, 175 Fifth Avenue, New York, NY 10010, USA

Andrew Davies is hereby identified as the author of this work as provided under Section 77 of the Copyright, Designs and Patents Act 1988.

British Library Cataloguing in Publication Data
A CIP catalogue record for this book is available from the British Library

ISBN 1 85567 144 1

Library of Congress Cataloging in Publication Data
A CIP catalog record for this book is available from the Library of Congress

Typeset by Mayhew Typesetting, Rhayader, Powys
Printed and bound in Great Britain by
Biddles Ltd., Guildford and King's Lynn

Contents

List of tables and figures   vi

Preface   vii

Acknowledgements   xii

1 Introduction   1

I   The first technological divide: analogue telecommunications   17

2 From competition to monopoly   19

3 National monopoly and the decentralised alternative   55

II   The telecommunications revolution   87

4 Corporations, communications and computers   89

5 Case studies: corporate information systems   117

III   The second technological divide: digital telecommunications   145

6 Restructuring the national monopolies   147

7 Restructuring the regional systems   179

8 Paths of modernisation   203

9 Conclusion   241

Bibliography   250

Index   261

Tables and Figures

Tables

1 Degree of digitisation in all telephone subscriber lines,
   1990   217
2 Average telephone costs per month, 1989   221
3 Telephone company efficiency, 1991   227
4 International comparison of telecommunications total
   factor productivity   235

Figures

1 Hierarchy or pyramid structure: public switched
   telephone network   22
2 High fixed-cost structure of the telephone infrastructure 24
3 Public integrated services digital network   211
4 Competing technological architectures   213

Preface

Nearly 10 years ago, Piore and Sable published *The Second Industrial Divide*. It argued that the twentieth-century trend towards mass production and ever larger corporations was not inevitable. Improvements in productivity did not require technologies which deskilled workers or necessitated large-scale organisations in order to operate them. Rather their growth must be explained by politics as much as by economics. Coalitions of power developed which had an interest in these mass forms of production – a new managerial class, national states, and after a time, the leadership of trade unions. These coalitions can be traced both in capitalist states and in the new socialist countries, and were more effective the weaker the traditional bases of resistance that were in a position to operate an alternative. In their early formulation, Piore and Sable saw the alternative as based on skilled labour, and networks of small and medium firms, artisans, and integrated regional economies.

The first 'divide' when there was a real choice between the alternatives came in the late nineteenth and early twentieth centuries. After that a set of integrated institutions were built up around 'Fordism' which allowed this path of development to realise its potential, and ruled out a similarly integrated alternative. From the 1970s, however, the Fordist 'regime of accumulation', to use the terms of the French regulation school, reached its limits. The world economic slow down of the past 20 years should be seen, the argument runs, as a crisis of transition from one industrial era to another. What replaces it, however, is open. There is a second industrial divide, which provides the possibility for a modernised version of Piore and Sable's original alternative to win out rather than a reshaped and globally extended neo-Fordism.

This was a bold thesis which has excited considerable controversy. Much of the empirical work inspired by it has been on manufacturing industry, from mechanical engineering to light industrial sectors such as clothing, furniture, shoes, and food processing. In this book Andrew Davies explores the argument in relation to a sector which on the face of it is less open to technological and organisational choices, namely telecommunications. This is a sector where central control by the telephone monopolies appears to have been determined by technology. Alfred Chandler argued the case, and drew on US telecommunications history to support his more general thesis on the growth of the 'visible hand' in economic organisation.

Andrew Davies here challenges this argument. In the early historical chapters, he shows how the political power of the old postal monopolies in Europe, and large-scale private interests in the United States, was instrumental in the adoption of the centralised telephone network. There was no technological necessity for such a regime. The technology was equally consistent with independent local telephone monopolies, connected to a separately run national and international system. In the United States a coalition of local telephone companies sought to develop their own national system, but were squeezed out by Bell Telephones and J.P. Morgan.

Where there was a different constellation of political forces, an alternative took root. The most notable case was in Finland, where a reaction to the Tsarist centralisation after Finnish independence in 1917, led to a telephone system which rested on a public long distance network and a mass of small local telephone companies.

For British, French and North American readers, the passages on the Finnish, Danish and Dutch systems are remarkable. In Finland there are still 49 independent local telephone companies, the majority of them co-operatives, and 80 per cent of all Finnish telephone subscribers hold shares in these co-ops. In the United Kingdom we know about municipal telephone networks through the example of Hull. This book shows it was a much wider phenomenon, cut off in Italy in 1907 by the power of the postal monopoly, in Holland by the Germans in the Second World War, but persisting strongly in the Nordic countries. In the latter there were no earlier indigenous postal monopolies. Instead strong associations of local telephone companies proved politically strong enough to resist programmes of centralised nationalisation.

Not only did the alternative exist, it was, on most measures, remarkably successful, from both a financial and a social point of view. Denmark and Finland are among the lowest cost providers of business communications in Europe. Denmark has the fourth highest telephone density in the world, and Finland, in spite of its dispersed population, has the fifth. A recent study of telecommunications found that conversion to digital switching had been undertaken more rapidly by the small telephone companies than by the large ones, and that their standards of service and efficiency were comparable. Finland is one of the top three countries in the number of mobile phones per capita.

The early chapters of the book establish the diversity of telephone regimes which arose from the first industrial divide. The later ones analyse a second 'digital divide'. From the 1970s onwards there has been increasing integration between data processing and telecommunications centred round the introduction of digital technology. Andrew Davies argues that the centralised telecommunications monopolies have found it difficult to realise the potential of the new technology. As far as the basic network is concerned, PTTs (with the notable exception of France) were reluctant to write off sunk costs in their analogue systems. They were also restricted in their capacity to develop peripheral equipment and new value added services, and resisted the opening of these markets to competition.

Yet it is these services that have been driving the new industrial revolution. Part 2 of the book shows how new information processing systems are playing a similar synthesising role in modern production to that played by Henry Ford's assembly line in an earlier industrial epoch. This has meant that telecommunications have become the key infrastructure of the late twentieth century. Their prime function, however, is no longer voice transmission, but the communication of a wide range of non-voice information. This meant a new relation between the telephone network and the providers of the information processing services, but because of the delayed response of the national telephone monopolies, large corporations have been forced to develop their own private systems.

The information revolution has thus rendered problematic the old monopoly forms of telephone organisation. What is to take their place? Davies identifies three alternative paths which have emerged: modernisation led by the public monopoly, but with competitive supplies of peripheral services (France); private, and in the medium term competitive supply of long distance and local lines (Britain and from 1994 Finland); and a decentralised system of regional telephone monopolies separated from long distance networks (the United States and Denmark). What is common to all three is the need to open up the supply of equipment and complementary services. Where they differ is the degree of decentralisation and competition within an overall connecting system. The new technology cannot avoid undercutting old organisational structures, but at the same time does not determine the new.

In line with modern organisational theory, Davies puts greatest theoretical weight on the concept of system economies. These he distinguishes from economies of scale and scope which have in the past been the foundation for arguments about firm concentration and a justification for public monopolies. System economies highlight questions of information and communications flow, common standards and system strategies. They may be realised through a single firm, but can equally well be undertaken by associations of producers, in conjunction with regulatory authorities. This is his theoretical explanation for the persistence of decentralised structures in the Nordic countries and their adoption today (in the demerging of AT&T in the United States for example). By separating the necessary range of systems from the size of the productive organisations within it, he can distinguish the scale required for the efficient operation of parts of the system (for example, national transmission) from alternative ways of co-ordinating the system as a whole.

For Davies the mark of strong systems is spaces for innovation, competition, and closeness to users. These are more important than issues of ownership. What is critical for the general interest is public control over the parameters of the system, its regulatory structures, and the securing of open access to key parts of the infrastructure. Some of the most interesting sections of the book are about the relative adequacy of different organisational forms: the value of municipal and user co-operatives in securing a locally oriented service, the weakness of the British regulatory body Oftel in controlling the still dominant privatised British Telecom, and, at the other extreme, the remarkable programme of digital innovation carried through by French Telecom.

His concern with systems also allows Davies to move beyond the binary oppositions of the traditional literature on industrial organisations: large/small; public/private; local/global; centralised/de-centralised; competition/co-operation. Davies suggests it is the balance between these oppositions that is important, and it is a balance which will be struck in different ways according to the country and the historical circumstances. It is one of the subtleties of this book that he suggests that if any of these oppositions is collapsed, by plumping for one of them, the system as a whole is likely to suffer. Thus the Danish regional networks co-operated at the same time as they competed. The pressure for global integration of telecommunications in no way undercuts the need for autonomous local operators. Public ownership may be necessary in some parts of the system to ensure the functioning of the whole. In short, he is seeking to shift the axis of current political debates away from ownership and deregulation, to systems and strategies.

For these reasons the current book is more than a treatise on the restructuring of a particular sector. It questions the dominant version of the link between technology and industrial organisation, and through the medium of a case study, provides a re-reading of twentieth-century industrial history, and of the alternatives now before us.

Robin Murray

Acknowledgements

I would like to thank Robin Murray for providing rigorous doctoral supervision and helping me develop the argument of this book. Thanks are due to my colleagues for helpful discussions including: Jens Arnbak, Francois Bar, Michael Borrus, Teddy Brett, Alan Cawson, Mick Dunford, David Gann, Nicholas Garnham, Michael Hobday, Christopher Freeman, Robin Mansell, Mark Matthews, Francis McGowan, Lois McNay, Ian Miles, Kevin Morgan, Keith Pavitt, Annemieke Roobeek, Andrew Sayer, Susanne Schmidt, Paul Slaa, Jack Spaapen, Rob Van Tulder and Tom Whiston. I would particularly like to thank Jari Karpakka and Marianne Mortensen for helping me set up my interviews in Finland and Denmark.

The empirical research undertaken to write this book conducted over the past six years involved a number of related projects: a doctorate in the 'Social Implications of Technical Change', Social and Political Thought graduate division, University of Sussex; participation in the OECD–BRIE Telecom-User Group Project between 1987 and 1989; and research into information and communication technologies in the Science Policy Research Unit, University of Sussex. The completion of my research as a book was made possible by a post-doctoral fellowship in the Department of Science and Technology Dynamics, University of Amsterdam.

1 Introduction

In November 1992 President-elect Bill Clinton outlined his vision of technology as the engine of American economic growth for the twenty-first century. Telecommunications policy was placed at the centre of Clinton's blueprint for technological renewal. Announced in February 1993, the development of advanced technology for 'information superhighways', or digital telecommunications networks, is one of Clinton's most ambitious and expensive policies.[1] Building on the existing High-Performance Computing and Communications programme, the new democratic administration has authorised an investment of $2 billion over five years for the creation of a high-speed information and communications network, connecting universities, private and public research laboratories, hospitals, schools and eventually homes, which could serve as a catalyst for growth in information services. A symbol of the national effort to regain world technological and economic leadership, in the words of Bill Clinton this digital information and communication infrastructure 'could do for the productivity of individuals at their places of work and learning what the interstate highway of the 1950s did for the productivity of the nation's travel and distribution system'.[2]

A more accurate historical analogy is between digital telecommunications and the telegraphs and telephones. By the beginning of the twenty-first century, a vast infrastructure of digital telecommunications will have the possibility of generating economic growth in new services, employment and manufacturing productivity in the way that the telegraph and telephone did in the second half of the nineteenth century. Between the 1840s and 1920s, the rise of the system of large-scale mass production in the United States and Western Europe depended on the elimination of spatial and temporal barriers made possible by the almost instantaneous communication of messages across large geographical distances through telegraph and telephone networks. First, the creation of a web of telegraph and telephone networks had the effect of compressing space. With the new electrical systems of telecommunication, corporations were able to place spatially dispersed units under centralised control and facilitate increases in production output by extending the geographical reach of mass markets. Second, communication by telegraph and telephone compressed time. Permitting a closer match between supply and demand, the new electric communication technologies accelerated the turnover time of capital: orders could be transmitted and supplies delivered with greater speed and regularity; and, with better access to information about market prices and supply conditions, the new systems of communication improved the scheduling of production, reduced dependence on large inventories and decreased working capital requirements.

Since the 1960s, radical technological change has slowly transformed the telephone infrastructure from a system for conveying written messages and the human voice by transmitting electrical signals in analogue waveform, to a system for communicating electronic digital signals of voice, data, moving images, and text made up of discrete pulses coded to represent information in the binary digits recognised by computers.[3] The computer is a device for both processing and communicating information: it moves information in digital code; it stores, processes and retrieves information; and it can be programmed to simulate reality and approximate human consciousness. The large growth since the 1970s in the number of computer terminals in use and the continuing decline in the costs of information processing and transmission have made the construction and organisation of the digital telecommunications highways one of the most pressing economic and political questions of the late twentieth-century. The purpose of this book is to examine the technological transformation of the telecommunications infrastructure from an analogue to a digital system, and explain the different ways in which the infrastructure can be organised to provide an efficient and equitable service for national societies.

Technological and institutional change

The revolution in telecommunications technology is connected to a more fundamental transformation in the production process of the economy as a whole. Since the middle of the nineteenth century, the history of industrial capitalism has been punctuated by two stages in the mechanisation of production. First, the development of the system of mass production – turning out large-volumes of low-cost standardised goods for mass-markets – depended in part on the improvements in the physical capacity and speed of output made possible by the introduction of steam-driven motors into the economy from the late 1840s and electrical motors from the 1890s. Second, since the late 1940s the shift from mass production to a system of flexible production – producing specialised products that are customised for large but constantly changing markets – is closely connected to the diffusion of electronic computer control technologies into production, where far-flung activities are integrated into digital systems of information and control.[4]

The way in which the rise of the system of large-scale mass production brought about the first technological revolution in communications is explained by Marx (1976: 505–506):

... the revolution in the modes of production of industry and agriculture made necessary a revolution in the general conditions of the social process of production, i.e. in the means of communication and transport. In a society whose pivot ... was small-scale agriculture, with its subsidiary domestic industries and urban handicrafts, the means of communication and transport were so utterly inadequate to the needs of production in the period of manufacture, with its extended division of social labour, its concentration of the instruments of labour and workers and its colonial markets, that they in fact became revolutionised. In the same way the means of communication and transport handed down from the period of manufacture soon became unbearable fetters on large-scale industry, given the feverish velocity with which it produces, its enormous extent, its constant flinging of capital and labour from one sphere of production into another and its newly created connections with the world market. Hence ... the means of communication and transport gradually adapted themselves to the mode of production of large-scale industry by means of a system of river steamers, railways, ocean steamers and telegraphs.

By the 1920s, the revolution in telecommunications which accompanied the expansion of mass production was completed by the creation of national postal, telegraph, and telephone systems.

The second technological revolution in telecommunications was initiated in the late 1940s when electronic data processing and control technologies began to transform the system of mass production. Whereas the rise of mass production since the mid-nineteenth century depended on improvements in the 'physical' capacity and speed of production, from the mid-twentieth century it has been changes brought about by improvements in the capacity to process, manipulate and communicate 'information' which have engendered the technological revolution in telecommunications. In the period of mass production, when information processing was conducted by clerks and electromechanical tabulated processing techniques, the telegraphs and telephones provided adequate systems of communication. From the late 1940s, however, a large number of industries slowly shifted from electromechanical to electronically controlled processes of production and began to transform the nature of work. Even more significant was the integration of the digital computer into the telecommunications networks of the corporation linking electronically controlled islands of production. Substantial increases in the capacity of data processing techniques called for a transformation in the technology, speed and capacity of telecommunications. Information processing and control between geographically dispersed corporate plants and offices had to be linked by transmission networks capable of communicating computer data as well as voice messages.

In the period of computer-controlled flexible production, information has become an even more significant source of power for nations and competitiveness for corporations. It is a central resource in the organisation of production, in the control of markets, and in the processing and executing of financial transactions through computer networks. In 1963 Honeywell first demonstrated the computer's potential for the international control of production by situating a terminal in Britain to control a computer in an American plant in Massachusetts, with signals being transmitted by telex. The first international computer networks were used mainly by service companies for stock-market quotations, banking and insurance transactions, and hotel and airline reservations. By the 1970s multinational manufacturing corporations in the United States, Europe and Japan had established computer networks through leased-lines as part of control and information systems. The mechanisation of production on flexible lines – using computer control technologies to produce a range of products and services for differentiated markets – has been accompanied by an expansion in the scale of the corporation to supply world markets. Global digital systems of information and control have been constructed to coordinate the newly-extended worldwide production activities of the corporation.

National telecommunication infrastructures engineered to carry analogue signals were to prove incompatible with the requirements of a period when information had to be processed and communicated in digital form, and transmitted across a worldwide infrastructure of copper and fibre optic cables, and satellite and radio transmission systems. Yet this shift to digital technology could not be accomplished without prolonged and uneven transformations in established institutional frameworks.

The history of technological and institutional changes in telecommunications – marked by the introduction of the telegraphs in the late 1830s, the telephones in the 1870s and digital telecommunications in the late twentieth century – has been characterised by what Schumpeter (1943: 83) called the dynamic process of 'creative destruction': 'the process of industrial mutation . . . that incessantly revolutionises the economic structure . . . incessantly destroying the old one, incessantly creating a new one'. During these times of industrial change, the technological and organisational choices made by governments and corporations contribute towards the restructuring of traditional methods of production and management practices, and a disruption of established industries, legal frameworks and political interests.[5] In his earlier work Schumpeter (1939: 315) drew a distinction between 'secondary competition' along an existing line of innovation and 'primary competition' which threatens the foundations of the old industry by substituting new product and process technologies, or new forms of productive organisation for the previous ways of doing things. Resenting the threat of primary competition, the old economic structure 'perceives possibilities of defence other than adaptation by a competitive struggle which generally means death for many of its units . . . Taking industry as a whole there is always an innovating sphere warring with an "old sphere", which sometimes tries to secure prohibition of the new ways of doing things' (Schumpeter 1939: 82). Faced with the threat of being dislodged by innovating firms and new industries, the introduction of new technologies eventually becomes a necessity for the survival of the established economic interests. Shorter phases of primary competition are separated by spans of comparative quiet while societies absorb the results of the revolution and perfect the utilisation of known technologies.

The institution of monopoly, or single seller, plays a pivotal role in the process of creative destruction, as both a stimulus to and consequence of primary competition.[6] A monopolistic position is a source of economic and institutional power that provides opportunities to command influence over the course of technological progress. By the 1870s, for example, after a period of adjustment when the technology and organisation of telegraph systems were perfected, these systems were administered by national monopolies. In the United States, the telegraph system was controlled by Western Union, a private monopoly. In Europe, the telegraph was placed in the hands of state-owned postal monopolies. The invention of the telephone in 1876, and its rapid development during the 1880s and 1890s, offered a superior communications technology which eventually superseded the telegraph. Established telegraph monopolies tried unsuccessfully to prevent the premature devaluation of their sunk capital in telegraph systems by resisting the introduction of telephone technology. Old investments had first to be adapted and later abandoned. Competition from new communications technologies, therefore, threatens to undermine the power of traditional monopolistic practices that aim at defending established positions, conserving fixed capital by delaying the adoption of radical technologies, and setting prices so as to maximise short-run profits. To overcome the obstacle of monopoly power the successful introduction of new technologies must be carried out by new firms or through the reorganisation of part or the whole of the established industry.[7] Yet some form of monopoly arises again in the process of creative destruction as cycles of economic concentration eliminate smaller producers, and private or public enterprises mobilise the cost-saving economies of large-scale production to serve expanding markets.[8] Despite Schumpeter's insistence that technological transformations of the economy are conditioned by the institutional environment, his assumption that economic evolution creates an institutional pattern in which control is vested with a centralised authority neglects the diverse social and political choices in the construction of different forms of productive technology and organisation.

These brief moments in industrial history when paths of technological development are open to change are what Piore and Sabel (1984) call 'technological divides'. Rare breakthroughs in the use of new technologies and production methods are followed by the expansion of the dominant form of productive organisation, which culminates in a crisis signifying the end of existing arrangements. During the short-lived interludes of experimentation and change, the choice of technology is neither a reflection of technical necessities nor the culmination of an evolutionary struggle for competitive survival which unfolds independently of the influence of politics and society. On the contrary, diverse new forms of technology and organisation are shaped by strategic decisions about potential markets and the historically-contingent balance of political power within societies. At these critical conjunctures, when technologies and institutional structures are in a state of flux, a combination of structural economic forces and political contests will determine the future direction and shape of technological progress for many decades.

Piore and Sabel challenge the assumption of a trend towards bigness in the organisation of mass production, and that a single solution – the large-scale mass production corporation – was or had to be the most successful route to industrial efficiency. The view that there is a single best model of productive organisation has prevented an explanation of the technological and organisational diversity under capitalism, and encouraged a neglect of the considerable variation in terms of production process, firm size, ownership, management and product mix (Rosenberg 1992: 193).

The first technological divide, from the mid-nineteenth century to the 1920s, was marked by the rise of the large-scale corporation, which deployed dedicated mass-production equipment and a semi-skilled workforce to produce large volumes of standardised products for mass markets in the United States and Western Europe. Yet there was an alternative model of industrialisation established in various regions of Western Europe based on a system of craft skill and flexible equipment which employed sophisticated general-purpose machinery to turn out a wide range of products or services for large and constantly changing markets. The efficiency of the craft system depended upon a combination of cooperation and competition: a network of specialised firms shared the costs of dynamic innovation, and created institutions to support their cooperative arrangements. Under slightly different historical conditions, cooperative systems of flexible production could have played a more important role in the economy. The second technological divide opened in the early 1970s when, according to Piore and Sabel (1984), the downturn in the world economy revealed the limits of the century-long model of industrialisation based on mass production. There are two possible paths of renewal: the first builds upon the principles of mass production, and the second suggests that the way forward is to emulate the decentralised principles of the craft system which were marginalised during the first divide.

The central thesis of this book is that we are living through a second technological divide in telecommunications. An understanding of the political options facing national governments in the period of digital technologies since the 1970s can be achieved by specifying the choices made in the past. An analysis of the conditions which led to the emergence of dominant forms of technology and organisation of the telephone infrastructure during the first technological divide between 1876 and the 1920s indicates the preconditions for the success of emerging alternatives in the current period.[9] I will examine the economy, technology and organisation of the telecommunications infrastructure, and the various forms of political intervention which shaped the historical development of telecommunications in particular countries. This comparative approach in political economy is used to bring out the distinctive structural features of the technology and economy of telecommunications more sharply and to show how technical characteristics set limits but do not determine possible ways of organising the system. Therefore, the telecommunications infrastructure is analysed both as a general technological and economic system of production and as a product of institutional conditions in particular countries which have given rise to differences in the way that the system is organised.

History and politics

Electrical telecommunications originated in 1837 with the invention of the telegraph: an electrical means of transmitting written messages which by the late 1840s had superseded the postal service as the favoured means of business communication. For Max Weber (1948: 212–214) the modern means of communication – the postal, railway and telegraph networks – which had to be administered in a collective way because they provided growing volumes of inter-regional traffic for public consumption, were among the pacemakers of the process of bureaucratisation behind the rise of the large-scale, centralised organisation. Weber regarded big bureaucracy as technically superior to other forms of organisation; especially decentralised systems of cooperative production.

The invention of the telephone in 1876 disrupted the monopolistic structure of established postal and telegraph interests and marked the beginning of the first technological divide in telecommunications. Within four decades, the telephone had substituted for telegraph as the preferred system of electrical communication. The economics of telephone systems dictated that both components of national telephone systems – local exchange operations and long-distance networks – formed a hierarchy of monopolies: local operations were geographical monopolies (which could be placed under independent ownership) interconnected to a single long-distance operator. The policy of private competition in the provision of the telephone helped to expand the system in the United States, but ultimately failed to provide a long-term solution. Competition promoted the unnecessary duplication of local telephone plant and equipment, and resulted in the problem of a private monopoly, which in the absence of competition failed to modernise the system.

Nationally integrated and standardised telephone systems which placed local and long-distance communications under the control of a national monopoly were being completed by the 1920s. The postal, telegraph and telephone sectors of the economy were distinguished by their being 'natural monopolies' and placed under centralised control. In the United States, after a period of private competition the provision of the telephone was dominated by a single private monopoly, American Telegraph and Telephone (AT&T). In most European countries, the state-owned telegraph monopolies had taken control of the telephone.

There was, however, an alternative to the centralised, national monopoly form of organisation. Telephone systems could be decentralised: local or regional exchange operations under independent control and ownership could be interworked with a single long-distance monopoly. In the United States and Europe, there were political struggles in the 1890s and early 1900s, to place the telephone system under municipal or cooperative ownership. In the Netherlands, Finland, Denmark and the municipalities of Hull and Guernsey in Britain, municipal and cooperative telephone systems were established. Elsewhere in the world, the decentralised model was abandoned. Under different historical circumstances the decentralised structure could have provided a viable model for the provision of national telecommunications. Municipal and cooperative systems were analogous to the craft systems which challenged the dominance of mass production. They were highly efficient and innovative: with the advantage of being close to customers within their geographical areas, decentralised organisations offered a range of services to satisfy the particular requirements of business and residential subscribers.

It was politics not economics which selected the national monopoly arrangement. In the United States, an alternative federated monopoly structure composed of independent local telephone companies interconnected to a jointly owned long-distance operator failed because the finance needed to build an independent long-distance network was blocked by a consortium of bankers who, in defence of their particular interests, supported the development of AT&T. AT&T's rise to dominance can, therefore, be only partially attributed to economic efficiency. In Europe, the development of municipal or regional systems was prevented by state-owned postal and telegraph monopolies, that exercised institutional power to have the telephone placed under the centralised control of state-owned postal and telegraph monopolies.

By the end of the 1970s, corporate demands for a revolution in telecommunications ushered in the second technological divide. Established telephone monopolies proved unable to accommodate corporate requirements for data transmission between computers. In the early 1980s national governments were examining ways of modernising and reorganising telephone infrastructures for the age of digital telecommunications. Efforts to introduce the new digital technologies by an innovating sphere of new firms met the resistance of the old monopoly interests. On the one hand, a new set of commercial interests led by corporate users and electronic manufacturers sought to dismantle closed monopolistic telecommunications markets. Competition, they argued, would increase the choice and flexibility of services and technologies needed to establish corporate information systems of data processing and telecommunications. On the other hand, the traditional coalition of national monopolies, telecommunications equipment suppliers and communication trade unions, sought to defend the existing arrangement and promote national and social requirements for universal telecommunications services.

Large corporate users were successful in realising their aims. Liberalisation of the telecommunications sector began in the United States during the 1950s, and was eventually emulated by Britain and Japan in the early 1980s. By the late 1980s, every country in North America, Western Europe and Japan had liberalised the telecommunications terminal equipment and computer information services markets. The task of integrating data processing and telecommunications was then accomplished by large corporations that built private digital communication networks to connect their dispersed activities.

Once governments have selected particular technological and organisational forms, huge investments in fixed capital which have to be amortised over several decades will set limits to the ways in which national telecommunications networks can be administered and operated during the twenty-first century. Although the shape of the different national forms of restructuring is currently being determined by political interests, the long-term viability of these solutions will be decided by the economic success of each organisational form. Rather than predict future developments, my aim in this book is to clarify the economic and political implications of each solution.

On the level of economics, the introduction of low-cost and high-capacity digital technologies produced a wave of deconcentration in the provision of telecommunications services during the 1970s and 1980s. Whereas a monopoly structure emerged in the nineteenth-century telegraph and telephone industries because a single firm or federated structure of companies owned the physical infrastructure and controlled and operated all the traffic carried over it, in the digital age the traffic in information services is supplied by numerous companies that do not necessarily own the underlying infrastructure. Data processing companies and new suppliers have entered the market to provide information services transmitted between computers, and many corporations have established private telecommunications networks and services which bypass the public network. Yet a drive towards economic concentration in the provision of national and international information and communication systems is now underway. The pattern of economic concentration and centralisation which was the outcome of private competition during the late nineteenth-century is being replicated in the current period. National telecommunications carriers and service providers are competing to satisfy the highly-profitable market in information services carried over worldwide corporate communication networks.

On the level of politics, government policies determine how national telecommunications systems are organised to deliver information services. By the 1920s, most national governments had adopted the social policy in favour of the provision of a universal telephone service for the population as a whole. Under state-ownership or state-regulation, telephone systems could be organised to promote national economic integration, and be placed in the hands of the military during times of national emergency. National monopolies attempted to serve the telecommunications needs of society as a whole, while offering specialised leased-lines and equipment to accommodate the private needs of large firms.

In the 1970s, however, a split emerged between the societal requirements for universal telephony and private demands for specialised digital services and technologies. Large corporations requiring a global telecommunications network capable of transmitting data between computers, at low cost, wanted greater control over terminal equipment attached to private networks and choice over the services transmitted between computer terminals. Corporate requirements for worldwide digital communications proved to be incompatible with traditional telecommunications policies of nation states. Consequently there was no longer a simple one-to-one geographical correspondence between political and economic organisation in the sphere of telecommunications. Since the 1980s, there has been an increasing 'territorial non-coincidence' between the telecommunications facilities of nation states and global information systems of large corporations.[10] A solution to this problem of national telecommunications provision has been complicated by a divergence in telecommunications needs: residential subscribers' and small businesses' demands for a universal telephone service at low prices within the territorial space of nation states, and large corporate demands for cheaper national and transnational digital capacity, terminal apparatus and services.

Although this general conflict has been resolved in particular countries by introducing a mix of public control and private competition in new telecommunications markets, there are two contrasting views over how the system should be controlled. On the one hand, liberals argue that during a period of rapid and dynamic technological change, private competition provides the greatest spur to the expansion and modernisation of the telecommunications system. Greater efficiency, they argue, is generated by private competition rather than static monopolies. In their view, government monopolies are unnecessarily bureaucratic and unresponsive to change. Under a regime of competition, private companies seek out new markets and realise latent but unsatisfied demand.

On the other hand, the traditional interests, including state monopolies and trade unions, have argued for the preservation of the national monopoly on the grounds of efficiency and social equity. Citing traditional arguments about the natural monopoly status of telecommunications, they argue that economies of scale and scope are so large in this sector that competing companies can never match the efficiency attained by a single company. The fundamental implication of opening up national telecommunications markets to competition is that it expands the power of transnational corporate interests at the expense of national control of telecommunications. In particular, the growing number of private networks which bypass the public network reduce the volume of traffic and increase the costs of services available to remaining residential and small business users of public systems. In doing so, the privatisation of telecommunications serves to weaken the power of state infrastructural policies aimed at promoting social equity and national economic development.

While those in favour of retaining the traditional arrangement clarify the essential problem with competition, I want to argue that a return to a national monopoly is untenable. There is a third path between monopoly and competition: a renewed regional model based on the decentralised arrangement of local and long-distance operators. This model maintains a balance between cooperation and competition in the provision of telecommunications services which generates efficiency and technological innovation, while adapting to the needs of local and long-distance users.

By the 1980s, then, national telephone administrations in the United States, Japan and every Western European country were challenged by the need to introduce new digital technologies. National monopolies were unable to furnish the range of equipment and services required by corporate customers. The monopoly walls surrounding the telecommunications industry – which were sanctioned by the nation state – had to be partially dismantled or broken down in order to expose the industry to competition, and allow it to undergo a process of dynamic technological change. Hence the process of modernising the infrastructure and reaching a new equilibrium could not be achieved without radically restructuring the technological and organisational stability of national telephone systems.

While by the early 1990s the United States, Japan and most European countries had liberalised terminal equipment and information services (in addition to voice telephony), the new digital telecommunications infrastructure was placed under three different organisational arrangements. First, in most mainland European countries, the state monopoly has been retained. Although some countries, notably the Netherlands, have announced plans to privatise national monopolies, the state has maintained control by holding the majority of the shares in the transformed utilities. Rather than introduce competition as a spur to efficiency in long-distance or local transmission, these Public Telecommunications Operators (PTOs) have introduced new forms of management structure to respond to the needs of large corporate customers. Second, from 1959 the private telephone monopoly in the United States was gradually exposed to competition in several markets. In 1984, a more radical policy of competition was implemented. AT&T's national monopoly was broken up. Regional monopolies under Federal regulation are now responsible for the provision of public telecommunications services, while AT&T is permitted to compete in the unregulated markets of long-distance and international information and communication technologies and services. In Britain and Japan, competition in telecommunications transmission was introduced by privatising the state monopolies and licensing competing common carriers. Third, the decentralised systems of local or regional monopolies interconnected with state-owned or competing long-distance carriers, which were marginalised during the first divide, have been resurrected as an alternative path of modernisation.

This book is divided into three parts. Part I examines the economic and political conditions which led to the formation of telephone systems under national monopoly control during the first divide in analogue technology. I will argue that it was politics rather than economics which selected the national monopoly organisation in preference to the decentralised alternative. Part II explains how the transformation of mass production generated demands for a revolution in corporate telecommunications. The failure of traditional telephone monopolies to accommodate corporate needs resulted in the widespread development of corporate digital networks. Part III shows how corporate pressures brought about the restructuring of the technology and organisation of national telephone networks during the second divide, and considers the economic viability of the three different paths of modernisation.

Notes

1. L. Kehoe (1992), 'Driving down a superhighway', *Financial Times*, 19 November 1992; N. Dunne (1993), 'Department gets enhanced role and a bigger budget', *Financial Times*, 19 February 1993.
2. Quoted in Kehoe, op. cit.
3. As distinguished from 'incremental' technological change which refers to changes in technique using known technologies (e.g. improvements in electromechanical technologies), 'radical' technological change refers to the introduction of an entirely new technology (e.g. the shift from electromechanical to digital technologies).
4. By contrast to Mandel's three technological revolutions, I have distinguished between physical and informational transformations in the technology of the production process. E. Mandel, p118 (1975), *Late Capitalism*, Verso, London.
5. As Freeman and Perez (1988) explain, the current transformation of entire economies brought about by the conversion to digital information and communication technologies has culminated in a 'structural crisis of adjustment, in which social and institutional changes are necessary to bring about a better "match" between the new technology and the system of social management of the economy – or "regime of regulation"'. C. Freeman and C. Perez (1988), 'Structural crises of adjustment, business cycles and investment behaviour', pp38–66, in *Technical Change and Economic Theory* (eds) G. Dosi, C. Freeman, R. Nelson, G. Silverberg and L. Soete, Pinter Publishers, London.
6. J.A. Schumpeter p87 (1943), *Capitalism, Socialism and Democracy*, George Allen and Unwin, London.
7. J.A. Schumpeter p306 (1939), *Business Cycles: A Theoretical, Historical and Statistical Analysis of the Capitalist Process*, abridged version (1964) R. Fels, Porcupine Press, Philadelphia. The fact that 'the telephone industry [in the United States] was not built up by the telegraph industry and has shown no tendency to be dominated by it' is a 'verification of the hypothesis of New Firms and New Men arising independently of the Old Firms and laying themselves alongside them'. In Europe, by contrast, armed with a legal monopoly, the state telegraph interests did, contrary to Schumpeter's new firm hypothesis, influence the nature of progress in telephone development.
8. Schumpeter p101 (1943), op. cit.
9. M.J. Piore and C.F. Sabel p4 (1984), *The Second Industrial Divide: Possibilities for Prosperity*, Basic Books, New York.
10. For a general discussion of the problem of territorial non-coincidence see R. Murray (1975), 'The Internationalisation of Capital and the Nation State', pp107–134 in *International Firms and Modern Imperialism* (ed.) H. Radice, Penguin, Harmondsworth.

Part I

The first technological divide: analogue telecommunications

2 From competition to monopoly

For the three decades following the invention of the telephone in 1876, there were possibilities for mixing the technology and organisation of the telephone infrastructure in a variety of ways. The 1920s, however, marked the end of the first technological divide in telecommunications history. Nationally integrated and standardised telephone infrastructures were being completed in Europe and the United States. In most European countries, politics determined the institutional structure created to operate telephone networks. The telephone was centrally operated and administered by state-owned postal and telegraph monopolies. This chapter focuses on the United States, the country which led the world in the development of telephone technology. Driven by private competition, early telephone development in the United States illuminates the technological and economic forces which led to the formation of monopoly in this industry.

By the 1920s, when a particular mix of technology and organisation had been selected in the United States, large investments in fixed capital, which had to be amortised over several decades, left little scope for major changes in the organisation of the telephone infrastructure. From the 1920s to the 1970s, the operation of the American telephone infrastructure was dominated by a single national monopoly. In common with other public utilities, like the railway and electric power industries, the telephone infrastructure was assumed to be a 'natural monopoly': an industry in which economies of scale and scope meant that the cheapest service could be provided by a single monopoly. This view is advocated by Alfred Chandler (1977) in his account of the monopolisation of the telephone industry by the first decade of the twentieth century.[1] In this chapter I want to examine the economics which produced a tendency towards monopoly in the provision of the telephone service. Contrary to the Chandlerian view, however, I will argue that the form of organisation cannot simply be read off from the underlying characteristics of the technology. The telephone system formed a hierarchy of monopolies composed of a long-distance network operated by a single monopoly, dovetailed into numerous local exchange operations under independent management or ownership, each with a geographical monopoly. This technological structure set limits to but did not determine forms of organisation.

During the 1880s and 1890s, the telephone system could be developed under three different organisational structures: private competition, national monopoly or a decentralised cooperative structure. While phases of competition stimulated the rapid expansion of the American telephone infrastructure, each phase resulted in a process of economic concentration. I will argue that the emergence of a national monopoly was not purely a reflection of the economic supremacy of this model of organisation. On the contrary, the dominance of the telephone system by American Telegraph and Telephone (AT&T), a single integrated local and long-distance national monopoly, was determined by powerful economic and political interests. An alternative decentralised arrangement, composed of a federation of independent local monopolies, represented a viable alternative to a single national monopoly. The federated model was prevented not because it was inefficient, but because the finance needed to fund the independent long-distance network was blocked by AT&T and a consortium of bankers. Under different historical circumstances the federated structure could have provided an efficient form of organisation.

1. Economy of the telephone infrastructure

The ways in which the evolving telephone technology could be organised, ranging from competition to monopoly, were defined by the economy of the telephone infrastructure as a large-scale system of production. An electrical system for two-way communication, the telephone transmitted the spoken word in analogue modulated waveform and reproduced it at a distance. The telephone infrastructure contained three types of equipment: at the receiving end of the system was *terminal equipment* (telephone apparatus); a *transmission system* sent messages from source to destination through a communications circuit; and, unless subscribers had direct private lines, *switches* routed calls from local exchange operations, through the main trunks linking larger regions, then back into the local exchange or distribution system to final destinations.

By the 1880s, telephone infrastructures formed a hierarchical structure consisting of three technological components (see figure 1). First, the telephone exchange, invented in 1878, was the main technology of the local telephone component of the network. The exchange or switchboard revolutionised telephony by placing each telephone subscriber in communication with any other subscriber connected to the same local exchange operation. Second, a long-distance telephone service was initiated in the 1880s, which eventually formed an intercity telephone network, linked by a hierarchy of high capacity trunk exchanges, connected to existing local exchanges. By the first decade of the twentieth century, nationally integrated networks were formed which joined together local exchanges in all the major centres of population and economic activity throughout national territories. Third, from the 1920s technical improvements in transmission connected national networks through gateway telephone exchanges to international networks linking countries throughout the world.

Economics of high fixed-cost telecommunications infrastructures

The construction of local and long-distance networks entailed large investments in fixed capital (in terminals, telephone exchanges and transmission equipment) which were characterised by very slow turnover periods. Sunk capital had to be recovered over many years, independent of the wear and tear of plant and equipment. High fixed costs had to be paid for even if the system was not operating or operating at low levels of capacity. Telephone companies were willing to incur high fixed costs on the expectation that, during the life span of the investment, costs would be recouped if the price of the telephone service remained above the variable costs of operating the system (the costs of wages and materials which varied with output).

Expenditures on new plant and equipment increased the ratio of fixed over variable costs. During its early development, the telephone system experienced an enormous thirst for expansion, since where it was possible to increase the volume of traffic, fixed costs declined.[2] Increases in efficiency lowered the costs of the telephone service and extended it to a wider circle of subscribers. As long as there was spare capacity in the system, there was an incentive to attract traffic by reducing rates. But production systems like the railway, telegraphs and telephones which incurred high fixed

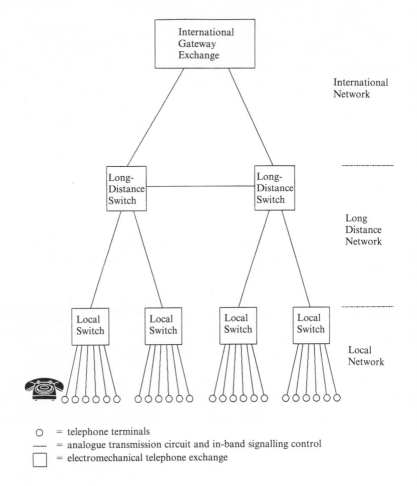

Figure 1: Hierarchy or pyramid structure: public switched telephone network

costs were always threatened by 'ruinous competition'. Driven by the imperative of recouping sunk capital, ruinous competition occurred when competition drove prices below variable costs, leaving companies saddled with fixed costs and forcing the closure of inefficient or financially weak companies. Three categories of economies (scale, scope and system) resulted from the requirement to accelerate the turnover time of fixed capital invested in the telephone infrastructure.

Economies of scale

The system was expanded and costs were reduced by the pursuit of two types of economies of scale. On the one hand, extensive economies of scale were obtained by increasing the number of subscribers with access to the system, either within existing areas or by extending the service to new geographical areas. New subscribers had to have a dedicated access line to the exchange. Additional subscribers could be provided with access to the network at low marginal costs because the same transmission circuits could be used more intensively.

Between 1877 and 1897, increases in the number of subscribers connected to telephone systems improved the utility of the service. Every increase in the number of people who could converse with one another over the same interconnected telecommunications system increased the value of the service to subscribers.[3] The early extensive development of the service did not, however, result in declining marginal costs. Manual telephone exchanges were more expensive to operate per subscriber as the total number of subscribers increased.[4] The source of extensive diseconomies of scale was not the fixed cost of plant and equipment, but the increasing variable costs of handling an ever widening circle of possible connections: as the number of subscribers increased, the number of circuits required to furnish connections increased more rapidly. This so-called 'switchboard problem' stemmed from the errors and operating time wasted in transferring calls between switchboards within the same office and between central exchanges in large metropolitan areas. As I will explain below, the switchboard problem was solved by improvements in the capacity of telephone exchanges.

Local exchange operations provided a telephone service in metropolitan areas, towns and villages. An exchange service was most efficient when operated by a geographical monopoly. Two companies operating in the same exchange area could only serve the same customers by duplicating plant and services, and without achieving the extensive economies of scale captured by a single supplier. Subscribers wishing to communicate with every other telephone customer in the area were forced to install the telephones of both companies, or accept an inferior service.

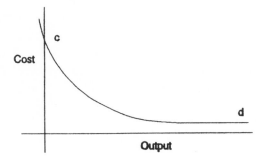

Figure 2: High fixed-cost structure of the telephone infrastructure

On the other hand, intensive economies of scale could be obtained by improvements in the capacity to handle a larger volume of traffic: fixed costs per message declined as the volume of traffic increased. Such improvements in transmission and switching capacity were achieved in two ways: in the short-run, by investments in additional plant and equipment (using existing technologies), and, in the long-run, by adopting new technologies and organisational methods which improved capacity utilisation in a given period of time.[5]

Empirical evidence shows that there were intensive economies of scale in long-distance transmission.[6] If the sunk capital in long-distance plant was divided by a growing volume of traffic it resulted in declining average costs. This cost-structure situation is depicted in figure 2, where cost is measured on the y-axis and output on the x-axis. The curve shows how average unit costs vary with output. As the volume of traffic handled increased, average costs declined rapidly from initial fixed costs indicated by point c, until full capacity utilisation was reached at point d.

The construction of additional transmission capacity reduced the costs of transmitting messages per circuit mile, since doubling the number of circuits more than doubled the capacity to handle traffic.[7] Consequently, two long-distance systems operating at scale x would be less efficient than a single system operating at double the capacity of x. The total number of messages carried over AT&T's long-distance network increased from about 3 million in 1900 to 50 million in 1930. With the growth in traffic volumes carried over higher-capacity long-distance lines, more circuits could be placed on the same pole lines, reducing the average costs per message transmitted.[8]

Intensive economies of scale associated with long-distance transmission depended not just on additional plant and equipment. The technological bottleneck associated with the switchboard problem was solved by improvements in capacity utilisation. A combination of organisational and technical innovations (such as better switchboard design, rapid signalling systems and the invention of the semi-automatic Strowger exchange), expanded the capacity and reduced the size of telephone exchanges, while minimising the number of long-distance trunk lines needed to handle peak-load traffic.[9]

The cost of sending a message increased the greater the distance covered. A number of inventions, including Michael Pupin's loading coil, the complex amplifier and repeater (based on the invention of the vacuum tube by DeForest), lowered transmission costs over long distances by reducing the physical thickness of wires and increasing carrying capacity. But improvements in transmission capacity in metropolitan areas were held back by the high costs incurred in constructing and maintaining wire-plant. Early telephone wires, made of galvanised iron, were noisy, prone to cross-talk and poor conductors of electricity. The introduction of copper wire, the underground conductor in 1887, and the implementation of the loading coil in 1902 improved cable construction and operation. The use of metallic cables economised on maintenance and plant construction, since smaller wires were used, and a less congested system furnished improvements in capacity utilisation. By 1920, telephone conversation in the United States was possible over 2,000 miles of cable, and a single, standard cable could carry a greater number of circuits (between 250 and 300).[10]

As subsequent technological improvements brought reductions in the average costs per telephone message transmitted, the telephone substituted for the telegraph. Investments in additional plant and facilities, better transmission, and improved techniques, contributed to a reduction in AT&T's rates for long-distance calls. In turn, lower prices stimulated an increase in the volume of traffic carried. Between 1923 and 1928 – the most rapid phase of growth – total long-distance telephone traffic increased by 67 per cent, and the volume of traffic between important business routes such as New York–Chicago increased by 194 per cent while transcontinental business grew by 430 per cent.[11]

Finally, local and long-distance operations were organised to accommodate the load factor on network capacity: this was the busiest hour of the day which represented a large proportion of the total daily traffic.[12] If traffic overwhelmed facilities, as it often did in Europe in the 1880s and 1890s, calls could be delayed for hours. Therefore, one of the essential requirements for high efficiency of service was constant provision of plant and capacity for future traffic. The intensive scale of capacity in the system – buildings, switchboards, conduits and cables – had to be greater than actual traffic requirements because requests for telephone service could exceed the capacity of the system to serve them. Plant had to be constructed with excess capacity to cope with the load factor. Network planning prevented congestion of plant, lack of facilities for future subscribers, and consequent loss of efficiency.

Economies of scope
Communication services were differentiated by distance (local, long-distance and international) and variety (postal, telegraph and telephone). Economies of scope were obtained by using the same plant and equipment to provide two or more services at lower costs than the total costs of providing each service separately.[13]

The integration of local and long-distance telephone services increased the volume of through traffic carried over a single system and reduced the costs of furnishing both local and long-distance calls. In the mid-1880s, for example, AT&T could not justify the construction of an isolated network dedicated to private-line long-distance communications. To raise the volume of traffic carried over such a large-scale investment, long-distance services were interconnected with local exchange operations.

The assumption behind the integration of the postal, telegraph and telephone systems in Europe was that a cheaper range of services could be furnished by sharing the same offices, labour and transmission plant. For example, cost savings associated with combining telegraph and telephone services would result from economies in the use of common plant and maintenance, since much of the work could be done jointly for both services. Moreover, it was claimed that to reap the cost reductions associated with the compositing of trunk telephone circuits for simultaneous telephone and telegraph transmission, both services had to be under centralised control. However, in the United States evidence to the contrary demonstrates that very effective coordination was accomplished between the telegraph and telephone services under separate control by contract, not common ownership.[14]

Economies of system

While the concepts of economies of scale and scope demonstrate the cost advantages of expanding the size of the infrastructure, they are not sufficient to explain the economics related to the control of the telephone system. The concept of 'economies of system' is required to explain cost reductions stemming from the centralisation of network management and control. The operation, management and maintenance required in routing traffic through communication circuits in the network between transmitting and receiving terminals is performed by network management and control. One of the main problems incurred in the operation of large-scale telecommunications systems is that of 'organisational complexity': as the number of interacting technological components in the system increase, the system's complexity and cost of control grow exponentially.[15] In consequence, techniques for managing an increasing number of interacting components as the system grows in size have been a focus for cost saving innovations – particularly during the recent period of digital technology. Economies of system refer to the ways in which central coordination of flows of traffic improves the utilisation of capacity and accelerates the turnover of fixed capital in a given period of time.

Prior to the development of long-distance operations, the geographically isolated local exchange operations obtained economies of system by controlling subscriber connections from a single centre. Once local and long-distance components of the infrastructure were integrated and standardised, network operation and control could be accomplished either by a single national monopoly, or by the joint control of local geographical monopolies responsible for the management of local traffic, and a single firm controlling long-lines. In either case, a centralised long-distance authority secured economies of system by controlling the through traffic carried over the long-distance network between exchange operations.

The long-distance service was best developed under centralised control because of the particular technological characteristics of the telephone service.[16] Hypothetically, a long-distance network could have been built up incrementally, in the same way as the railway, by numerous agreements to establish physical interconnection between autonomous exchange companies operating in adjacent local areas. However, the transmission of a telephone message was different from the physical connection involved in the transportation of people or commodities. When a railway company transported freight to its destination, all the property, facilities and operation remained under the control of the owning company. During the transportation of the freight, the facilities of this company were not put to the exclusive use of another company. The principle of the telephone service was quite different.

A telephone company neither distributed commodities, nor transmitted and delivered messages like telegraph companies. The product of the telephone system was a through service over a circuit which enabled one subscriber to communicate almost instantaneously with another regardless of the intervening distance. It was uneconomical to establish more than one long-distance service, since in order to provide a circuit carrying through traffic, local exchange and long-distance services had to be coordinated into one telephone service, using much the same equipment and labour utilised in the operation of both services. To enable one subscriber to communicate with another over long-distance lines, a circuit used exclusively for these two subscribers had to be established which was continuous for the duration of the call. The whole circuit embracing the calling and the called persons' instruments and the complete line connecting them had to be in use for each call. Although all parts of the circuit had to be technically harmonious, local and long-distance components of national infrastructures could be operated by different owners.[17]

Operators along the various stages of the line had to have absolute control of the circuit between the points of communication. Operators had to work in unity because differences in operators' techniques decreased efficiency by delaying connection time. Physical connection depended upon the exclusive use by one company of part of the facilities of another, irrespective of the latter's use of such facilities. In those cases where local exchange operations were duplicated, diseconomies of system resulted from the increasing organisational complexity of controlling traffic through competing networks and maintaining the technical integrity of the service to prevent fraudulent operation.

But economies of system obtained by centralised control of through traffic did not depend on the combination of local and long-distance operations under single ownership. Physical inter-connection between Bell's long-distance network and the independently owned local operating companies proved that a through service could be effected by contract between autonomous firms. System economies could be obtained through bilateral contractual relations between independent owners who had a collective incentive to cooperate because autonomous owners of parts of the system could be held directly accountable for their individual actions on other parts of the system.[18] This is indeed how coordination was effected between the Bell System and independent telephone companies, and between the Post Office and the municipality of Hull in Britain.

Organisation of the monopoly

According to Chandler (1977), a single national monopoly integrating local and long-distance operations resulted from this early period of telephone competition because this was the most efficient organisational structure. The large-scale corporation emerged at the end of the nineteenth-century in those industries, like the railways, telegraphs, and telephones, which were charac-terised by the use of new technologies (allowing revolutionary increases in output) and expanding markets. Chandler makes the important distinction between the new transportation and com-munication industries of the nineteenth century, and the older infrastructures of canals and road systems. Whereas the state usually built and maintained the canals and roads, it rarely operated all the canal boats, stage lines and mail routes carried by the infrastructures. By contrast, the telegraph and telephone companies erected their own wires and operated the traffic in messages carried over communication infrastructures. Exclusive monopolies came to dominate national telegraph and telephone infrastructures because, he argues, single companies could attain economies of scale and scope by operating high volumes of through traffic flowing on top of unified communication systems.

Thus with reference to the telephone infrastructure Chandler's (1977: 202–203) central argument is that:

The speed and volume of messages made possible by the new electric technology forced the building of a carefully defined administrative organisation, operated by salaried managers, to coordinate their flow and to maintain and expand transmitting facilities. The first enterprise to create a national organisation to handle through traffic obtained an almost unassailable position. To achieve that position, however, required more careful planning in the building of the telephone system than in the creating of the telegraph system, because through traffic for the telephone was for many years only a technological potential.

Control of through traffic prevented small independent companies from growing large through acquisition and growth. With a monopoly of long-lines – the nerves of the system – Bell's competition was geographically isolated.

Integration of local exchange operations and the long-distance network permitted the flow of traffic between such activities to be administratively coordinated and routinised. Improvements in productivity depended on the formation of a managerial hierarchy to coordinate and control through traffic, and the imposition of highly rationalised labour processes throughout this centralised operation. Chandler (1977) assumes that by routinising transactions between local and long-distance operations, the costs of these transactions were lowered.[19] Consequently, a more effective scheduling of traffic in messages between local and long-distance operations enabled a more intensive use of telephone facilities and workforce, so increasing productivity and reducing costs.

While a central administration was required to control long-distance lines and obtain economies of scale by operating high volumes of traffic, I want to argue that contrary to Chandler's assumption this did not depend on centralised control and integrated ownership of local exchange operations. Chandler invokes a form of technological determinism: he assumes that the technological requirements of the telephone called for one solution – a single national monopoly under the control of a centralised managerial hierarchy.

The central problem with Chandler's thesis is that it equates progress with technological change: a teleological assumption which implies that industrial history is purposefully moving technology and organisation along a fixed road towards the most successful solution.[20] Competition promotes a uniformity in technique by forcing firms to pursue industrial efficiency, eliminating inefficient technologies, and selecting the most advanced solution. In contrast to this 'narrow-track' view of technological development, a more appropriate conception is one that recognises that technological change can evolve in several directions, like a branching tree.[21]

Industrial history is composed of suppressed but viable technological and organisational arrangements to the paths that are finally selected.[22]

This many-worlds view of history differs in two important respects from the Chandlerian perspective. First, there is no guarantee that competition drives technology towards the goal of universal efficiency. In the many-worlds view, one mix of technology and organisation competes with another. The pattern of technological and organisational change can evolve in various directions of progress, under forms of private or public ownership, and with different aims. Although movement in one particular direction eliminates experiments with alternative arrangements, it does not necessarily mean that the chosen path is the most efficient. Rival firms may adopt the preferred approach rather than risk finding an alternative arrangement. Eventually, however, the transition from competition to monopoly imposed by the economic logic of high fixed-cost technological systems entails increasing fixed capital investments, whose amortisation over many years discourages and finally prohibits further experiments with alternative technological solutions. This tendency towards technological stability is only reversed when the introduction of radical technologies makes it economically possible to disregard sunk capital and technically feasible to follow new paths of development.

Second, in the Chandlerian world, technology is driven solely by economic imperatives. Politics has little or no influence over technological progress. In the many-worlds view, by contrast, technological choices depend on the distribution of power in society. In this respect the direction of technological development is not necessarily enforced by competition. On the contrary, dominant economic and political institutions have the power to select new technologies and shape developments to serve their own interests. The 'selection' of competing technological and organisational forms is, therefore, no indication that the surviving form is the strongest among several possibilities.[23] Since the nation state is able to support or penalise different interest groups, there is considerable scope for political intervention in the construction and organisation of technology.

From the many-worlds perspective, technologies set limits to possible organisational arrangements, but do not determine them.[24] A distinction should, therefore, be made between (i) the *technological and economic* structure of particular systems of production, and (ii) the *organisational form* set up to operate the system, including the industrial structure (from competition to monopoly), pattern of public or private ownership, organisation of the labour process, and management style (centralised or decentralised). Thus structurally determined economic conditions favouring technological scale and monopoly must be distinguished from the historically contingent construction of organisational forms. Economies of scale, scope and system in telephone operations may only apply to parts of the system, such as long-lines, not the whole system. It is, therefore, necessary to analyse where economies affect the whole productive system or parts of it, and where they do not, in order to reveal possibilities for varying the organisation of some of the parts.

My argument is that for two to three decades after its invention, the telephone was at a branching point in its history. Competition discarded some possibilities, and moved telephone technology towards a nationally integrated and standardised network. Most national systems operated using American telephone technology based on Bell and Edison patents. Technologically, there were few alternative ways of operating the system. It was designed according to a hierarchical structure, which in the late nineteenth century was the preferred engineering solution for most large technical systems, including electric power.[25] The high cost of switching relative to transmission was reflected in the pyramid or hierarchical structure of telephone technology. Millions of telephone terminals were linked vertically through a hierarchy of increasingly complex and higher-capacity local and toll exchanges, to a smaller number of trunk exchanges at the apex of the hierarchy.

Although there was little variation in the technological architecture of telephone systems, there was, however, considerable choice over how the provision of the service was organised. The control over telephone systems could be accomplished by introducing one of three different organisational forms: private competition, national monopoly under public or private owner-ship, and decentralisation – a cooperative structure of independent local and long-distance monopolies. While private competition fuelled the expansion of the telephone system, it was a temporary organisational solution which led to economic concentration and monopoly. The national monopoly paradigm succeeded in the United States and most European countries not because it was superior in terms of efficiency but because it protected and promoted the interests of established or dominant communication monopolies.

If the system had been decomposed into a hierarchy of monopolies, there are no economic reasons why a decentralised cooperative structure could not have matched the efficiency of a single monopoly. This decentralised and cooperative form of organisation represents a third path of development lying between the ideal-types of national monopoly and private competition.[26] It depended on the creation of a service involving the cooperation of autonomous companies. A decentralised system of independent local monopolies could operate a through service in a unified manner as long as each independent company cooperated with the long-distance monopoly over the implementation of standardised interfaces, operating procedures and pricing.[27] Moreover, in those examples where the system was decomposed into smaller parts, local operators were able to innovate rapidly and adjust to local market circumstances. Under independent control, local exchange operations had the authority and flexibility required to operate in local territories, while an independent long-distance operator provided through traffic and specialised services for large business subscribers.

2. Cycles of economic concentration

The American telephone industry underwent three cycles of economic concentration. In each cycle, competition or the threat of competition stimulated the expansion of the system.[28] According to the Chandlerian *a priori* thesis, the growth of the Bell system, which was driven by the pursuit of industrial efficiency, reflected and promoted the realisation of a natural monopoly. On the contrary, my argument is that while the pursuit of economies of high fixed-cost technologies substituted monopoly for private competition, the final shape of the monopoly arrangement was determined by powerful private interests, not industrial efficiency. AT&T did have a choice over how to attain a dominant position and used its financial and political power to achieve it.

In the first cycle (1876–1879), an initial period of competition between the Bell Company and Western Union, the dominant telegraph carrier, resulted in an agreement which divided American electrical communications into a duopoly, with Bell controlling local telephone operations, and the telegraph operator monopolising the long-distance message market. During the second cycle (1880–1894), under the protection of a patent monopoly, the Bell Company sought to consolidate its control over local and long-distance operations in anticipation of competition after the expiration of basic telephone patents. In the third cycle – lasting from the expiration of the basic telephone patents in 1893 and 1894 to 1913 – Bell's dominant position was challenged by a large influx of new competition, and attempts to form a rival federated organisation capable of challenging Bell's domination of the market.

Invention and early competition (1876–1879)

On 7 March 1876, Alexander Graham Bell patented the telephone. Telephony was founded upon the principle that electromagnetism could be used to reproduce voice at a distance. It was a radical invention which inaugurated an entirely new technological system, and eventually eclipsed the existing telegraphic means of communication.[29]

Differences in technological principles generated different patterns of competition in the infant telegraph and telephone industries.[30] Although the basic operating principle of telegraphy – electromagnetism reproduced at a distance – was unpatentable, patents could be secured on the numerous applications of telegraphy, and these formed the basis for competing companies. By contrast, the telephone was based on a technical principle unknown prior to the invention of the instrument, and there were only a few ways in which the principle could be applied to transmit sound. Despite a flood of imitations after 1878, the possessors of the telephone patent were protected from widespread competition because unlike the telegraph the principle itself, rather than just the application, was patentable. Whereas a monopoly in the telegraph service only emerged after an intense competitive struggle between many small companies, initial competition in telephony was primarily confined to two companies: Bell, which held rights to the telephone patents, and Western Union, the dominant telegraph company, which held rights over Gray's alternative telephone patent.

Western Union – in the shape of a potential telegraph and telephone concern – was a powerful competitor to Bell.[31] Faced with this threat, the problems of financing and commercialising a product with uncertain demand, and Western Union's decision not to purchase the Bell patents, the Bell associates developed the system by contracting suppliers and operators.[32]

In 1877, a small, unincorporated organisation was formed, called the Bell Telephone Company of Massachusetts. To undertake the manufacture and operation of the telephone service, Bell would have been forced to raise large amounts of capital, build an organisation, and solve production and development problems. Instead, the best alternative for the Bell Company was to farm out the manufacture of telephones by contract and lease instruments to Bell licensed operating companies.

From 1877, with the support of Boston financiers, Bell developed the telephone by granting short-term licences to operating companies for use of telephone facilities in different territories. The contracts were made for five or ten years and contained clauses which enabled the Bell organisation to purchase the property of the licensees when the contracts expired. The Bell organisation would then lease – not sell – the telephone apparatus used by operating companies. A group of telephone companies operating under patents owned and controlled by the Bell organisation, operated in defined territories throughout the United States.

Bell licensed independent manufacturers of electrical equipment to produce, under the Bell patents, telephone apparatus solely for the Bell licensed operating agents. In 1880 a contract was made with the Western Electric Company for the manufacture of standard equipment for the Bell operating companies. In the face of growing telephone demand and competition from Western Union's telephone operations, Bell was forced to expand its capacity by licensing four additional manufacturers. Bell made profits by charging royalties on the manufacture of telephone apparatus and by leasing telephones to the licensed operating companies. Subscribers paid more in the form of rentals than the purchase price of the telephones.

Such contractual arrangements furnished the Bell organisation with a steady cash flow with which to build and expand its operations.[33] With little access to working capital the Bell associates used the policy of leasing to encourage local agents to take responsibility for the expansion of the telephone service, including the construction and operating costs of telephone plant. Under the control of a general manager, Theodore Vail – formerly a superintendent on the United States Rail Mail Service – and William Forbes – one of the Bell directors – a consolidated National Bell Telephone Company was formed in 1879, and a managerial strategy was devised which emulated the managerial techniques and cost accounting used in the railways.

Between 1878 and 1880, two rival telephone companies, Bell and Western Union's subsidiary, American Speaking Telephone Company formed in December 1877 (armed with Gray's alternative telephone patents), engaged in a 'race to occupy the field'. Western Union was compelled to enter the field after its highly profitable telegraph subsidiary, the Gold and Stock Company, started losing customers to the telephone, who preferred two-way verbal communication.[34]

Prior to 1883, and the introduction of long-lines, there was no technological or economic imperative for a national monopoly. But technological scale did promote local monopolies.[35] The invention of the central exchange in 1878 transformed the telephone service. Previously, local agents sold a simple, point-to-point service mainly to business customers. The exchange gave each customer access to the phones of all other subscribers in the same exchange area. When competition resulted in the construction of more than one exchange, the advantage obtained by the first company to establish an exchange was lost. Subscribers had to pay for access to more than one service to have complete coverage, and telephone plant was unnecessarily duplicated. The first company to establish a working exchange often secured a monopoly position, because its customers were connected to a larger number of subscribers.

The high fixed costs of setting-up central exchanges enlarged the capital requirements and risks of entering the local exchange service. Whereas fixed costs on private-line operations were often recovered as soon as customers purchased the equipment, local exchange operations represented a permanent capital investment, only a portion of which was recouped through monthly service charges. Saddled with high fixed costs – which did not vary with the amount of traffic carried – local agents had an incentive to operate central exchanges at or near full capacity. Uncontrolled competition for local traffic was ruinous, since rate reductions, which frequently fell below the variable costs of transmitting messages, reduced total revenues.[36] Rival local telephone companies could only retain traffic by making comparable cuts in rates.[37] By 1880, the fixed costs of constructing central exchanges exceeded, often by several times, the original estimates. The cost of providing exchange connections was rising more rapidly than the revenues collected under the prevailing flat rate schedule, resulting in extensive diseconomies of scale.[38] To a certain extent rates were adjusted to compensate for high variable costs of operation. But returns on investments generally remained low.

The first cycle of concentration ended on 10 November 1879, when National Bell and Western Union reached a settlement, which cannot be explained by technological or economic imperatives.[39] The dominant telegraph company agreed not to enter the field of telephony for a seventeen-year period. Given the infeasibility of a long-distance telephone service, the settlement divided the American telecommunications market into a 'natural duopoly' with a local service controlled by Bell, and long-distance electrical communications operated by Western Union.[40]

Patent monopoly era (1880–1894)

The 1879 settlement eliminated Bell's strongest competitor, and left the company in the position of a protected monopoly until 1893 and 1894, when the basic telephone patents expired. The race to occupy new markets had accelerated the pace of telephone development. By 1880, 61,000 telephones had been installed and there was an exchange service in 998 American cities. However, there was no single technological system. Telephone operations were geographically isolated, unconnected exchange operations.

In 1879 Vail forecast that Bell's monopoly could only be defended against the threat of competition if the company's strategy focused on the still-to-be-created long-distance traffic.[41] The Bell organisation continued to generate and protect new telephone patents, and increase its stock ownership in operating and equipment companies. But the main way in which the Bell System consolidated its monopoly position during this period was by controlling through-traffic between local exchange operations which prevented small rival telephone companies from growing large through internalisation.[42]

Although the 1879 settlement was mainly about patents rights – the source of Bell's negotiating strength and legal basis for a monopoly – the most difficult part of the negotiations concerned long-distance operations. But Western Union did not recognise the competitive threat posed by the new communications technology in the long-distance market for business messages since it perceived the telephone to be an instrument of 'personal' rather than commercial communications.[43] Consequently, the settlement gave Bell a free hand to develop long-distance voice transmission.

In the early 1880s, toll lines were constructed between adjacent local telephone operations, starting with the twenty-eight-mile Boston–Lowell line. During the early 1880s, the expansion of toll lines proceeded rapidly: in 1883, 10,616 miles of toll wires were added to the Bell system, more than tripling the capacity of Bell's long-distance transmission plant.

Technically, AT&T faced a choice of developing a private-line, point-to-point long-distance service or building a long-distance interexchange network.[44] The latter strategy was chosen because the Bell management believed that a separate private-line long-distance system would not generate sufficient traffic volumes to recover initial fixed costs. AT&T calculated that fixed capital expenditures would be minimised if the capacity of existing exchanges and toll lines in Bell's local operations were used as feeders of traffic into an interexchange long-distance system. However, the problem of integrating AT&T's higher capacity long-distance network with older local plant operations contributed to a poor service, little demand and low returns.[45] During the late 1880s, the costs of operating long-lines were particularly high: accounting for 85 per cent of total income in 1888, and 80 per cent in 1889. AT&T's management continued to inject new capital in the construction of long-lines on the expectation that large profits would follow the creation of the system after the expiration of the basic telephone patents.[46]

During the patent monopoly period, the Bell Company abandoned its policy of leasing and licensing, and embarked on a strategy of integration under the slogan 'one system, one policy, universal service'. Integration of local companies was accomplished by substituting permanent contracts for temporary ones, on the condition that Bell took out an equity position in the company, usually less than 35 per cent. Under permanent contracts, Bell companies were obliged to operate in territories decided by the parent company, their performance was closely monitored by the central organisation, and they were required to make exclusive use of Western Electric equipment.

In order to prevent rival interests from acquiring parts of the Bell System, the central organisation began to acquire majority shares of the voting stock in adjacent independent companies. The Bell interests maintained that the adjacent local companies and toll lines had to be combined into larger units, to eliminate the duplication of organisation and to bring about a closer coordination of licensees.

For example, in 1882 the many local companies in New York State were reorganised into several larger systems.

From 1885, the development of long-lines introduced a new logic of system formation: economies of system obtained from centralised control of a through service depended upon technically standardised interconnections between local and long-lines. However, exchange operations had been constructed with no consideration of the compatibility required to connect with a standardised long-distance network. Local operating companies used single, grounded iron wires, which were unsuitable for connection with AT&T's higher-grade, two-circuit metallic long-distance network. While many local companies introduced the necessary upgrades in plant, other smaller companies could not raise sufficient capital to modernise local plant in line with the development of long-lines. By acquiring an equity position in the local companies, the central organisation secured greater leverage over local companies, in order to guarantee their technical cooperation in the construction of long-lines.[47]

Exchange and transmission equipment, which previously developed outside Bell's control on site in the local operating companies or independent manufacturers, resulted in considerable 'design chaos' and lack of standardisation. Ownership of equipment supply helped to guarantee quality control over production of standardised exchange technologies. However, backward integration was not a prerequisite for high quality and cheap supplies of standardised equipment. After the expiration of the basic patents, independent manufacturers of telephone equipment also captured economies of scale in the production of standardised equipment by supplying the growing market of independent telephone operations. The main reason why Bell System sought ownership of its equipment manufacturing source had little to do with economies of scale. Rather, it was a monopolistic strategy to protect telephone patents.[48] If Bell continued its licensing policy, there would be nothing to prevent Bell's contracted manufacturers from supplying rival telephone companies after the expiration of the basic patents. In 1881, Bell purchased 40 per cent of the stock of Western Union, which was soon wholly owned by Bell. Backward integration forced Bell's competitors to obtain their own sources of supply after 1893.

In 1885, American Telegraph and Telephone, AT&T, was created as a wholly owned subsidiary of American Bell to construct and operate long-distance lines. It was organised largely to overcome the obstacles the Bell System was experiencing in raising the capital to construct long-lines. Later, in 1899, AT&T acquired all the assets of the American Bell Telephone Company. A central administration was established to provide a national telephone service, and evaluate and monitor the performance of operating companies and the company as a whole.

AT&T formed an engineering department which was responsible for coordinating research activities, raising capital to develop and introduce costly new equipment, and making improvements in traffic methods, operation and design of the system. Local companies had exclusive rights to use all inventions owned and controlled by AT&T's long-lines department. AT&T had a workforce of specialists which advised local companies in such matters as general engineering, plant, traffic, operating, administrative, accounts, and legal issues, which were necessary for the efficient operation of the system. Efforts to standardise the national network, and harmonise operating procedures, depended on the formation of a centralised authority.

However, the administrative function of the managerial hierarchy set up by AT&T never attained the level of centralisation posited in Chandler's (1977) preferred paradigm of organisation. By the late 1880s, the Bell Company had cultivated a decentralised culture founded upon an entrepreneurial class of local capitalists who managed local exchange operations. Bell's management faced a dilemma: it could either continue to follow the traditional policy of allowing local agents to plan, construct and manage their operations, or introduce greater centralisation. There were two schools of thought: those who wanted to form a simple holding company, leaving scope for administrative and financial responsibility at the local level; and, those in the 'Think Big' school, like Vail and Forbes, who envisioned the country covered by telephone lines under centralised control.

At the end of the patent monopoly era the main source of revenue was still the local exchange operations. But it was the long-distance monopoly, constructed at considerable expense, that guaranteed American Bell's dominant position during the subsequent phase of competition.

Competition and consolidation (1894–1913)

After the expiration of the basic telephone patents, the local, long-distance and manufacturing arms of the Bell System were exposed to competition from companies attracted by monopoly profits earned by Bell. At the beginning of this final cycle of concentration, the telephone industry experienced widespread economic decentralisation. The number of new independent telephone subscribers grew rapidly, rising from 30,000 in 1894 to 656,000 in 1899. There were three kinds of local telephone competition: first, new local operating companies, including municipal authorities; second, mutual systems owned cooperatively by subscribers themselves and organised into exchanges with a central switchboard; third, informally organised telephone exchanges called 'farmer lines', connecting households and farms in rural areas with single or multiple lines. The independent telephone companies acquired their equipment from a variety of new manufacturers, rather than Bell's integrated manufacturing supplier.

Demand for the services of independent telephone companies grew rapidly. In 1894 eighty commercial systems and seven mutual systems were established, and 15,000 independent telephones had been installed accounting for 5 per cent of the market. The success of the early rivals to the Bell System stimulated widespread telephone competition and a growth in the telephone service. At the end of the patent monopoly there were 266,431 telephones in operation, all owned by Bell.[49] By the end of 1902, however, 3,057 non-Bell local telephone systems and 988 mutual systems had been established. In the same year, Bell operated 1,317,178 telephones in comparison with 1,053,866 telephones operated by the independent companies. The proportions of market share were the same in 1907, when Bell maintained approximately 3.1 million telephones compared to 3 million owned by the independents. By the beginning of the twentieth century, the extensive spatial development of the telephone service was largely complete; there were few remaining 'virgin territories' – locations where there was no telephone but enough people to make it profitable. Companies subsequently concentrated on the intensive spatial development of telephone markets, driven by direct competition between two or more telephone systems in the same area. Overall the drive to realise new markets forced substantial rate reductions, and brought the telephone service within reach of new and larger markets.[50]

Competition eroded Bell's monopoly profits and encouraged Bell to accelerate its programme of investment in a nationwide exchange system. This raised Bell's fixed capital requirements and provided a further incentive to minimise costs. From 1890 to 1895, the value of Bell-related telephone plant and equipment increased from $53.5

million to $70.1 million; mainly due to the heavy fixed costs of constructing long-lines.[51] The dilemma facing Bell was that although the number of subscribers connected to the network increased rapidly after 1894, the company's marginal return of capital fell dramatically. Rate reductions induced by price competition with the independents led to a decline in net earnings on individual telephone stations from $34 in 1893 to $20 in 1900.[52]

To finance the expansion of American Bell, the company was forced to move from the localised and entrepreneurial environment of Massachusetts to the newly centralised capital markets of New York. Because the New York charter of AT&T offered better opportunities for access to national financial capital, American Bell transferred its assets to AT&T, and in the course of transactions doubled Bell's capitalisation. From 1900, AT&T continued to operate long-distance lines, and became the parent company for the Bell System as a whole. The moment AT&T started to fund growth with outside capital was the time when external financiers began to exercise control over the direction of the company.[53] The move to New York symbolised the fusion of AT&T's big-business interests with those of investment bankers. In early 1907, after a review of AT&T's management and organisation, investment bankers on the company's board selected Theodore Vail, who had resigned in 1887, to become AT&T's president. Vail was closely allied with the Morgan Banking Group: both had the same vision of a nationwide system of communications.

From the late 1880s, a centralised management structure was introduced incrementally. The idea of 'system performance' began to take hold amongst the managers in Bell and the local companies. Engineering meetings and conferences were the means by which technical standards were agreed amongst the Bell officials. A particularly important administrative change was the uniform accounting system devised by Thomas Sherwin, which provided a comparison of depreciation charges, toll service accounts, assets and local operating expenses. This accounting method improved the flow of accurate information concerning operating and revenue statistics from local agents to Bell's headquarters.

A special committee was set up by Fish, president of AT&T between 1901 and 1906, which studied management structures in other major corporations such as US Steel and the railways. The committee recommended that the traditional territorial management structure, with local services under the control of local capitalists, be replaced by a highly rationalised, centralised management structure specialised along functional lines. After 1907, with the support of the Morgan Banking Group, Vail's strategy was to restore AT&T's dominant position in the market by reasserting his belief in the single objective: 'one system, one policy, universal service'. Vail considered the territorial configuration to be the main obstacle to a nationwide interconnected system.

Frederick W. Taylor's scientific management techniques were adopted by Bell management in an attempt to replace the old territorial structure with a functional organisation. First, a managerial structure was created which divided the task of providing the telephone service into specialised sub-units of labour under plant, traffic and commercial activities. Second, a single authority was instituted to coordinate these discrete functions. General corporate functions were separated from the day-to-day provision of the telephone service, so that top management could concentrate on the provision of system oriented solutions, rather than geographically focused ones. By 1910, the central administration had ten regional divisions which supervised the local districts, a structure Bell retained until the 1980s. The engineering activities of Western Electric and AT&T were consolidated to eliminate diversity in the equipment of local and long-distance operations. Licensees were required to implement compatible equipment to conform with system-wide production requirements.

AT&T emulated the highly centralised management structure established in the railways. Chandler (1977) maintains that the communications firm was only involved in handling a single kind of traffic, and therefore never became as complex to manage as the railways which had to coordinate flows of passengers, goods and messages. In consequence, rather than invent their own administrative structure, managers in AT&T adopted the centralised style of railway management.[54]

Although the telephone furnished a through service, there were in fact two kinds of traffic: in 1907, for example, long-distance traffic accounted for 3.1 per cent of Bell's total volume of messages, and the remaining 96.9 per cent were local calls. Bell's operations controlling local traffic were difficult to reorganise along specialised functional lines: firstly, because of long-standing traditions of local company autonomy; secondly, due to AT&T's lack of complete ownership of the operating companies; and, thirdly, because efficiencies in specialisation could only be achieved in large local operations. Tighter centralised control and rationalisation of smaller local operations did not increase efficiency and reduce costs.[55] Not surprisingly, the influence of Taylorism amongst AT&T's executives and engineers never took hold in small local companies.

Hence the management structure for local operations, finally implemented in October 1909, was a compromise between centralisation and decentralisation. AT&T's headquarters had broad responsibility for financial planning and policy issues, and local companies had to implement corporate standards and policies. The new organisation introduced specialisation of tasks into local operations: whereas under the old territorial structure district managers were 'generalists', under the functional organisation managers became specialists in plant, traffic and commercial activities. Although this uniform management structure and technical standardisation slowly spread throughout Bell's operations, local operations remained decentralised in the sense that local managers retained considerable latitude in the organisation of specialised tasks, and the flexibility to deal with local markets and regulatory conditions.

With the incorporation of AT&T, the basic organisational form of the modern Bell System was established: vertically integrated supply, a horizontal network of local operating companies, and overall coordination of the whole system by the parent company. However, the Bell System did not fully conform to the principles of industrial efficiency proposed by Chandler (1977). Bell managed a network it did not entirely own. Indeed it is probable that the relatively decentralised management style of the early Bell System, which was composed of licensed operators and interconnected to independently owned companies, enhanced efficiency by avoiding the creation of a top-heavy centralised bureaucracy.[56] As we will now see from an alternative view of the historical development of the system, the technological scale of the telephone service could have been organised differently, based on a federal system composed of independent operators linked to a single independent long-lines company.

Failure of independent competition and Bell's monopoly tactics
The formation of an alternative federal organisation of independent telephone companies failed, not because this organisational form was less efficient, but because it was blocked by the monopoly strategies of AT&T and its financiers. Thus the defence of the

national monopoly paradigm depended on monopolistic tactics akin to robber barons (characteristic of many monopolies during the late nineteenth-century period in American industrial history), rather than efficiency decisions of Bell's management.[57]

New independent companies with only a few subscribers, and no long-distance service, found it difficult to attract customers. Their main competitive strategy was to offer lower rates. In the beginning, those independent companies engaged in intensive competition in Bell operating territories were successful with isolated systems because they could undercut Bell's high prices. For some independent companies, this was a disastrous policy. It led to under-maintenance, poor service and bankruptcy. Like the earlier phase of competition, dramatic reductions in rates offered by independents attracted so many subscribers that average costs increased and the independents were forced to increase rates and seek additional capital for expansion.[58]

Many independent companies offered strong competition, lasting for several decades, in the local telephone service, and frequently operated a profitable service. The well-organised independent companies were highly innovative and able to provide a high quality service while adapting to changing market conditions and increasing traffic volumes over time. Independents often furnished a more modern and better service at comparable or lower rates than the Bell companies.[59] Some of the Bell companies met competition by improvements in service and reductions in rates. The rapid innovation and ability to tailor services to local requirements realised under independent ownership often outweighed the organisational economies of scale attributed to Bell's integrated network of operating companies. Again, competition in local exchange areas resulted in a duplication of telephone plant and service, and eventually favoured the re-establishment of geographical monopolies.[60] However, the main advantage of the Bell System had nothing to do with greater efficiency. Composed of many exchanges, the Bell System lowered rates in one territory to meet competition, while losses could be recovered in exchange areas where no competition existed.[61]

Independent competition was weakened by one fundamental problem: the companies lacked long-distance facilities comparable to those of the Bell System. Subscribers of independent exchanges demanded interconnection with the 'outside world', and in the absence of interconnection with the Bell System, the independents were forced to build their own long-distance facilities. Competition exposed the disadvantages of isolated exchanges, and encouraged the independents to seek mutual assistance in fighting the Bell companies. In 1897, the independent companies organised a federal association called the National Association of Independent Telephone Exchanges. The association aimed to form a union of independent companies in the United States for mutual protection, cooperation and development, and to establish long-distance facilities between independent exchanges throughout the country. A further step by the association to form an independent long-distance network was taken in 1899 when the Telephone, Telegraph and Cable Company (TTCC) was organised with an authorised capital of $30 million.

This independent long-distance service would have had a good chance of succeeding in competition with AT&T, if the association had not faced difficulties in raising capital. When they did not attract the support of the large investment bankers, William C. Whitney and J.P. Morgan, other financial concerns refused to participate in the venture. The finance was blocked because J.P. Morgan and his associates, who later financed the growth of AT&T, displayed their preference for the Bell System by refusing to help the independent rival.[62] In spite of the lack of capital, the TTCC provided strong competition to the Bell System in seven states.[63]

At the same time, another rival organisation was being established in the Middle West. It was set up by Bell licensees and provided an internal competitive threat to the centralised authority of AT&T. It was outside the central control of the Bell System because AT&T only had a minority interest in these operating companies. The Erie Telephone and Telegraph Company, a holding company, had obtained stock control of five Bell licensees: the Cleveland Telephone Company, the Northwest Telephone Exchange Company, the Michigan Telephone Company, the Southwest Telephone and Telegraph Company, and the Wisconsin Telephone Company. They operated about 15 per cent of the total number of lines in the Bell System. In granting licences to these companies AT&T had agreed not to compete in their territories.

When the independent interests behind the TTCC obtained control of the Erie Telephone and Telegraph Company, the federal association secured control of operating companies which used Bell patents and were protected against Bell competition. A large independent, nationwide system of long-lines might have been erected which would have created the basis for efficient competition, and might have broken Bell's monopoly.[64] But the federal association exhausted its limited resources in acquiring control of the Erie company, and could not furnish the capital needed to develop long-distance facilities. C.W. Morse, one of the directors of the TTCC, was engaged by the Bell interests to purchase two-thirds of the stock of the TTCC, at half the price the stockholders had paid, without revealing that he represented the Bell interests, and that his funds were supplied by the Bell organisation.[65] The Erie company was initially reorganised, its assets acquired by a company controlled by AT&T, before finally being dissolved.

Lacking a long-distance system, local independent companies, even if they were highly efficient, could not match the extensive service offered by the Bell System. The competition between the independents and the Bell companies continued actively until 1914. From 1907 to 1913, under Vail's leadership, the Bell System embarked on a programme of horizontal mergers. The Bell organisation established a policy to purchase competing exchanges. In 1909, AT&T purchased 30 per cent of Western Union's stock, which restored the link between the telegraph and telephone broken by the 1879 settlement. The policy of mergers aroused criticism from the independents, who eventually took their complaints to the Federal Department of Justice.

The independents complained that the Bell System had deliberately set about attaining a national monopoly by unfair means. First, the Bell System purchased competing lines to destroy competition which otherwise provided a better service at lower rates. Second, it refused to interconnect its long-distance facilities with the local lines of independent companies. Third, in those instances where interconnection was granted, Bell furnished poor interconnections, which discouraged subscribers of the independent system and drove them into the Bell System. Under mounting political pressure and the threat of action under the Sherman anti-trust law, Nathan Kingsbury, the vice-president of AT&T, entered into negotiations with the attorney general which resulted in the 'Kingsbury Commitment' of 13 December 1913. Under this commitment AT&T agreed to dispose of its stock of Western Union, allow interconnection with all remaining independent companies, and refrain from seeking acquisitions of directly competing companies.

Agreement to interconnect reduced competition between Bell and the independents. In many territories, the new policy still resulted in a duplication of telephone service which was uneconomical and wasteful, and tended to raise the cost of the service to subscribers. In the following years, the duplicate situations were adjusted to create local monopolies: in one territory the Bell company acquired the property of the independent; in another the independent acquired the property of the Bell company. The Bell organisation continued to merge with independents after 1913, but at a slower rate. By 1932, the Bell System accounted for 79 per cent of the market share for telephones.

The Kingsbury Commitment transformed the telephone industry from one evenly divided between Bell and the independents, with direct competition, into an interconnected system dominated by Bell, with no direct competition. Because there was only one long-distance system with every local exchange connected to it, and every local company had a geographical monopoly, the national service could be operated in a unified way as if it were under a single company's control. In 1934, there were 16,800,000 telephones installed in the United States, of which 13,378,103 were operated by the Bell companies, the remainder being operated by 6,700 connecting companies and 25,300 rural lines.[66]

Conclusion

In this chapter I have argued that the early development of the telephone under competitive conditions was driven by the desire to obtain economies of high fixed-cost telecommunications systems by sustaining high levels of capacity utilisation. By the 1920s, the cycles of competition culminated in mergers and consolidation. Most of the telephones in the United States were operated by AT&T and its twenty-four associated companies. Technically, the telephone system consisted of a hierarchy of monopolies: including a single long-distance service under centralised administration, interworked with numerous exchange operations administered by local monopolies. An efficient and economical national telephone system depended upon the economies of system associated with the standardisation, common administration and operation, and coordination of research activities undertaken by a centralised long-distance operator.

Yet a natural monopoly was not inevitable. The technology of the telephone system merely sets limits to the possible organisational forms. Indeed the organisational arrangement that eventually dominated the Bell System was more decentralised than Chandler's (1977) ideal form of industrial efficiency. Bell dominated a system it did not entirely own, and the management style was relatively decentralised during these early years. Moreover, the national monopoly organisational form was not the product of inexorable technological progress towards the most efficient solution. The Bell interests, supported by powerful financial institutions, eliminated competition from rival long-distance operators by preventing the alternative systems from receiving financial support. Under slightly different historical conditions it is possible that a federation of autonomous telephone companies could have matched the advantages attributed to an integrated monopoly. As we will see in chapter 3, the organisation of national telephone systems in the United States and Europe was also shaped by the intervention of the nation state.

Notes

1. Alfred D. Chandler (1977); *The Visible Hand: The Managerial Revolution in American Business*, Belknap Press, Harvard University Press, Cambridge, Mass. Chandler's work is located in the industrial organisation school of economics concerned with the relationship between the strategy and structure of industry. It is worth concentrating on the Chandlerian view that integration was the key to industrial efficiency because this assumption has become influential amongst communication researchers. His findings were cited by AT&T management in defence of the efficiency of the national monopoly and to support internal reorganisations in the late 1970s. Two important Chandlerian accounts of early telephone history include George D. Smith (1985), *The Anatomy of Business Enterprise: Bell, Western Electric, and the Origins of the American Telephone Industry*, Johns Hopkins University Press, Baltimore; and G.W. Garnett (1985), *The Telephone Enterprise: The Evolution of the Bell System's Horizontal Structure, 1876–1909*, Johns Hopkins University Press, Baltimore.

2. The importance of carrying large volumes of traffic to recover sunk capital infrastructural investments is explained by K. Marx pp529–531 (1973), *Grundrisse: Foundations of the Critique of Political Economy*, Penguin, Harmondsworth.

3. Improvements in the service which derive from the growing number of subscribers interconnected to a single network are called network externalities. Users of one system can only use the facilities of another if network technologies are compatible. If networks are incompatible, users of the larger system benefit from access to a greater number of subscribers. See M.L. Katz and C. Shapiro (1985), 'Network

Externalities. Competition and Compatibility', pp424–440, *American Economic Review*, Vol. 75, No. 3.

4. M. Mueller (1989), 'The Switchboard Problem: Scale, Signalling, and Organisation in Manual Telephone Switching, 1877–1897', pp534–560, *Technology and Culture*, Vol. 30, No. 3.

5. A.D. Chandler, chapter two (1990), *Scale and Scope: The Dynamics of Industrial Capitalism*, Belknap Press, Cambridge, Mass.

6. The long-run average cost curve is L-shaped; after initially falling, costs remained constant. S.C. Littlechild p57 (1979), *Elements of Telecommunications Economics*, IEE, Peregrinus, London.

7. p28. ibid. For more general discussion of this aspect of scale see B. Gold p12 (1981), 'Changing Perspectives on Size, Scale and Returns: An Interpretive Survey', pp5–33, *Journal of Economic Literature*, Vol. 14.

8. J.M. Herring and G.C. Cross, p200 (1936), *Telecommunications: Economics and Regulation*, McGraw-Hill, New York.

9. Mueller, p550, op. cit.

10. Herring and Cross, p54, op. cit.

11. p55, ibid.

12. The load on a network is defined as the call arrivals per second times the average call duration in seconds. The unit of load calculated in this way is known as the erlang, after A.K. Erlang, the inventor of traffic theory.

13. J.C. Panzar and R.D. Willig (1982), 'Economies of Scope', pp268–272, *American Economic Review*, Vol. 71, No. 2.

14. Herring and Cross, p200, op. cit.

15. The general concept of organisational complexity is described by D. Bell p29 (1976), *The Coming of Post-Industrial Society: A Venture in Social Forecasting*, Basic Books, New York.

16. Herring and Cross, pp189–190.

17. Frank Gill (1922), 'Inaugural Address', *The Institution of Electrical Engineers*, IEE Journal, Vol. 61, No. 313.

18. This situation is analogous to the technology of electric power systems. If parts of power systems are owned by different firms, externality problems may arise (i.e., the effects of positive or negative actions of one individual actor on another) *unless* those firms can be made to bear the consequences of their actions. See P.L. Joskow and R. Schmalensee (1983), *Markets for Power: An Analysis of Electric Utility Deregulation*, MIT Press, Cambridge, Mass.

19. Garnett, p171, op. cit., provides the following definition of the horizontal integration of the Bell System: 'All of the parts of business performing a similar function (e.g., distribution) are said to be horizontally related to each other, and that relationship, marked by lines of corporate oversight and authority, defines the horizontal structure of the business. Thus the corporate ties encompassing the management of the twenty-three local Bell Telephone companies that together delivered local exchange services across the country and AT&T represent the horizontal structure of the business.'

20. Chandler adopts the 'classical synthesis' of political economists like

Smith and Marx. His argument is that the logic of industrial efficiency is founded upon improvements in productivity through investments in new technologies and specialised resources, resulting in lower unit costs, which in turn is a stimulus to a growth in demand. See M.J. Piore and C.F. Sabel, pp38–39 (1984), *The Second Industrial Divide: Possibilities for Prosperity*. Basic Books, New York.

21. P.A. David (1992), 'Heroes, Herds and Hysteresis in Technological History: Thomas Edison and the "Battle of the Systems" Reconsidered', pp129–180, *Industrial and Corporate Change*, Vol. 1, No. 1.

22. The underlying theoretical perspective in this chapter refers to the work of Roberto Unger who emphasises the multiple pathways, or branching points that societies face at specific conjunctures. He recognises the importance of identifying the origins and causes of institutional forms, and the possibility of alternative arrangements in history. See (1987), *False Necessity*, Cambridge University Press, Cambridge.

23. Max Weber put it this way: 'The fact that a given specific social relationship has been eliminated for reasons peculiar to a particular situation, proves nothing about "its fitness to survive" in general terms', p135 (1964), *The Theory of Social and Economic Organisation*, The Free Press, New York.

24. Thomas P. Hughes, who is critical of Chandler's technological determinism, argues that although the organisational form follows from technological structure, the technological system is reciprocally influenced by organisational decisions. See Hughes (1983), *Networks of Power: Electrification in Western Society, 1880–1930*, Johns Hopkins University Press, Baltimore. See other articles by Hughes: 'The Order of the Technological World', *History of Technology*, Fifth Annual Volume (1980) (eds) A. Rupert Hall and N. Smith, Mansell Publishing, London.

25. T.P. Hughes, p55 (1987), 'The Evolution of Large Technological Systems', pp51–82 in *The Social Construction of Technological Systems: New Directions in the Sociology and History of Technology* (eds) W.E. Bijker, T.P. Hughes and T.J. Pinch, MIT Press, Cambridge, Mass.

26. On the differences between monopoly, competition and cooperation see G.B. Richardson (1972), 'The Organisation of Industry', pp883–896, *Economic Journal*, September 1972.

27. Gill, op. cit.

28. G.W. Brock (1981), *The Telecommunications Industry: The Dynamics of Market Structure*. Harvard University Press, Cambridge, Mass.

29. According to Hughes, p.57 (1987), op. cit., inventions can either be radical or conservative: 'Those occurring during the invention phase are radical because they inaugurate a new system; conservative inventions predominate during the phase of competition and system growth, for they improve or expand existing systems'.

30 E.P. Douglas, pp487–488 (1971), *The Coming of Age of American Business: Three Centuries of Enterprise, 1600–1900*, University of North Carolina Press, Chapel Hill.

31. In 1877, telephone technology could have been organised to complement rather than compete with the telegraph system. Between

1878 and 1880, the telephone was limited to transmission of about twenty miles. Although a web of long-distance telegraph lines straddled the American continent in the late 1870s, a local telegraph service was only profitable for a certain class of business customers. The notable example was Western Union's subsidiary, Gold and Stock Telegraph, which transmitted price quotations from the stock exchange to brokers' offices. The local telephone direct private-line service was less cumbersome to operate than local telegraphs. The telegraphs needed expert operators, and encoded messages had to be retranscribed at the receiving end. The telephone only needed an operator to connect subscribers, and it provided the additional benefit of almost instantaneous voice communications. If the two communications systems had been joined together, local communication needs could have been furnished by the telephone, and long-distance by the telegraph. See Brock, pp91, 97, op. cit.

32. There are three possible reasons for Western Union's decision: that experience had shown that many rival telegraph inventions turned out to be insignificant, that the telephone posed no direct threat to Western Union's lucrative long-distance message service for business users, and that Western Union had its own claims over a telephone patent. p92, ibid.

33. Garnett, p15, op. cit.

34. H. Coon, p38 (1939), *American Tel & Tel: The Story of a Great Monopoly*, Longman, Green, New York.

35. Garnett, p23, op. cit.

36. Garnett, p23, op. cit.

37. Bell attempted to help its local affiliates meet the competition from Western Union by a number of means: providing phones rent-free, reducing the price charged for transmitters, and sometimes by taking responsibility for the costs of connecting a certain number of subscribers to Bell licensed exchange operations.

38. Garnett, p57, op. cit. Mueller, p541, op. cit., explains that the 'biggest exchanges needed twice as many operators to handle a given number of subscribers as the medium-sized exchanges, and three or four times that of the small exchanges'.

39. There are several possible contingent explanations. (i) Bell was in the process of filing a patent suit, filed in September 1879, against Western Union. Bell had a very strong patent position which drew Western Union into accommodation. (ii) Western Union sought a rapid solution to the telephone problem so that it was free to meet intensified telegraph competition from Atlantic and Pacific Telegraph in 1879. Western Union was particularly concerned about Bell joining forces with the rival telegraph company to form a combined telegraph and telephone power. (iii) The desire to protect its monopoly over telegraphy, particularly the lucrative business market for long-distance communications, and the unlikelihood of long-distance telephony emerging in the foreseeable future, made Western Union less interested in the new market for telephonic communications.

40. Western Union agreed to withdraw from the telephone service for

seventeen years, sell its network of 56,000 telephones in fifty-five Cities to Bell, transfer its telephone patent rights to Bell, and pay 20 per cent of the cost of all new Bell telephone patents for the seventeen year period. In return, Bell agreed to stay out of the telegraph business, turn over to Western Union all telegraph messages that came under its control, and pay 20 per cent of its rental from telephones to Western Union.

41. Chandler, p201 (1977), op. cit. In 1879, Vail believed that interconnection of local exchanges provided the foundations of Bell's monopoly: 'the status of the telephone patent was a little uncertain. What we wanted to do was to get possession of the field in such a way that, patent or no patent, we could control it. No exchange could exist without being tied up with every other exchange', Vail quoted in Coon, p60, op. cit.
42. Chandler, p201 (1977), op. cit.
43. As long as its highly profitable long-distance telegraph monopoly remained intact, Western Union was not opposed to opening up the long-distance market to telephone competition, particularly since the amplification of voice over large distances seemed a remote possibility at this time.
44. Garnett, p77, op. cit
45. In 1880 AT&T's net income was only $21,768 on revenues of $146,555; in 1889 its net return increased, but was still only 1.75 per cent on a capital investment valued at $3 million. Garnett, p81, op. cit.
46. Vail maintained that profits should be reinvested in the expansion of the long-distance system. In a disagreement with Bell's management Vail resigned in September 1887 because he believed that American Bell's stockholders were too greedy for cash returns. See Coon, p66, op. cit.
47. Garnett, pp74–89, op. cit.
48. Smith, pp96–120, op. cit.
49. See R. Gabel (1969), 'The Early Competitive Era in Telephone Communication, 1893–1920', *Law and Contemporary Problems*, Vol. 34.
50. p345, ibid.
51. Garnett, p103, op. cit.
52. In part this decline was counterbalanced by decreasing per station costs from $58 in 1895 to $44 in 1905. p108, ibid.
53. After 1907, J.P. Morgan, chairman of the AT&T board of directors, exercised influence behind the scenes, possibly through Vail. See J. Brooks, p128 (1975), *Telephone: The First Hundred Years*, Harper and Row, New York.
54. Chandler, p189, op. cit.
55. Garnett, p138, op. cit. explains: 'For small district operations manned by no more than a handful of employees, the straightforward adoption of the new, three-column structure would almost certainly add to existing staff. Local managers remained skeptical concerning the thin prospects of realizing gains in economy and efficiency under these conditions.'
56. Douglas, op. cit.

57. M. Josephson (1934), *The Robber Barons: The Great American Capitalists*, Harcourt, Brace and Co., New York.
58. Mueller, p558, op. cit.
59. Herring and Cross, p63, op. cit.
60. Brooks, p104, op. cit.: 'A citizen who wished to be in touch with all other telephone users needed to have two phones and two directories: before making a call, he had to know which system the person being called was a subscriber to'.
61. Herring and Cross, op. cit.
62. Coon, p86, op. cit.
63. ibid.
64. pp87–88, ibid; Herring and Cross, p64, op. cit.
65. Coon, p88, op. cit.
66. Herring and Cross, p67, op. cit., from the Annual Report of AT&T, 1934, p18.

3 National monopoly and the decentralised alternative

The organisation of telephone systems depended on the balance of political and economic interests in particular nation states. This power relation determined the various forms of state intervention in the telephone industry.[1] The pattern of monopoly ownership in each country was shaped by the power of the state to privilege or penalise economic and institutional interests. Struggles over the shape of the institutional structure took place between central and municipal governments, between state telegraph monopolies and private telephone companies offering competing long-distance services, and in local exchange operations between municipal, private and state-owned operations.

By the 1920s the policy of telephone competition had failed. Competition resulted in private monopolies, and while it endured, it led to a wasteful duplication of plant and equipment. The national monopoly became the dominant form of organisation, with local and long-distance services centrally operated as a single system under state-ownership or state-regulation. In Europe, the legal monopoly held by state telegraphic administrations was extended to the telephone from the late 1870s. Even in countries like Britain and France, where private telephone capital was given the opportunity to develop under franchise agreements, the activities of private telephone companies were always constrained by the legal power invoked by state-owned telegraph monopolies. By the 1920s, state-owned national monopolies administered local and long-distance operations in most European countries. In the United States the provision of the telephone service was dominated by a state-regulated private monopoly. The American government made one attempt to place the early telephone system under a public monopoly. When the United States entered the First World War in 1917 mounting political pressure to nationalise the telephone industry was – after a short-lived episode in government ownership – resisted by the private Bell monopoly, and this marked the end of further experiments in telephone nationalisation.

There was, however, an alternative to the national monopoly.[2] In the United States and in Europe, there were municipal and local movements in favour of placing local telephone monopolies in the hands of local authorities or private enterprises, leaving long-lines under the control of a state monopoly. Although telephone localism was largely defeated by the regulatory solution in the United States and the statist solution in most of Europe, it survived and continued to exist after the 1920s in Denmark, Finland, the Netherlands, and the municipality of Hull in Britain. For many historians of telephony, the regional system is merely a curiosity; an organisational relic of little significance.[3] On the contrary, these exceptions illustrate the possibility that under different historical circumstances an institutional structure composed of independent local monopolies could have been a viable alternative to the national monopoly model.

1. The United States: national monopoly under private ownership

In the United States, the national monopoly structure of the telegraphs and telephones was designed, constructed, operated and financed by private enterprise. By the 1930s independent operators controlled less than 20 per cent of telephones. Political struggles to place telephone operations under municipal or state ownership had been defeated. A compromise was reached between AT&T and the American government which preserved private ownership of the national telephone monopoly. Federal regulation was accepted and the telephone monopoly was allowed to retain private ownership and centralised control over much of the American telephone network.

When the telephone was commercialised in the United States in 1877 there was no state-owned telegraph agency.[4] In Europe, state telegraph administrations, motivated by the aim to protect sunk capital invested in public telegraphs, deliberately restricted the infant telephone industry. It was the absence of an existing public communications utility which marked the fundamental difference between telephone development in the United States and Europe. With little government interference, private economic interests struggled over the control of the American telephone system. After the expiration of the basic Bell patents, a regime of competition between Bell and the independents soon passed into a phase of consolidation after 1907 as Bell re-established a private monopoly position.

By 1930, the $5 billion Bell system had become the world's biggest monopoly, a giant combination of financial and industrial power, with 454,000 employees, and the largest concentration of capital controlled by a single company in the history of private enterprise; all held together by centralised control.[5] Composed of 200 separate companies, the Bell System operated 83 per cent of telephone stations in service, 91 per cent of plant, controlled 98 per cent of long-distance wires, and accounted for 90 per cent of the total telephone revenues in the United States. Through the vertically integrated manufacturing subsidiary, the Western Electric Company, the Bell System manufactured more than 90 per cent of telephone equipment for the American market.

The perfection of long-distance voice transmission during the first decade of the twentieth century made the telephone a matter of Federal interest, in the same way as the integration of regional railways had in the 1880s. The formation of the national telephone system under private control was accompanied by a struggle between economic power and political power. AT&T had become sufficiently powerful to exercise influence over the American state.[6] This conflict between private and public interests resulted in what became known as the 'monopoly question': should economic power control government, or government dominate economic power? While the American state made no attempts to dominate private telephone interests by breaking up the Bell System into competing groups, there was political sentiment in favour of placing the Bell System under public ownership or Federal regulation. Although AT&T continued to pursue a national private monopoly through the programme of mergers after 1907, some justification of this monopolistic behaviour was needed to avoid the threat of government ownership or anti-trust action.

Eventually a compromise was reached. In 1907, AT&T recognised that a private unregulated monopoly would not be accepted without some form of public control. AT&T's market power was threatened by three kinds of political intervention. First, between 1907 and 1912 many independent companies had filed charges against AT&T under state anti-trust laws which prevented some of Bell's proposed mergers. However, AT&T was more concerned about Federal anti-trust action under the Sherman Act, because successful prosecutions of Standard Oil and American Tobacco proved that Federal government was prepared to break up monopolies. Second, in the first decade of the twentieth century, there was widespread support for both municipal and government ownership of the telephone system. Third, by 1907 there was increasing political support for state and Federal regulation of private monopolies. Railways had been regulated by the Interstate Commerce Commission (ICC) for almost two decades, and by this time, twelve states had a regulatory commission with varying degrees of authority over telephone rates and operations.

From 1907, a growing number of regulatory commissions were established by individual states. AT&T aimed to avoid the growing threat of municipal ownership by accepting the authority of the state utility commissions. On the West Coast the radical movement for 'home rule' and municipal ownership by local councils competed with the more conservative state regulatory agencies for control over telephone operations. Claims for municipal control were dismissed by state agencies because the latter argued that telephone operations were integrated by the long-distance lines of the Pacific Telephone Company which extended across several states.[7]

Under Vail's direction AT&T decided to welcome state and Federal regulation, and in this way reduced the risk that the Bell System would be dismantled by anti-trust action or placed under public ownership. With the agreement of Bell and the independents, the Interstate Commerce Commission Act was amended by the Mann–Elkins Act of 1910 which placed interstate telephone companies under the Federal jurisdiction of the ICC. The ICC only had nominal power over interstate telephone operations, confined to prescribing accounting systems and investigating complaints. In 1913 the Department of Justice began monitoring the activities of AT&T after independent local companies lodged complaints regarding AT&T's policies of purchasing competing companies and refusing to interconnect with independently owned local operations. Under pressure to negotiate with the public authorities, AT&T reached a compromise with Federal government under the Kingsbury Commitment of 1913.

Regulation served as a check – in the absence of the check of competition – on the abuse of monopoly power. This compromise served Bell's interests: not only did it prevent loss of market control effected by the other two forms of intervention, it allowed AT&T to influence state and Federal regulation. State regulatory commissions had not been effective in controlling telephone companies, and the experience of Federal regulation of the railways demonstrated that regulation had not reduced profitability. AT&T used regulation to support its claim for monopoly control of national telephony. In the hope that public regulatory authorities would permit a combination of Bell and the independent competitors, Vail began advocating the benefits of regulation.

Vail claimed that a regulated large-scale monopoly would furnish a cheaper and better service than competition or public ownership. Moreover, if Federal regulation was imposed, and the Bell System was required to serve the whole community, it should be protected from competitors serving only profitable telephone markets. Vail intended to realise his technological vision of a telephone infrastructure provided as 'one system, one policy, universal service'. A centrally managed national system under public regulation would avoid redundancy in telephone operations, and the decline in quality incurred by uncontrolled competition.

Public ownership of the American telephone system was brought to the fore by the nationalisation of the telephone in Britain on 1 January 1912. There was growing public support in favour of the 'postalisation' of the telegraph and telephone, placing both systems under the control of the government-operated and owned postal service. The leading advocate of government ownership was Congressman Lewis. He argued that government ownership was necessary when monopoly rather than competition determined price. Lewis criticised the 'institutional efficiency' of the Bell System, on the basis that the number of phone calls per employee per year was below capacity. To improve rates, plant capacity utilisation had to be improved. In response to such criticism AT&T claimed that the institutional efficiency of the Bell service was not only superior in quality compared with any other government-operated systems, it was cheaper and more extensive. In spite of AT&T's counter-evidence, the views of Lewis won the support of Postmaster-General Burleson, who on 25 November 1913 issued a report advocating government ownership of the telephones and telegraphs.

Political support of government ownership was rendered expedient by the entry of the United States into the First World War in 1917. The resources of the Bell System were mobilised in the service of the nation the moment war was declared. The contribution of the Bell System to the war effort showed that government ownership of telecommunications was not necessary in times of military emergency. The year of 1918 was, however, the most difficult in Bell's early history. Wartime demand for exchanges built in cantonments, aviation fields and naval yards, together with 14,000 of Bell's employees in war service, made it difficult to operate the American telephone network.

Advocates of postalisation pointed to the inconsistency of having the government take over the railways while leaving the telegraphs and telephones under private control. On 11 July 1918, Congress passed a resolution enabling Postmaster-General Burleson to administer the telegraphs and telephones. However, during the one-year period of federal control the telephone service operated at a deficit. Telephone rates were raised to cover increases in the costs of operation. On 29 April 1919, Burleson recommended the return of the telegraphs and telephones to the original private owners. Nevertheless, the experience of Federal operation proves nothing on the subject of public ownership of the telephones.[8] The one-year experiment was not an indication of government inefficiency because the Bell companies remained in charge of operations. Finally, AT&T was powerful enough to negotiate a favourable contract with government over the terms of compensation, executed on 5 October 1918.

Postalisation of the telephone was raised in Congress a number of times during the 1920s, but the Bell System was subject to greater Federal regulation rather than government ownership. In 1934, a committee of the Roosevelt administration recommended that AT&T be placed under strengthened and centralised regulation. In the same year, Congress established the Federal Communications Commission (FCC). The Communications Act of 1934 was an early New Deal measure which broadened the powers of the FCC. Whereas the FCC controlled the interstate telephone service, local telephone companies operated as geographical monopolies under state regulatory authorities.

Regulation gave the Bell System the legitimacy of a public utility. From 1934 to 1956, the Bell System operated as a quasi-public national monopoly. Yet a decentralised telephone system could have been more widespread, based on physical interconnection between a long-distance monopoly and connecting independent companies. But this institutional structure did not emerge as a substantial alternative to the national monopoly form. A national monopoly was successfully defended because of the financial and economic power of AT&T in the American political system. In 1956 the structure of the American telephone industry was virtually the same as in 1934. AT&T was the dominant company, controlling 80 per cent of the telephones and operating the only long-distance network. During the period, protection from competition was guaranteed by Federal regulation, and regulatory decisions substituted for the pressures of the market.

2. Europe: national monopolies under state ownership

National telephone monopolies under centralised operation and administration also became the dominant form of telephone organisation in Europe. However, in Europe this paradigm of telephone organisation was imposed by the state. Telephone systems were placed under state ownership in Germany, Russia, Switzerland, France, Britain, Hungary, Austria and Italy by the second decade of the twentieth century. The fundamental cause bringing about a transition to the state monopoly form was that the telegraphs were already in the hands of government. In order to protect telegraph revenues, most European state postal authorities either directly placed the telephone under public ownership, or deliberately restricted private telephone development before finally taking complete responsibility for the new system. State telephone monopolies inherited the highly centralised and bureaucratic structures of the traditional postal monopolies.

Origins of state communication monopolies: posts and telegraphs

The invention and development of all new means of communication were closely controlled and administered by European states from the seventeenth century. While not having the legal status of a state monopoly, postal systems were established by governments to provide state sovereigns with a rapid means of issuing military and political intelligence. Mail was sent by special messengers on horseback. The first state monopoly of the posts was established in Britain in 1609. A state postal service was created in Prussia in 1614. It was the need to have access to correspondence of suspected persons, and to open and read all foreign mails entering Britain, which provided the original motive behind the setting-up of the state monopoly in Britain.[9] During the next two centuries, the monopoly was more and more necessary to protect Post Office revenues from private competition. Poor service and high postal rates offered by the state system stimulated illicit rival postal systems. Private attempts to circumvent the state monopoly did not cease until the formation of the penny post in 1840, which cheapened and extended the state service.

Once institutionalised, state postal administrations displayed an active interest in controlling further improvements in communications, in the form of the telegraphs in the late 1830s and telephones in the late 1870s.[10] The telegraph came to be administered by the traditional postal monopolies in every European country by the 1860s. But there was considerable variation in the form of state intervention in the early telegraph industry in Europe. In Germany, France and Prussia, the state immediately controlled the telegraph to exploit its military and political potential. In smaller European countries the state was concerned with the social value of the telegraph and its use in integrating remote rural communities.

In Britain the economic motive of private enterprise guided telegraph development for twenty years before the state stepped in and nationalised the industry. Prior to 1864, there was no state intervention and no central planning of a coordinated telegraph network. The British telegraph industry was based on an invention patented by Edward Cooke and Charles Wheatstone in 1837, four months earlier than the Morse patent application in the United States. Although military–strategic factors were not used to justify state ownership of the telegraphs, the Telegraph Act of 1846 gave the Home Secretary the right to take possession of private telegraph interests in times of civil disturbance and national emergency. Such powers were exercised in 1848 when central government took control over the wires of the Electric Telegraph Company in order to obstruct lines of telegraphic communication among members of the revolutionary working class Chartist movement.

Arguments for the postalisation of the telegraph in Britain gained wider political acceptance after 1854. Support for nationalisation came from business users, especially the newspaper owners who believed they could receive a better service at lower rates if the telegraphs were administered by the British Post Office rather than private companies. But the strongest movement for public ownership came from the established state postal monopoly. The Scudamore Report released by the Postmaster-General in July 1866 was in favour of the purchase of the telegraphs by the Post Office.[11]

The Telegraph Act of 1 August 1869 placed all telegraph wires under a state monopoly. This was the first time the British government had intervened in the activities of private enterprise. Previously political intervention was confined to a controlling and checking power. A select committee in 1868, investigating the viability of postalisation, reiterated the justification for Post Office control of the telegraphs made by the Postmaster-General. The report argued that only under Post Office ownership could the telegraph be extended to unprofitable outlying areas, where low traffic volumes could not yield an adequate return for private companies. In order to furnish economies of scale and lower rates, the telegraph service had to be offered at uniform rate under centralised operation, using shared plant such as combined telegraph and post offices. In fact the comparison between the telegraphs and the postal system was exaggerated to furnish a rationale for ownership of the telegraphs by the Post Office. Whereas in the case of the penny post increases in the volume of traffic could be operated at low marginal costs, such economies of scale did not result from an expansion in the telegraph system.[12]

In those European nations like Prussia, Russia and France where the threat of war was continuous in the nineteenth century, the state-owned postal monopolies used the telegraph to improve the rapidity with which military and political information could be transmitted.[13] In France, for example, on the eve of the 1848 revolution, the Minister of the Interior declared to the Chamber of Deputies, on 12 July 1847, that the telegraph must remain exclusively a political instrument, denied to the general public. Private enterprise showed little interest in developing the electric telegraph in these countries. Even where no central government prevented private development of the telegraph – as was the case in Southern Germany – there were few attempts to exploit the commercial potential of the telegraph. Public ownership of the telegraphs was forced upon government in Southern Germany – and indeed most Continental European countries – due to the scarcity of private capital prepared to undertake such ventures.

Unlike Britain where the telegraph was used for business and residential purposes from its inauguration, the major Continental European countries did not open the telegraph service to the public until the 1850s. Yet state owned postal monopolies reserved the right of precedence over their own telegraph dispatches and exercised close control over the use of the telegraph by private individuals. In the smaller European states, which did not face the persistent danger of national wars or internal revolts, such as

Switzerland and Norway, the motive behind state ownership was primarily to facilitate communication between urban centres and outlying rural areas. For example, the main purpose of Switzerland's Law of 1851, which placed the telegraph under the direction of the government postal monopoly, was to extend telegraphic communications into remote rural areas.

State ownership of national telephone monopolies

In 1878 and 1879, American speculators entered Europe to establish private telephone companies working with Bell's patents or Edison's invention based on an improved transmitter. In 1879, for example, two private companies gained concessions to establish a local exchange service in London. However, the political circumstances which led to the postalisation of the telegraphs were repeated when the telephone was introduced into Europe. The decisive cause of the public ownership of the telephones in Europe was related to the institutional power vested in existing state postal monopolies, which controlled national telegraph networks and successfully extended their authority over the telephone. In comparison to the United States, the task of bringing about public ownership of the telephones in Europe was made easier by the strength of state postal administrations and the relative weakness of opposing private telephone interests.[14]

When the telephone first made its appearance, state postal monopolies were still under obligation to prove their capacity for the management of telegraph systems. The British Post Office, for example, proved unable to manage the telegraphs with economy and efficiency during the 1870s. The advantage of centralised management of the telegraphs on a large scale was under close public scrutiny. Alternative ways of organising the long-distance and local telephone operations were experimented with and introduced in various countries. State postal authorities had to realise the advantages of centralised management of the telegraphs, while taking steps to introduce the telephone, in order to justify the continuance of the policy of state ownership of communication monopolies.

Few European states sought to exploit the telephone for its military and political significance.[15] One exception was Austria, where the telephone was introduced in 1879 by the war department to facilitate the communication of military orders at the military headquarters in Cracow. In every European country governments retained the legal right to repossess the telephone in the event of war. In Britain, a clause in the Telegraph Act of 1878 allowing the government to control the telegraphs in times of national emergency, was applied to the telephone. One of the few countries to invoke military authority over the telephone on a permanent basis was the Nazi regime in Germany.[16] The Telegraph Law of 1892 had been amended under the Telecommunications Act of 1927, which placed the property rights of the telephone in the hands of the military. The law was enforced by the Nazi government to support its military and political command structure used to control the German population and occupied territories between 1933 and 1945.

In Germany and Switzerland, the policy of public telephone ownership was adopted as early as 1878 and 1880 respectively. Heinrich von Stephan was the prescient Postmaster-General in Germany who recognised the potential of the telephone, and in 1877 placed the new device under the control of the imperial telegraph service, so creating the world's first public telephone service. In 1877 the telephone rather than the telegraph was used in rural post offices to which the telegraph had not been extended, and by 1880 telephones were utilised in the German urban telegraph service. In Switzerland, the Federal Council issued an ordinance on 18 February 1878 which declared that the telephone came within the scope of the public telegraph monopoly. By 1880 demand for local telephone services in Zurich proved that the exchange business would be a profitable venture. The postal administration quickened the development of local and long-distance state telephones and extended the telephone service into rural communities.

Outside of Germany and Switzerland, the preliminary experimentation and introduction of the telephone in Europe was entrusted to private enterprise under licence obtained from state telegraph agencies. No other European telegraph administration was prepared to assume the initial risks of building telephone systems. The general institutional pattern in Europe was to place the telephone under the legal monopoly held by state telegraphs: the telephone was declared within the scope of the public telegraph monopoly in France in 1879, in Britain in 1880, in Belgium in 1883, and concessions to private companies were revised and placed on a uniform basis in Italy in 1883. State postal authorities offered highly restrictive licences allowing private companies the opportunity of developing the telephone business. The policy of private competition under licence offered advantages for state telegraph monopolies: state authorities avoided the risk of sinking public money into unsuccessful investments, and later when the telephone proved to be a substitute for the telegraphs, the state took the service back into public hands after paying private speculators a recompense. In some countries, private competition under licence was short-lived, and quickly replaced by a policy of public ownership in Austria in 1887, in Hungary in 1880, and in Belgium in 1893.

The terms of the concessions offered by the European postal authorities to private telephone business were designed to protect and conserve state telegraphs. Policies to shift the risk of the introduction of the telephone to the shoulders of private enterprise were abandoned when long-distance telephony proved to be a substitute for state telegraph systems. The development of long-distance telephony was held hostage to the state telegraph interests: from the mid-1880s government agencies were concerned to protect sunk capital invested in the telegraphs from the increasingly superior means of long-distance communication furnished by the telephone.

France: the selection of the national monopoly form
In France, the state telegraph administration took possession of the telephones in 1889 after a period of private competition.[17] On 26 June 1879, the minister of the postal and telegraph service issued a *cahier des charges* or model franchise, prescribing the conditions for private telephone companies. The conditions restricted the infant telephone industry and protected the government telegraphs. The franchise was limited to five years, without a definite provision for further prolongation or state purchase once the franchise had elapsed. Concessionaires were obliged to pay the government a prohibitive royalty of 10 per cent of their gross receipts. Three private telephone companies were amalgamated on 10 December 1880 into a single private monopoly called Société générale des téléphones. In 1882 the telegraph authorities, still unconvinced of the potential complementary relationship between the telegraphs and telephones, decided to gain experience in telephone operations by establishing government telephone exchanges. In 1885, the state telegraph authorities began the construction of long-distance lines between Paris and provincial cities. The telegraph authorities prevented the Société générale from developing long-distance telephony because this would introduce direct competition with the state telegraphs.

The development of long-distance telephone lines raised the question of the advisability of public ownership. Since the railways were already in the hands of the state, nationalisation was an option. But the form of state ownership was contested. Alternatives to a state national monopoly under centralised management were given serious consideration. On 18 January 1887, M. Granet, the minister in charge of the telegraph service, introduced a bill in parliament under which the monopoly held by Société générale was to be broken up into a number of local operations under separate management. It proposed that existing government-owned local exchange operations should be controlled by the private company and placed under separate local management, while the state telegraph authorities should retain complete control of long-distance lines. The private company would be granted a concession running for thirty-five years when the entire plant could be purchased by the state without cost. A second plan was introduced by M. Coulon, who replaced Granet at the head of the postal and telegraph administration. In a special report Coulon recommended the division of the telephone business outside Paris into six sections. In each section the activities of the telephone monopoly should be farmed out to a private company, and a special company should be created to manage Paris. This proposal was similar to the French solution to the development of the railways prior to their conversion to state ownership.

It was the desire to prevent destructive competition between the telephones and public telegraphs which convinced the French government of the need for complete state ownership of the telephones. On 16 July 1889, the French parliament rejected the Granet plan and Coulon's alternative, passing an act providing for the purchase of the private company's plant. Possession of private telephones was taken by force after the private monopoly refused to surrender its plant. Subsequently, the postal and telegraph administration assumed complete control of the telephones.

Britain: the failure to choose between organisational forms
Under Gladstone's Liberal cabinet, the British government rejected the policy recommended by the Post Office of developing the telephone as a national service in close connection with the state telegraphs. Adhering to laissez-faire principles, the British state of the 1880s and 1890s was reluctant to intervene in the economy, preferring to supplement, not replace, private enterprise. Although

the favoured institutional model for the development of the infant industry was private competition, the state telegraph monopoly was neither surrendered nor dismantled. The preference for liberal policies held by various British governments did not coincide with the interests of the Post Office whose purpose was to safeguard state telegraphs. During the 1880s and 1890s, while the telephone was developed according to the principle of competition, successive Postmaster-Generals introduced policies which – designed to protect state telegraph interests while making concessions to private and municipal interests – severely restricted telephone development under private and municipal control. Finally, the failure of competition provided the rationale for the nationalisation of the telephones in 1912.[18]

Potential private interests in Britain resisted the inclusion of the telephones under the state telegraph monopoly. While the Postmaster-General was personally inclined to adopt a liberal policy towards the telephone, he was hampered by fiscal difficulties in the telegraph activities, and forced to protect telegraph revenues from telephone competition. In consequence, the initial task of introducing the telephone into Britain was thus declined by the Postmaster-General.

By 1878 the Postmaster-General had become aware of the possibility of the future growth of the telephone. A clause was inserted in a telegraph bill to place the telephones in the hands of the telegraph monopoly. The House of Commons struck out this clause, preferring that the telephone be undertaken by private enterprise. By May 1880, competition between the rival Bell and Edison companies was ended by an amalgamation into the United Telephone Company. With a large investment in public telegraphs to protect and the threat of competing with the private telephone monopoly, the Postmaster-General aimed to extend the scope of the telegraph monopoly by appealing to the courts. The defendants were the United Telephone Company, who claimed that the telephone differed essentially from the telegraph. In December 1880, a High Court ruling determined that a telephone and a telephone conversation transmitted by electrical signals was a telegraph within the meaning of the Telegraph Act of 1869. In consequence, during the experimental period of British telephone development in the 1880s and 1890s, various private companies operated under licence from the Postmaster-General.

The policy of the Post Office towards the telephone was

influenced by the necessity to conserve and protect public money sunk in the state telegraphs.[19] Competition from the telephones would result in the premature devaluation of sunk capital in state-owned telegraphs and heavy losses for the Post Office. Consequently, in April 1881 the Postmaster-General granted licences to the United Telephone Company and its provincial subsidiaries under restrictive conditions designed to obstruct competition and protect telegraph revenues.[20] The licensees were authorised to operate an exchange system within a radius of two to five miles of an exchange, but they were refused statutory powers to erect poles and wires on public highways or private property, and were required to pay the Post Office a royalty of 10 per cent of the gross revenues. Each licence was to run for thirty-one years, and could be terminated at the discretion of the Post Office in 1890 or thereafter at seven-year intervals.

This 'policy of strangulation', as it became known in parliament, had constrained telephone development by 1884. For example, the refusal to permit private companies to operate inter-urban trunk lines retarded the development of long-distance telephony. Under public pressure for a more liberal telephone policy, the Postmaster-General announced a new plan of universal competition.[21] This policy gave companies the rights to build long-distance telephone lines, and removed all restrictions on the services to subscribers outside local areas. However, licensees still obtained no statutory rights to secure wayleaves for the construction of their lines. From 1884, the expansion of the inter-urban telephone trunk lines contributed to a larger deficit in telegraph revenues. While a reduction in the minimum rate on telegrams stimulated use of the telegraph, it was not sufficient to increase telegraph revenues.

Universal competition, however, resulted in a new problem for the Post Office; a private telephone monopoly. The Bell and Edison patents were due to expire in 1890 and 1891, respectively. In anticipation of the competition expected after the expiration, the three main telephone companies, including the United Telephone Company, were amalgamated in 1888 to form the National Telephone Company. But the inefficiency of the National Telephone Company's system, which conducted at least 93 per cent of Britain's telephone service, was widely recognised and condemned by public opinion. Transmission plant and office switchboards were not based on modern apparatus, and the National Company was reaping very large monopoly profits by charging high telephone rates.

Following the creation of a telephone 'trust' there was a renewed agitation for government ownership of the trunk lines and exchange systems.[22] For example, in 1888, the Associated Chambers of Commerce voted for a national telephone system, and the *Economist* preferred a state to a private monopoly.[23] Rather than place the telephones under government ownership, the British government compromised with the private monopoly. This new proposal of public cooperation with private monopoly was presented in a Treasury Minute, on 23 May 1892, and embodied in the Telegraph Act of 1892. The state took complete control of long-distance lines, purchased for £1 million, and private telephone companies were confined to local areas. This policy was devised to place long-distance telephone operations under the control of the Post Office to protect public revenues obtained from the telegraphs, whilst at the same time using competition – which remained the favoured institutional solution – to improve the telephone service in local areas. The government of the day believed that after the expiration of the patents new competitors in local exchange operations would force improvements in service provided by the private monopoly.

But the policy of partnership with private companies did not stimulate competition. It resulted in a national duopoly: by 1895 the Post Office controlled 2,651 miles of trunk lines and the private companies, dominated by the National Company, had the local profits. Sixteen days before the passage of the 1892 Act, the National Telephone Company entered into a contract with its only major competitor, the New Telephone Company. The latter agreed not to construct a line or open an exchange in competition with the National. After 1892 the new improved and cheapened state telegraph service was still operating at a deficit. But, telegraph losses due to long-distance telephone service – which was taking away from the telegraph the most profitable traffic between neighbouring cities – were now absorbed by the Post Office.

By the late 1890s the problem of devising an adequate telephone policy had taken a new form. Again the means of improving the telephone service was competition rather than complete nationalisation. But this time the source of competition was the municipal authorities. A Select Committee of 1895 recommended the establishment of municipal telephones.

While the trunk service developed by the state had become one of the most extensive in Europe, the local exchange service under private ownership lagged behind many Continental European countries. Under private monopoly, the exchange service was costly, inefficient, excluded working-class subscribers, and was limited to populous areas. The government rejected proposals to nationalise local exchange systems, preferring that local systems, which accounted for 98 per cent of total telephone traffic, should be undertaken by local authorities rather than the Post Office.[24] Municipal competition was expected to reduce the high prices charged by the National Telephone Company.

Introduced at this late stage, when a private monopoly dominated the field, municipal competition could not be successful. The advantage of being first in the field, the accumulated experience in telephone operations, together with the ability to cross-subsidise operations, enabled the private monopoly to provide a cheaper service than most of the local authorities.[25] Of 1,334 municipalities able under the 1899 Act to take out licences, only six constructed exchanges. By 1906, Tunbridge Wells, Swansea, Glasgow, and Brighton had sold their municipal systems to the Postmaster-General. Portsmouth sold out in 1912. Hull was the only municipality to keep its exchange system after nationalisation in 1912.

Municipal competition failed to stimulate improvements in the local telephone service. The National Company warned the government in 1898 that due to the necessity of recouping the company's sunk costs before 1911, when its licence was due to expire, it would be unwilling to extend its local service to new districts. Under the national agreement made between the Post Office and the private monopoly on 2 February 1905, the state purchased the National Company's plant and equipment. On 1 January 1912, the entire telephone system in Britain, with the exception of the municipality of Hull, was purchased by the state for £12.5 million and placed under the central administration of the state postal and telegraph monopoly.

Successive policies to promote competition in Britain's telephone service failed because the state neglected to select a clearly defined organisational path. Consequently, with a legal monopoly including the telephones, the Post Office restricted private telephone competition in order to protect state telegraph investment. Nationalisation of trunk lines in 1892 limited competition to local areas and enabled the Post Office to appropriate the surplus from long-distance telephone revenues while continuing to develop its telegraph service.

Several reasons were put forward to reject competition and to justify the nationalisation of Britain's telephone infrastructure. First, it was argued that a national monopoly was the appropriate institutional structure for telephone administration because a private monopoly had emerged before the state had nationalised trunk lines. The national form depended on economies of scale: the larger the system, the cheaper and more extensive the service. This avoided the duplication of plant and staff associated with the so-called 'hugger-mugger' system of telephone competition.[26] Moreover, it was uneconomical to have separate transmission and buildings for the telegraph and telephone. Second, centralised control of the telephone system was required in order to trace to its source any imperfection in the service, an organisational task rendered increasingly complex between competing telephone systems.[27] Third, the familiar argument made for state control of the posts and telegraphs was applied to the telephones: the telephone service could only be extended to rural areas if undertaken by a government monopoly below cost price. By the 1930s, these various rationales, summarised as the need for 'unity of control', were used to support the argument that telephony constituted a natural monopoly: the main justification for the domination of the telephone by a national operator throughout the twentieth century.[28]

Elsewhere in Europe, similar claims were invoked to support the formation of public communications utilities which were integrated into government Postal, Telegraph and Telephone (PTT) agencies. Although the causes which led to operation of telephone systems by the state were complex, the one unifying theme was the intention of state telegraph authorities to conserve their sunk capital while at first restricting private telephone enterprise, before finally taking possession of the telephones.

3. The decentralised alternative

State-owned PTT authorities argued that alternative institutional arrangements were inefficient. In Britain, the national monopoly was justified by reference to the waste, duplication and inefficiency of competition and private monopoly. There was, however, a viable alternative which did not depend on the principle of free competition. Several small European countries, including Denmark, Finland and the Netherlands, established regional systems, composed of a single state-owned long-distance network, interworked by local monopolies owned or managed by municipal authorities or local private monopolies.

In Germany, the Bavarian and Bad-Württemberg authorities sought to control the management of the telephones.[29] While the constitution of 1871 placed the administration of the telegraphs under the centralised control of the state telegraphs, a later section permitted Bavaria and Bad-Württemberg to retain independent management of intra-state telegraphs and could be invoked to municipalise the telephones. However, to defend the embryonic national telephone monopoly, Postmaster-General von Stephan issued an order in 1880 forbidding all municipal telephones.

In Italy, there was widespread support for municipal ownership at the turn of the twentieth century, especially in the northern cities.[30] In an attempt to stimulate the growth of Italy's underdeveloped telephone service, an Act of 1903 ruled that the telephone was an appropriate system for municipal ownership. The plan was to create a composite system of public ownership, with long-distance lines owned by the state telegraph authorities, and local exchanges owned by municipalities. However, only one municipality entered into the provision of local telephony. The municipal model failed in Italy because the minister in charge of the postal and telegraph authorities successfully argued that the telephones should not be in private hands to nullify the threat that private telephone ownership posed to state telegraph investments. On 15 July 1907, Italy's telephones were nationalised.

The growth of telephone localism in Britain was led by the city of Glasgow, the stronghold of municipalism, where the water, gas, electric light, and street railway were already undertaken by the town council. In an attempt to discourage the National Telephone Company from establishing an exchange service in the city, Glasgow Council refused to grant the company the rights to dig up the streets to install metallic circuits underground. In 1897, a special commissioner reported against municipal competition. But this decision was reversed in 1898 by a Select Committee, whose recommendations that the Post Office or local authorities compete with the monopoly of the National Telephone Company were contained in the Telegraph Act of 1899. The Act gave the Postmaster-General £2 million to extend the trunk service and construct local exchanges, and it encouraged local authorities to apply for funds to establish telephone systems.

Although municipal ownership of the telephones was not a

success in Britain, Guernsey and the municipality of Hull have the distinction of having provided efficient local telephone services under the direction of the local authorities. The Hull system demonstrates the viability of municipal telephones; it still operates in the late twentieth century as a sub-system within the national telecommunications network.

While the National Telephone Company made an abortive attempt to introduce a private telephone system, there was still no public telephone system in Guernsey in 1896. The agitation which led to the introduction of a local telephone system coincided with the movement for telephone municipalism in the rest of Britain. The system in Guernsey was similar to the systems established by the municipalities in terms of ownership and management. It was interconnected with the national service of the British Post Office by submarine cables laid for war purposes, and opened for public use on 1 May 1915. By 31 December 1921, the Guernsey States Telephone Department had the reputation for providing the best service in the British Empire: the number of direct exchange lines was 2,393 out of a population of 37,914.[31]

After being petitioned by local business telephone users, Hull City Council secured a licence to operate a municipal telephone system on 8 August 1902. The municipality set up a telephone system in competition with the National Telephone Company. Elsewhere competition between the private company and the municipalities resulted in price wars, sabotage and an erosion in the quality of service. Hull's municipal telephone survived because rather than engage in direct competition, the council used its wayleave powers as a bargaining lever to reach a cooperative agreement, whereby the municipal system was interconnected to subscribers of the National Telephone Company exchange.[32] On 5 January 1914, the city purchased the National plant from the Post Office. After paying working expenses, royalty and interest on sunk capital, the Hull system increased its profitability during the first decade of operation.[33] Hull, therefore, confirmed the possibility of municipal ownership as an alternative to nationalisation.

In the Nordic region of Europe, the telephone service was managed and owned by various local initiatives rather than centralised public institutions. What distinguishes telephone development in countries like Sweden, Norway and Finland from other European countries is that their governments had no legal monopoly of the telegraphs when the telephones were first introduced, and, therefore, were unable to exercise the same constraints over the infant telephone industry. These were fertile conditions for local enterprise. With less political interference, the telephone was developed rapidly by private and local initiatives, and reached a higher level of development than in the rest of Europe.[34] However, by the first decade of the twentieth century, state telegraph administrations were formed in Norway and Sweden, and the state gradually acquired a de facto monopoly over national telephone systems. In Denmark and Finland, by contrast, the regional systems survived intact for most of the twentieth century.

In Norway, local enterprise was the driving force behind the rapid expansion of the telephone business.[35] In towns and villages throughout Norway, communities took over the responsibility of providing four different kinds of local telephone service: first, small joint-stock companies were formed, in which each subscriber in the village possessed a share; second, there were mutual associations which assumed the initial costs of construction; third, cooperative societies were established in which each member purchased his or her telephone line and instrument, and shared with other members the cost of constructing the central exchange; fourth, local authorities invested in village exchange systems at the public expense, for the use of local communities as a whole. In Sweden during the 1880s the same kind of public-spirited local initiatives were flourishing. By the late 1880s, local telephone services existed in settlements throughout Norway.

But diverse local systems were constructed with no consideration of the need to secure intercommunication with neighbouring towns and villages. The formation of the municipal telephone organisation depended on the creation of an institutional arrangement providing central coordination. After 1890 local authorities successfully cooperated with both each other and the state telegraph authorities in welding local telephone systems into an interconnected national system. Although the expansion of the system on a larger scale depended on centralised supervision (but not unified ownership), many local systems resisted immediate absorption by the local and long-distance state and private companies.

In Denmark the telephone was introduced by private enterprise.[36] A local exchange system was initiated in Denmark by the International Bell Telephone Company in 1881. The Copenhagen Telephone Company was formed in 1882 when the Bell Company was taken over by private Danish owners. The director of the

Telegraph Directorate, which operated the state-owned telegraphs throughout Denmark, declined to intervene in the infant telephone industry because he failed to anticipate the future potential of the telephone, and considered it no competitive threat to state telegraphs.

There was a rapid period of system building in Denmark during the 1880s and 1890s when the telephones were undertaken by numerous private initiatives. The lead was taken by the Copenhagen Telephone Company which quickly secured a large number of subscribers, and paid high dividends to the shareholders. The development of the telephone soon spread from the large cities to smaller towns and rural areas. By 1890 this phase of private enterprise resulted in fifty-seven local telephone companies. The same forces of local private and public initiative witnessed in Norway and Sweden accelerated the growth of the telephone, and resulted in local geographical telephone monopolies, controlled by well-organised stock companies. When long-distance telephony became feasible in the 1890s, the Telegraph Directorate began to establish a telephone system for international traffic and a trunk network to interconnect the local telephone systems.

The Danish state did not intervene in the legal structure of the industry until the Telegraphs and Telephones Act of 11 May 1897 placed the telephones as well as the telegraphs under a state monopoly. In practice, however, the law merely extended state control of rates and regulation, and granted the right to develop the regional telephone business to eleven private monopolies, one for the peninsula of Jutland, and one for each of the main islands of Denmark.

The organisation of the Finnish decentralised telephone system during the twentieth century must be seen in the context of the historical watershed marked by the birth of the Finnish nation state in 1917.[37] From 1809 to 1917, Finland was an autonomous grand duchy of the Russian Empire. When first introduced in Finland in 1877, the telephone was undertaken by private individuals who built point-to-point private lines between merchant houses and railway stations, warehouses and harbours. The Russian authorities had no incentive to build telephone lines because, unlike the Finnish telegraph service which was operated by the Russian authorities to control armies and local officials in geographically remote regions, the telephone had no comparable military or administrative significance because transmission was limited to local calls.[38]

Under the Imperial Decree of 1886, the local Finnish Senate issued a 'Declaration of the terms on which telephone lines can be installed and used' in the name of Czar Alexander III. This Declaration became the legal foundation for the regulation of the Finnish telephone system for the next century. In a successful attempt to resist the Russian domination of Finnish telecommunications, the Finnish Senate sought to enhance domestic control of the telephones by granting as many concessions as possible to local companies prior to 1917, rather than by establishing a Finnish state telephone agency. This made the threat of Russian control of the telephones less likely because of the difficulty and expense of purchasing the numerous independent telephone companies, in comparison to the relatively simple option of buying-out a single government telephone agency.[39]

In the absence of political intervention, local telephone systems were rapidly constructed in urban areas of southern Finland. Beginning in Helsinki and larger southern towns, the number of independent local companies grew from 250 in 1910 to 850 in 1938. Although the local companies were developed under various local initiatives – including private individuals, limited liability companies, economic associations, and municipalities – the dominant form of enterprise in this period was cooperative ownership. Under the cooperative form, subscribers exercised democratic control over local telephone operations, services and tariffs because they were the main shareholders in the company. Subscribers invested a sum of capital in return for a share in the company and access to a telephone line. In a country with limited credit available for investment, this model of ownership mobilised scarce start-up capital from the customer. Because profits were passed on to subscribers in the form of lower rates and new investment, the cooperatives provided new telephone services, adequate standards and low tariffs to meet the requirements of local customers.

After national independence in 1917, the new Finnish state assumed control of the Russian telegraph service. The Telegraph Act of 1919 placed the telegraphs under a state monopoly, and the new state telegraph agency immediately began the construction and operation of government-owned local, long-distance and international telephone services. In 1927, the Telegraph Office was merged with the Post Office to form a single organisation, the Administration of Posts and Telegraphs (P&T), with a monopoly of the telegraphs and all international traffic. Lack of funds, however, prevented the Finnish state from purchasing existing private local telephone companies (which dominated the field), and emulating the European model of an integrated local, long-distance and international telephone operator.

Established in 1894, the Long Distance Telephone Company of Southern Finland began to build a private system along high-volume long-distance routes carrying business traffic between Helsinki and adjacent urban centres. Built to maximise short-run profits, the Long Distance Company provided a poor-quality service. In 1930, the Swedish company L.M. Ericsson purchased the majority of shares in the Long Distance Company and acquired shares in several local telephone companies in Southern Finland. Ericsson proposed a compromise with the Finnish government. In return for constructing a nationwide telephone network for Finland, Ericsson wanted a monopoly of long-distance and international traffic for forty years.

In 1935 the Finnish parliament rejected Ericsson's proposal and nationalised the private Long Distance Company, placing the private company's plant, equipment and employees under the control of the P&T.[40] For the next fifty years, the operation of Finnish telecommunications was divided into two groups: the P&T was the monopoly provider of all nationwide telephone services and a few local systems in remote areas to meet universal service obligations; and local systems were dominated by private local companies.

In the Netherlands the decentralised model was also developed, as an efficient alternative to national monopoly. Here the telegraph was a state monopoly by the law of 7 March 1852.[41] When the telephone was introduced it was assumed to lie within the scope of the state telegraph monopoly. The telegraph authority granted concessions for the development of local and long-distance operations by private companies. When the licences of long-distance operations expired in 1897, the state repossessed this part of the telephone business.

In the main commercial areas, telephone subscribers were dissatisfied with the poor local telephone service provided by the private companies, who were more interested in short-term profitability than quality or efficiency of service. Since the telegraph authorities declined to engage in the provision of local telephone services, local telephone users demanded municipal ownership of the telephones. Telephone subscribers believed that the municipalities could protect the interest of local users from the high charges and inefficient service offered by private companies. The state telegraph authority – whose primary concern during the 1890s was deficits from the operation of the telegraphs – willingly relinquished to the municipalities the task of safeguarding the interests of local subscribers.

From 1896, Dutch municipalities began to take direct control of the local telephone business. In the cities of Amsterdam and Rotterdam, dissatisfaction with the service of the private companies was so great that the city authorities refused to purchase or use the poor-quality plant of the Bell Telephone Company when the concessions expired on 30 October 1896. On the following day, these authorities began the construction of entirely new municipal telephones. The Hague established a municipal system in 1903. By 1904, twenty-two municipalities operated local telephone systems. From 1894 to 1904, the number of local exchanges increased from thirty-three to sixty, and most were under municipal ownership.

In comparison to the private companies, municipal systems provided substantial improvements in services and greater reductions in rates, especially in the larger cities. In Amsterdam and Rotterdam, for example, the Bell rate was approximately $47.20 in 1894, for a direct line with unlimited use; and this was the only rate and only service available. A decade later, after the substitution of municipal for private ownership, telephone rates were significantly lower, and services were differentiated according to business and residential subscriptions. Business rates had been reduced to $36 and residential to $26.40.

Under the policy of municipal ownership, the Dutch munici-palities succeeded in realising significant improvements in the local telephone service. Municipal authorities furnished the capital needed to fund the growth and modernisation of local telephone operations.[42] The municipal model of telephone organisation in the Netherlands survived until the German occupation during the Second World War, when the Dutch system was nationalised (a structure retained after the war) and interconnected to the highly centralised command and control telephone network interconnecting occupied territories.

In summary, then, the policy of local ownership and decentralised management in Europe demonstrates the advantages of utilising local initiative to provide an innovative, low-cost local telephone service. In comparison to the centralised national monopoly framework, the localised form of telephone organisation emphasises the advantages to be obtained from the decentralisation of ownership and operation. This alternative organisational form survived longest in those countries where localism was strong politically, or, as in most of the Nordic countries, where when the telephone was introduced there were no state telegraph monopolies with the power to constrain and shape telephone development.

Conclusion

By the early twentieth century, the prevailing model of telephone organisation was a national monopoly under centralised control. The reason for the different pattern of ownership in Europe and the United States was that in the latter – where private economic power was strong relative to the nation state, competition produced a large-scale private monopoly which subsequently resisted attempts to place the telephone under public ownership. In Europe, by contrast, where private economic power was less concentrated, large state postal administrations formed during the seventeenth century were the source of institutional power which retarded the private development of telephony and shaped the national monopoly form in their own interests.

The best measure of comparative telephone development is the number of population per telephone station (connected with public exchange systems).[43] Those countries which adopted clearly defined organisational paths exhibited the highest levels of telephone development. In Germany and Switzerland, where the telephone was nationalised from the start, telephone development grew rapidly. In 1895, for example, the ratio of telephones were capita was 1:129 in Switzerland and 1:397 in Germany.[44] But it was in those European countries where the impetus behind telephone development was from local initiatives, without state telegraph interference, that telephony grew most rapidly. In 1895, the fastest growth in telephone development in Europe was in Scandinavia: in Norway and Sweden the ratio of telephones per capita was 1:115.[45] It was, however, in the United States under the regime of private competition and absence of state telegraph monopolies that telephone development was the most rapid in the world.[46] In 1902, there was one telephone for every thirty-four persons in the United States. Driven by competition between AT&T and the independent companies, American telephone development accelerated after 1893. However, competition was only temporary: it resulted in a duplication of local plant and service, and in an unregulated private monopoly.

Telephone development lagged behind in those countries where neither public ownership, local initiative nor pure competition were adopted at the outset. For example, the failure to select a clearly defined organisational path combined with policies designed to protect telegraph interests stunted telephone development in Britain. Initial mistakes were rectified in 1912 with nationalisation, after which telephone development accelerated. Similarly, in the Netherlands, the adoption of an efficient organisational form was postponed until 1896, when the substitution of municipal organisation for private monopoly led to the rapid development of telephone service.

National monopoly, whether under state ownership or state regulation, was superior to the inefficiency of private monopoly. The supremacy of the national monopoly was underpinned by advantages of centralised operation and economies of scale. But the implementation of the dominant model sacrificed the benefits associated with local initiatives: namely the provision of a low-cost, innovative service, tailored more closely to match local business and residential user needs. Moreover, the advantages of centralisation associated with national monopolies were later obtained by regional systems. Once heterogeneous local systems were welded together to form national infrastructures, a degree of centralisation was required to operate through traffic between interconnected local networks under independent control. Despite the dominance of the national monopoly form, the local or regional systems were viable institutional alternatives. Under different historical conditions – in a political and institutional environment which favoured the decentralised model – interconnected regional monopolies might have become more widespread. While this decentralised organisational form was suppressed by the 1920s, it re-emerged in the 1970s as a possible alternative to monopoly and competition.

Notes

1. Forms of state interventionism vary between countries, and are not reducible to a simple economic logic that the state intervenes in domains that are unprofitable to private capital. See N. Poulantzas (1978), pp180–189 *State, Power, Socialism*, Verso, London.
2. An analysis of suppressed organisational forms and the institutional diversity contained in industrial history is provided by C. Sabel and J.

Zeitlin (1985), 'Historical Alternatives to Mass Production: Politics, Markets and Technology in Nineteenth-Century Industrialisation', pp133–176, *Past and Present*, no. 108.

3. See for example J.H. Robertson (1947), *The Story of the Telephone: A History of the Telecommunications Industry of Britain*, Pitman and Sons, London.

4. The close relationship between the postal and telegraph services was, however, recognised at an early stage by the Federal government. The first electric telegraph invented by Samuel Morse was used to transmit a public message for the United States government over a line between Washington and Baltimore in 1844. The telegraph was administered by the Postmaster-General, and royalties were placed in the Treasury of the United States for the Post Office Department. In December 1844, Morse appealed to Congress to place the telegraph under a government monopoly. In 1845 Postmaster-General Johnson argued to retain control of the telegraph as a permanent part of the postal service, referring to the potential of the telegraph in facilitating business transactions, and its military value to government during time of war. However, the Washington–Baltimore telegraph attracted little demand and was not self-supporting. Congress reluctantly made appropriations for the maintenance of this line, and was opposed to the government takeover of such a risky investment. From 1846, the Morse patentees abandoned attempts to obtain a government takeover and enlisted private capital to develop the telegraph. R.L. Thompson, p33 (1947), *Wiring a Continent: The History of the Telegraph Industry in the United States, 1832–1866*, Princeton, New Jersey.

5. A.A. Berle and G.C. Means, p3 (1935), *The Modern Corporation and Private Property*, Macmillan, New York.

6. H. Coon, p260 (1939), *American Tel & Tel: The Story of a Great Monopoly*, Longman, Green, New York.

7. State institutions maintained that the interstate nature of telephony dictated that the system be regulated as a whole, not in portions. Telephone municipalism, particularly strong in Los Angeles, Seattle, Spokane, and San Francisco, gradually lost the struggle for authority over the telephone as the state commissions asserted their jurisdiction over rates and operations.

8. p154, ibid.

9. E. Murray, chapter 1 (1927), *The Post Office*, Putnam's Sons, London.

10. A.N. Holcombe (1911), *Public Ownership of the Telephones on the Continent of Europe*, Houghton and Mifflin, London.

11. To justify national ownership the report compared the private telegraphs with the postal service. It argued that if the telegraphs were operated under a uniform rate like the one-shilling rate of the penny post established in 1840, lower prices would increase telegraph business. Moreover, the main cost of the telegraphs was related to the construction of lines. If a wire could be used more intensively or laid more cheaply, fixed costs per message would fall. According to the Scudamore findings, economies of scale could only be realised if the telegraph was operated as a unified and coordinated system. The report

also emphasised that under private ownership the telegraph had not been made available in remote locations. J. Kieve (1973), *The Electrical Telegraph: A Social and Economic History*, David and Charles, Newton Abbot.

12. p184, ibid. What was not foreseen were the rising variable costs of operating expenses, particularly wages, which converted anticipated profits into permanent deficit. As Kieve (1973) explains 'Telegrams had still to be individually received and transmitted; every increase in traffic involved increased expense in nearly the same ratio for many items'.

13. In late eighteenth-century France, the medieval courier, equipped with saddle bags of messages carried by relays of fast horses, could not transmit military or political communications with sufficient speed or reliability. Efforts were made to furnish a mechanical substitute for the postal service. The optical telegraph, invented by Claude Chappe in 1793, was devised to help the French military dispatch orders with greater speed than the postal system. The optical telegraph consisted of towers built at intervals of several miles, each equipped with a visual signalling device which used sunlight as the medium for telegraphic transmission. However, the optical telegraph was prone to delays and failure in transmission. It could not be operated at night or in weather conditions of poor visibility.

14. H.L. Webb (1910), *The Development of the Telephone in Europe*, Electrical Press, London; Holcombe makes this point in (1911) op. cit. and in 'The Telephone in Great Britain', pp96–135, *Quarterly Journal of Economics*, November, 1906.

15. When it was first developed in the late 1870s and early 1880s, the telephone could not transmit voice over large distances. The telegraph was well established by this time, and remained the only feasible means of transmitting intelligence over the long-lines of communication required by military and political command structures. Nevertheless, departments of government set up private telephone networks which excluded the public, and hence were able to transmit messages in secret with less risk of transmission failure and crossed lines. There was, therefore, little incentive for the state to undertake control of the telephone for strategic military and political exigencies.

16. F. Thomas (1988), 'The Politics of Growth: The German Telephone System' in *The Development of Large Technical Systems* (eds) R. Mayntz and T.P. Hughes, Campus Verlag, Frankfurt am Main.

17. Holcombe, pp267–280 (1911), op. cit.

18. Webb, p27, op. cit.

19. In expectation of high profits, the price paid for the telegraphs had been swelled from an original valuation of £3,000,000 to the huge sum of £8,000,000. Over £2,000,000 was spent on the immediate expansion of the telegraph system. However, the extension of the system to rural communities, and the introduction of a flat rate for all distances, resulted in low profits. By 1880 the Post Office had not paid the interest on sunk capital in the telegraphs, amounting to £326,417. Holcombe, p100 (1906), op. cit. and F.G.C. Baldwin, p561 (1938), *The History of The Telephone in the United Kingdom*, Chapman & Hall, London.

20. *Hansard*, summary of telephone development in speech of Dr. Cameron, 19 March 1892.
21. Holcombe, p107 (1906), op. cit.
22. Baldwin, p575, op. cit.
23. J.H. Clapham, p392 (1938), *An Economic History of Modern Britain*, Cambridge University Press, Cambridge.
24. Baldwin, p588, op. cit.
25. E. Murray, p124, op. cit. According to Baldwin, p382, op. cit.: 'As public authorities, the Corporations (municipalities) possessed a number of advantages over the National Telephone Company ... but the National Company was financially powerful, its organisation was strong, it was served by a large and experienced staff and it was accustomed to meet with opposition.'
26. *Hansard* (1905a), speech of John Burns. Telephone Agreement.
27. *Hansard* (1905b), speech of Austen Chamberlain. Telephone Agreement.
28. Robertson, op. cit., refers extensively to the principle of unity of control as the basis of modern telephone systems.
29. Holcombe, p28 (1911), op. cit.
30. pp366–373, ibid.
31. Baldwin, p384, op. cit.
32. 'The History and Development of Kingston Communications (Hull) PLC, 1904 to Present Day', Kingston Communications, circa 1990.
33. Baldwin, p378, op. cit.
34. Webb, p73, op. cit.
35. Holcombe, pp374–382 (1911), op. cit.
36. Webb, p74, op. cit, and Holcombe, pp390–391 (1911), op. cit.
37. Professor S.J. Halme (1992), University of Technology, Helsinki, interview by A. Davies, 30 November 1992.
38. In 1855, during the Crimean War, the Russian state constructed a telegraph line on the southern coast of Finland running from Helsinki to St Petersburg, which was used to support Russian military and administrative priorities in the war against Britain. Telegraph lines and services were placed under monopoly ownership and centralised control of the Russian Empire, although the line was later used for commercial and private messages.
39. World Bank Report (1992), 'The Study of Alternative Solutions for the Provision of Telecommunications Services in Developing Countries: Case Study based on Regulatory and Organisational Structures in Finland', pp11–18, November 1992, prepared by Telecon. Ltd for Finnish International Development Agency, Ministry of Transport and Communications of Finland, and The World Bank.
40. For a combination of reasons, Ericsson's proposed deal failed to be passed as a bill in the Finnish parliament: there was political resistance to handing over national telecommunications to foreign control during a time of growing Finnish nationalism; the military relied upon national control of telecommunications in a period increasingly under the threat of war; a universal service on a non-discriminatory basis in unprofitable remote regions could not be guaranteed by a commercial company;

and, the eventual bankruptcy of the main Swedish shareholder in Ericsson forced the issue of a government takeover.

41. Holcombe, pp358–363 (1911), op. cit.
42. The directors of the municipal service managed the telephone system according to the same principle as they did the municipal water supply. There were no advertising expenses. All resources were deployed to provide a satisfactory service for local users. In 1907 a new method of charge was introduced in Rotterdam based on the measured-service rate, which supplemented the existing flat rate for an unlimited service. The municipalities introduced the most modern telephone equipment, to provide additional capacity in anticipation of future demand. In The Hague, for example, battery switchboards with lamp signals were introduced as early as 1903.
43. It is, however, important not to draw too strong conclusions from such statistics because comparative telephone development is influenced not simply by state policies, but also by other factors including the strength of national economies, the existence of rapid and reliable postal and telegraph systems, physical and human geography, etc.
44. Holcombe, p421 (1911), op. cit.
45. By 1906, Scandinavia still led Europe in terms of telephone use: the number of telephones per 100 inhabitants had reached 2.57 in Sweden, 2.44 in Denmark, 2.03 in Norway. pp425–426, ibid.
46. This was partly due to conditions peculiar to the United States: the huge business demand from the most advanced industrial economy in the world during the late nineteenth century, the absence of protective state monopolies, and the need to unite spatially dispersed national markets.

Part II

The telecommunications revolution

4 Corporations, communications and computers

By the 1920s, the rise of a system of industrialisation founded on mass production was supported by national postal, telegraph and telephone infrastructures. After information had been organised into meaningful aggregates and processed by large-scale corporations, it was transmitted and retrieved over telegraph and telephone wires linking geographically dispersed corporate activities. The spatial integration of local and national markets required by the expanding system of mass production was aided by successive improvements in the capacity to transmit messages over long-distances. Until the 1950s, the capacity and speed of telegraph and telephone systems was in advance of information processing. Timely information about supply and demand conditions, orders and production plans accumulated more quickly than it could be processed.

From the late 1940s onwards, the transformation in mass production and creation of a system of flexible production depended on improvements in the capacity to manipulate and transmit cheaper flows of information using electronic control technologies. This transformation in the mode of production culminated in a revolution in the technology of telecommunications. The incorporation of electronic control and data processing technologies into all aspects of corporate operations – such as accounts, inventory control and financial monitoring – increased the speed with which information could be compiled into utilisable aggregates. Subsequent improvements in the capacity and performance of computer processing (accompanied by dramatic reductions in equipment costs) created a stimulus for changes elsewhere in the speed and capacity of data transmission. And the spatial expansion and internationalisation of plants and offices after 1945 fuelled corporate demands for a worldwide telecommunications infrastructure.

Telephone networks had become one of the components in an increasingly interdependent system of information processing and telecommunications. Yet the telephone component of the system was lagging behind advances in the capacity of information processing. Telephone networks were not technically engineered for efficient transmission of computerised information. Corporate demand for high-speed data transmission was, therefore, the major stimulus to the development of digital telecommunications. The imbalance in the capacity of telecommunications was an inducement to corrective actions and complementary radical innovation which eventually brought about the convergence of digital systems of information processing and communications.[1] However, this technological upheaval could take place only after a prolonged phase of institutional transformation. Since telephone monopolies were slow in furnishing integrated computing and telecommunications facilities, corporations campaigned for the liberalisation of terminal equipment and computer information services, and built their own private digital networks linking up data processing operations.

1. Mass production and analogue telecommunications

From the 1840s to the 1940s, mass production firms established new administrative structures, processed large quantities of information and used telegraph and telephone networks to transmit high volumes of messages. The central characteristic of this period was a clear separation between the technology of telecommunications and information processing. Corporate requirements for telecommunications were satisfied by a combination of national telegraph and telephone infrastructures, and privately operated leased-line networks.

Information, communication and mass production

All production processes perform two activities (Porter and Millar 1985). First, physical processing activities are required to transform raw materials into a product. Second, informational activities encompass the various steps required in the storage, manipulation and transmission of information necessary to perform physical activities. Information is used in scheduling production and distribution, planning production to ensure timely supplies of inputs, and in generating data regarding changes in supply and market conditions which companies use to revise product designs and manufacturing techniques. Information systems within corporations perform two functions: messages are communicated and retrieved; and information is processed into useful aggregates to serve business requirements. In each line of industry, there are different combinations of physical and informational conditions. For example, whereas transactions processed by banks are oriented towards informational activities, the production of machinery or clothing consists mainly of physical processing activities.

During the period of mass production, technological and organisational change progressed more rapidly in physical processing than in information activities. Mass production techniques involved the use of purpose-built machinery and a semi-skilled workforce to secure economies of scale through the production of large volumes of standardised products at low unit costs. In addition, what Chandler (1977) has called 'economies of speed', resulted from high-volumes of throughputs of materials in production and rapid turnover of stocks in distribution in a given period of time. Physical improvements in energy and materials intensity were generated by the substitution of machines for labour-power. Increases in the physical capacity to mass produce and mass distribute unprecedented levels of output threatened to exceed society's capacity to contain them. This 'crisis of control', as Beniger (1986) calls it, was solved by innovations in information activities: including the new electric technologies of telecommunications and data processing.

Therefore, the rise of mass production in the second half of the nineteenth century depended on the speed, volume and certainty in the transmission of messages over geographical space made possible by the new telegraph and telephone infrastructures. Wired telecommunications established new connections which extended the geographical reach of mass markets supplied by high volume producers and tied together far-flung activities of the large-scale modern corporation.[2] The drive to abolish spatial barriers between large-scale production and an extending circle of buyers is put forcefully by Marx (1973: 524) as the 'creation of physical conditions of exchange – of the means of communication and transport – the annihilation of space by time'. Once the system of mass production was freed from certain spatial constraints by the creation of national telecommunication networks, its advance was self-sustaining as increases in efficiency enlarged the market by lowering production costs, thus bringing cheaper products within reach of bigger and more distant markets.

Two fundamental conditions of large-scale production led to the creation of facilities for information processing and rapid communication within the firm. First, while in small firms a single office informally managed a single plant, store, laboratory, financial operation or sales activity, the increasing volume of output and technological complexity of large firms led to the creation of a formal administrative structure based on headquarters and specialised operating units. Information and data flowed through lines of communication and authority between the offices and supervisors. The operating units were responsible for a single function, for example sales, manufacturing, purchasing or engineering, and for transmitting accurate and detailed data to the headquarters. Under the corporate hierarchical system there was an inherent separation between the making of business decisions and communicating information – a separation which was less pronounced in smaller firms.

Second, the geographical dispersal of large firms – involving the establishment of a network of distribution offices in distant places and from the late 1920s the trend for final assembly to be carried out in decentralised branch plants – depended on the creation of an organisation at central headquarters and electric communications to administer scattered units. Copying the pyramid command-and-control structure developed by the army, the information activities of large firms were built around a centralised bureaucracy and information exchanges followed vertical lines of communication. Consisting of layers of specialised decision-making, orders were communicated down through the ranks of middle management in the corporate hierarchy to remote operating units. Wired communication gave centralised authorities the intelligence and authority needed to govern production plants and remote distribution outlets from a single headquarters.

By the 1890s many American industries were dominated by a few large firms, which manufactured goods, sold them directly to retailers or ultimate consumers, and purchased or produced their own materials or supplies. Vertically integrated mass production operations tended to be concentrated in single large-scale plants. This centralising tendency was symbolised by the Ford Motor Company's River Rouge plant in Detroit, which by the mid-1920s employed 75,000 workers producing basic raw materials, parts and components, as well as carrying on the final assembly. A fundamental problem facing mass producers and mass distributors was how to control and coordinate the flow of vast quantities of incoming raw materials and semi-finished components entering factories located at one site and distribute large volumes of outgoing standardised products to national and world markets. To enable mass production plants to operate at a predetermined scale, rather than depend on daily supplies of raw materials, large buffer stocks were held in reserve. To satisfy fluctuations in demand or changing customer specifications stocks of finished goods on-hand-for-sale were greater in size than average demand. However, while readiness of buffer stocks and inventories was a condition for the uninterrupted flow of mass production plants, it represented lapsed time during which capital existed in a latent state without functioning productively.

To minimise the costs incurred in buying, selling, storing and distributing products, there was an incentive to keep the time between purchase and sale to a minimum. This was accomplished by the 'marketing revolution', based on the railways and telegraph. During the 'telegraph decade' of the 1850s, entrepreneurs set up telegraph lines between major industrial and financial centres in the United States supplying price information for businesses: 'Business merchants, farmers, bankers, shippers and others . . . could thus regulate their trade and commerce everyday by the actual conditions of the markets at remote and distant points' (DuBoff 1983: 257).

Telegraphic and telephonic communications permitted a closer coordination between supply and demand. Timely information about orders and prices enabled 'manufacturers to sell directly to wholesalers, reduced requirements for working capital and the risk of having unsold goods for long periods of time in the hands of commission merchants. Reduced risks and lower credit costs encouraged further investment in plant, machinery, and other fixed capital' (Chandler 1977: 245). In producer-goods industries such networks facilitated the prompt delivery of fabricated shapes and forms to a variety of specifications. In mass consumer-goods industries, which supplied high volumes of goods not based on specific orders, the flow had to be directed and coordinated to meet fluctuations in demand. By the turn of the twentieth century, for example:

the meat packers, with their heavy investment in distributing and purchasing as well as in the processing of all kinds of meats, had pioneered in such coordination by developing telegraphic communications between branch houses, the packing plants, and the stockyards. Both the branch houses and the buyers in the stockyards were in constant telegraphic communication with the central offices in Chicago. And with such information the central office could allocate supply to demand almost instantaneously (Chandler 1962: 389).

The speed and reliability with which orders could be telecommunicated helped to reduce the size of stocks. This enabled mass producers to accelerate their rate of throughput of materials, and large retailers, department stores and wholesalers to speed-up the rate of stock-turn. It allowed producers and distributors to keep inventories to a minimum, while realising the demands of long-distance markets.

Following the wave of vertical integration in the 1890s – when manufacturing firms carried out the procuring of supplies, wholesaling, and the production of raw materials – the role of the centralised administrative unit proved more important in coordinating various operating units. Diversification into a new range of products (and the complexity of information flows required in monitoring and controlling such activities), rather than the expansion of existing product lines, forced the emergence of the new multidivisional administrative form. Growth by horizontal integration brought a variety of products under the aegis of a single firm. It became increasingly difficult to coordinate diverse lines of business and diversified patterns of demand within the existing centralised structure. The administrative structure was overcentralised. A few managers were unable to execute the great number of decisions required in the coordination, planning and appraisal of numerous operating activities.

Created in the 1920s, the multidivisional structure was pioneered by Du Pont, General Motors, Standard Oil Company, and Roebuck and Company, and later emulated by many other firms including the Ford Motor Company and the Chrysler Corporation after 1945. Different types of information regarding specific product lines had to be processed. New channels of communication and authority, as well as the processing of data flowing through these lines, had to be created to match the diversified activities of the firm. Operating divisions were established and the executives in command of such divisions handled the organisation and profitability of one major line of products or services over a wide geographical area. The line of authority ran from the general office at the top (responsible for corporate goals and policies), through central offices, departmental headquarters, down to field units where managers were personally involved in supervising day-to-day activities.

Information-processing and telecommunications

The use of information in business decision-making and mass productive operations involved the posting, retrieval and organisation of data into meaningful aggregates. Records of sales, orders, debts, credits, and inventories increased in importance with the rise of centralised bureaucracies in large corporations. Increasingly complex and detailed information used in the coordination of multidivisional firms, and the mountains of data which piled up inside the firm as a result of the speed of telegraphic and telephonic communications, had to be refined and screened before management could make effective business decisions. This was achieved by organisational and technological advances in data processing: by the 1920s, information-processing activities had undergone two stages of mechanisation.

First, by the 1890s, information-processing was entirely paper-based. Large armies of clerks and bookkeepers posted figures by hand, and undertook the responsibility of screening and retrieving reports. Second, the introduction of electromechanical punchcard and tabulating machinery improved the organisation of data into aggregates. Entries were punched on cards which could be retrieved by sorting machines and aggregated into totals by tabulating machines. While the new method was faster than manual work in retrieval and tabulation, what was gained in more rapid posting of data was lost in accuracy. The semi-skilled operator could never gain the accuracy previously achieved by the skilled clerk in screening and determining whether an entry made sense before posting. Data processing activities were located in close proximity to the large plants and departmental offices they served. The centralisation of data processing activities within local areas minimised the need to transmit aggregates of data recorded on paper and sent by mail over long distances.

The speed and reliability of corporate communications were successively revolutionised in the nineteenth-century. Slow and uncertain postal systems of communication were displaced by the rapid communication of mail transported by rail. But the break-through came with invention of the telegraph and the possibility of almost instantaneous telecommunication of messages regardless of the intervening space. Indeed, because of its timely arrival in the 1850s – the moment firms needed to extend their span of control – the telegraph contributed more than the telephone to the origins of the modern corporation (Porter 1973: 43).

The use made of the telegraph in railway operations was the earliest and most important solution to the problem of controlling and coordinating geographically dispersed activities. Without rapid and certain telegraphic communications railway companies could not carry volumes of traffic at the new speed of steam power in safety and with efficiency. Following a collision between two passenger trains on the Western Railroad in the United States on 5 October 1841, the Western management introduced bureaucratic administrative control and telegraphic communications. The Western Railroad was the first company to use the telegraph to extend its control beyond the span of a single manager's close personal contacts – a range estimated to be 50 to 100 miles in the early railways.[3]

As a prototype of the large-scale corporation, Western Railroad's command and control system supported by telegraphic intelligence represented 'the first modern, carefully defined, internal organisational structure used by an American business enterprise' (Chandler 1977: 97). Some functions of control required to coordinate the entire Western line became centralised in the Springfield, Massachusetts, headquarters which was linked by a hierarchical chain of communications to regional offices. Yet control had to be relatively decentralised to allow prompt treatment of circumstances by station-masters. Attempts were made to re-establish system-wide control under the direction of the general superintendent, by creating lines of feedback control from subordinates to superiors: 'Conductors and station agents began to report hourly, via telegraph, on the location of trains and reasons for any delays, accidents or breakdowns' (Beniger 1986: 230). Rapid signalling over telegraph lines which helped determine the position of trains on the tracks improved the scheduling and safety of railway operations.

Having used telegraphic systems to improve safety, accurate telegraphic information was applied to improve railway efficiency through closer monitoring of the movement of rail freight over complex nationwide systems.[4] In the United States, the telegraph and railways marched across the American continent in the 1840s and 1850s like 'siamese twins of commerce': the telegraph companies used the railway for right-of-way privileges, and the railway used the telegraph services to coordinate flows of traffic.[5]

In addition to contracts with most of the large railways in the United States, some of the biggest users of Western Union's telegraph facilities were the press associations. Agents of these associations transmitted local news to the central office in New York. The central office would then give the news to New York papers and would retransmit it to subscriber papers after the information had been reorganised to suit local tastes and interests in particular regional markets. By 1870, almost all the news published in the United States was transmitted by Western Union. In 1869, the aggregate amount of news transmitted to the newspapers over Western Union lines was 369,503,630 words.[6]

From the 1850s, when telegraph technology and organisation was perfected, the utility of the telegraph for large business customers lay in long-distance communication between dispersed sites rather than the local transmission of messages. Because of economies of scale, which raised message capacity and lowered the fixed costs of handling large traffic volumes, it was often cheaper even for the largest users, like the railways, to share long-distance facilities with other users.[7] While the commercial message services accounted for the largest proportion of telegraph traffic, many large corporations and government departments leased telegraph circuits for private use. In 1884, Western Union began leasing its own wires to brokers, large retailers, banks, and press associations. Business customers employed their own operators to furnish a private service. In 1929 AT&T's telegraph operations supplied 1,200,000 telegraph circuits for private use of which one-third were used by press associations and newspapers, and the rest by corporate and financial institutions.

Yet from the 1890s, when voice transmission was technically perfected over large distances, the telegraph was soon eclipsed by the telephone as the favoured means of business telecommunication. In 1879, for example, the Pennsylvania Railroad became the first railway to install a telephone. By 1910 its private telephone system had 175 exchanges, 400 operators, 13,000 phones, and 20,000 miles of wire.[8] The most important technological development in the local exchange service which adapted the telephone service to the requirements of large business customers was the private branch-exchange (PBX) service. Located in the premises of the business customer, the PBX was usually operated by employees of the customer. It gave the subscribers control of the operation of private systems. The service enabled one business extension to call another in the firm without going through the public exchange, but was connected to the whole public network through the PBX. Such private exchange operations ranged in size from small systems with a few extensions, to large systems operated by corporations (often having as many extensions as the smaller American independent local telephone companies). In 1936, the PBX installations in the Bell System accounted for 20 per cent of its total number of telephones, and in operating such systems private subscribers employed 100,000 operators.

The leased-wire telegraph service was abandoned by many firms, including railway offices, and replaced with long-distance leased-line telephone facilities. The private telephone service over long-distance lines gave subscribers exclusive use of a circuit on a permanent basis or for a portion of the business day. Subscribers had complete control of the operation of this service and devised operating procedures tailored to individual requirements. To furnish almost instantaneous voice contact between officers, department heads, sales executives and other managers in modern corporations, permanent voice telephone lines connected offices, plants, and other dispersed units. In the mid-1930s, AT&T provided almost 1,000 private-wire telephone services; 250 of these were used by financial houses. Leased circuits emanated from all the major commercial centres: there were 200 between New York and Philadelphia, and many longer circuits between New York and Chicago and New York and the Pacific Coast.

By the 1920s, then, nationally integrated and standardised telephone infrastructures were being completed in the United States and in Europe. Operated and controlled by state-owned Postal, Telegraph and Telephone agencies (PTTs) in Europe and a state-regulated monopoly in the United States, telephone infrastructures were gradually extended to reach the entire population. National telephone monopolies attempted to satisfy specialised corporate requirements for terminal and transmission equipment. Until the 1970s, national telephone infrastructures formed one of the 'general conditions of production'; a service used collectively by a large number of corporations and industries, and organised to serve the municipal, regional and national requirements of societies as a whole, rather than a particular firm's profitability.[9]

2. Flexible production and digital telecommunications

In the period of mass production, the speed and capacity of tele-communications was in advance of data processing. From the 1950s, however, the capacity of information processing was multiplied by the invention of the computer. By the 1970s all kinds of information including data, text and video images could be converted into digital form and transmitted. In this period of information-intensive flexible production, improvements in the capacity of data processing were ahead of telecommunications. Analogue telecommunications systems had to be technologically upgraded for digital transmission. This marked the beginning of the convergence of data processing and telecommunications, and the formation of digital information systems.

Demands for new conditions of communications

From the 1950s, the spatial expansion of mass production and adoption of computerised automation technologies fuelled the growth in corporate demands for a modernised telecommunications infrastructure capable of transmitting information in digital form.[10] First, the rise of the multidivisional firm and continued geographical dispersal of activities – especially after 1945 – increased the requirements for telecommunications over long distances. Driven by the need to gain access to new sources of labour, raw materials, low-cost sites of production, and new geographical markets, the highly concentrated plant typical of early mass producers was superseded by scattered, decentralised plants and offices. Consequently, larger volumes of accurate and detailed data flowed along corporate lines of communication connecting remote plants in various operating divisions.

For example, in the 1950s, General Motors began shifting car assembly operations out of Michigan. By the 1980s, General Motors had 147 plants within the United States. Between 1947 and 1977, the aggregate number of domestic multi-unit manufacturing enterprises in the United States increased from 35,202 in 1947 to 81,241 in 1977, in comparison with a growth in single-unit firms from 205,605 to 278,687 over the same period. This trend towards multi-unit corporations affected all sectors of the American economy, including manufacturing, services and primary industries. For example, while the number of banks in the United States remained constant at about 14,000 between 1946 and 1979, the number of affiliated branches multiplied tenfold.

Second, the telephone system had to be technically upgraded to carry large volumes of data in addition to voice messages. In fact, the need to transmit data preceded the introduction of computerised data processing facilities. Electromechanical punched card information processing facilities, including accounting, payroll and production control, were incorporated in many business activities by the turn of the twentieth century. A decade prior to the commercial application of computing in the mid-1950s, General Electric and IBM obtained a licence to build a microwave network for data transmission between Washington, New York City, and Schenectady.

Electromechanical data processing techniques were superseded by the introduction of the computer, or electronic data processing, in the early 1950s.[11] The computer combines the binary form of mathematics (which uses only 1 and 0) with the power and switching capabilities of electronics. Electronic data processing increased both the speed with which data could be compiled and the range of possible aggregates. Computers were used to automate routine activities in the plant, such as devices used in controlling the temperature, pressure, speed and other physical conditions of production. During the 1960s and 1970s, computerisation extended to numerous corporate activities in the office ranging from simple record keeping to sophisticated forms of sales inventory control, accounting and credit authorisation.

When first introduced in 1951 by the Census Bureau in the United States the computer utilised vacuum tubes. At their inception computers cost more than $2 million each. In a second phase of development the computer operated with transistors, and in a third, semiconductors. New technologies made computers more compact, cheaper, modular, and increased their computational speed and capacity. For example, whereas the cost to the customer of performing 100,000 multiplications was $1.38 using the early vacuum tube computer; with the transistorised models the cost was 25 cents; and by the late 1960s with micro-miniature circuits the cost was reduced to 3.5 cents or less.[12]

The geographical dispersal of plants and offices depended on suitable data communications between remote information-processing activities. In the mid-1950s, oil companies, large retailers and motor vehicle and computer companies in the United States required circuits for the transmission of data and computer programs. For example, with a centralised IBM data processing computer at a single location, Montgomery Ward, the retail distribution company, operated a service to three midwestern states using the high-speed computer for rapid delivery of orders which enabled retailers to cut back on inventories.

During the 1960s, centralised computer processing units within each firm were used to control a number of remote terminals in factories, branches of banks, and sales outlets. Such timesharing terminals had little or no independent processing capacity: rather they shared the centralised capacity of mainframe computers. Information about the performance of dispersed corporate productive activities was then transmitted over data transmission circuits to the mainframe computer and batch processed overnight. Improvements in the capacity of remote terminals and data networks during the 1970s permitted the transmission of information to central mainframes in real time. Connected with on-line information, which was analysed and supplied almost instantaneously, corporate management obtained minute-by-minute control over geographically dispersed branches.

Timesharing computer systems were eclipsed by the advent of distributed computing in the late 1970s. In distributed computer processing systems, control no longer necessarily resides in a single point: it is distributed throughout the computer network and involves intelligent operations carried out by terminals at remote locations with local processing power. Microcomputer machines, containing several central processing units, raised processing capacity beyond the power of traditional mainframe computers. After a further round of miniaturisation afforded by smaller more powerful semiconductors, dispersed microcomputers and personal computer workstations were introduced in the 1980s. But dispersion did not result in stand-alone data processing operations. On the contrary, the capacity and performance of personal computers depended on their interconnection over digital transmission and digital switches. Using personal computers, the tasks of data analysis and the storage and manipulation of information could be conducted by remote branches of corporations rather than centralised computers.

Corporate information systems

The development of electronic data processing did not merely increase the speed with which large quantities of data could be processed, it paved the way for the transformation of all information activities within the production process, including research and development, design, engineering, financial accounts and the control of production output. For the first time in the history of industrial capitalism, the rate of technological change in information activities surpassed that of physical production.

Computers provided a means of instantaneously retrieving, sorting and aggregating large quantities of data. The improved flexibility of the computer broadened the informational activities performed by electronic data processing. When the first computer was introduced into corporate operations it was used for such routine tasks as billing, payrolls, and accounting. By the early 1970s, with the introduction of small desk-size computers, purchased for a few thousand dollars and capable of thousands of calculations per second, electronic data processing was extended to numerous other decision-making areas of business including sales analyses, and monitoring of stock and inventory to reduce working capital requirements. Programmed to match corporate operations, electronic data processing furnished management with instantaneous information about:

which products, and even which models, designs, colours, and so on, are selling best and in which geographic areas; it can show the inventory status of the rapidly selling versus the lagging items, thus enabling management to make prompt adjustments in factory production; it can enable management to keep on top of the progress of a new or experimental model, permitting the prompt discontinuance of an unsuccessful item before heavy losses are incurred; it can show which is the most successful of different advertising programmes, sales approaches, or advertising media; it can reveal which dealers and which types of distributorship have the best – and the poorest – performance records in moving the company's products (Blair 1972: 149).

As the cost of computing declined, and the capacity of such equipment multiplied with further developments in miniaturisation, computers were applied to all aspects of day-to-day decision-making in the firm.

Previously distinct domains of physical and informational activities have been merged into a single interactive information system under centralised control. Computer communications have transformed the ways in which the modern corporation monitors and controls the process of production and distribution.[13] First, computer systems of information and communication have enhanced centralised control over the performance of each business unit belonging to the company: flows of accountancy data, forecasts, and financial information are transmitted from business units to the head office. Second, such systems improve the coordination of flows of raw materials and semi-finished components among interrelated units involved in the production of finished products.

Electronic processing and communication technologies have automated the interface between physical and information components of the production process. While the computerisation of information tasks has proceeded more rapidly than physical activities, many electronic devices are used to measure, record and control physical production processes. Such technological advances in physical activities resulted in islands of automation within plants and offices such as computer aided design (CAD), computer aided engineering (CAE) and computer aided manufacture (CAM).

Islands of automation are being connected by data communication networks; providing the potential for the fusion of productive activities into a single, flexible system of production. The digital logic of computers provides a common language for controlling the physical volumes, throughputs and outputs of machines to produce a variety of products for segmented markets. Information systems offer the firm the advantages that the assembly line under mass production gave the plant. The firm and its related customers and suppliers become a continuous flow of activities, information, evaluations and decisions. But, as Perez (1985: 454) clarifies, 'there is a crucial difference: whereas the assembly line was based on the constant repetition of the same sequence of events, information technology is based on a system of feedback loops for the optimisation of the most diverse – and changing – activities'. Flows of accurate, instantaneous information – about which line of products, designs, colours are selling in which markets; variations in exchange rates; inventory status of rapidly selling or lagging items of stock; and orders and deliveries – help centralised corporate management coordinate interconnected systems of flexible production.

Digital technologies have been used to enhance the informational characteristics of the product, and create new products or services. For example, information networks have created new financial services such as electronic funds transfer at the point of sale (EFT/

POS). This system furnishes the calculations and transactions involved in the instantaneous transfer of cash in retail shops. There are many types of information services including airline reservation systems, the transmission of stock market quotations, and banking transactions over the global SWIFT system owned by a cooperative of banks.

Telecommunication networks are used to coordinate the purchase of supplies and match output with market demand. Companies have attempted to improve their productive efficiency by installing computerised systems of communication to coordinate the delivery of raw materials and semi-finished inputs. Electronic order-entry systems have reduced to a few seconds the time taken to exchange documents when ordering supplies. The potential for flexibility in production is enhanced by the ability to re-direct supplies to different production plants. Sudden variations in the prices of raw materials and components, which can significantly raise the costs of inputs, have been kept to a minimum by the capability to order needed supplies almost instantaneously over digital networks. Where long-term contractual relationships with suppliers exist, electronic networks may replace traditional voice and mail communications with suppliers. This form of 'electronic quasi-integration' has helped to reduce stocks of inventories, lowered working capital requirements, and improved the scheduling of production processes.

3. Digital information and communication systems

During the 1960s and 1970s, therefore, the technological revolution in telecommunications was driven by the growth of electronically-controlled information activities in the production process. Improvements in the capacity and flexibility of computerised data processing generated pressures to transform the traditional telephone system. The provision of a relatively standardised telephone service by traditional PTT monopolies was no longer compatible with corporate communication requirements in the period of digital telecommunications. From the 1950s, as demands for improved telecommunications swelled, there emerged new technological means of supplying corporate communication needs.

In part, PTTs were slow to respond to corporate demands because they were primarily concerned with realising their public service obligations. Preoccupied with the task of providing sufficient capacity to accommodate a growth in voice traffic of 10 to 15 per cent a year during the 1960s and 1970s, PTTs and traditional equipment suppliers found it difficult to keep pace with requirements for data transmission. For example, with 2 million unsatisfied orders at the end of World War Two, AT&T focused on expanding its service to cope with the post-war demand for voice telephony: by 1956 the number of telephones in service in the United States had doubled and over 70 per cent of American households had telephones. But, more importantly, like the telegraph monopolies of the 1870s which attempted to preserve lumpy investments in telegraph equipment rather than embrace the new telephone technologies, so the telephone monopolies in the 1970s were reluctant to incur the massive devaluation of sunk capital entailed in transforming the whole telephone system from analogue to digital transmission. And because the monopoly held by telephone administrations was sanctioned by the nation state, there was no incentive for PTTs to make the conversion.

Technological transformation

The transition from analogue to digital transmission depended on further technological developments. Although computing and telecommunications developed as largely separate industries in the 1950s, there were important similarities in the design of the internal operations of the two technologies which suggested that they could converge. Digital signals in a computer were switched and multiplexed (the combination of a number of channels over a single physical path) over data channels between the central processing unit and peripheral devices, just as voice signals were multiplexed and switched to their destination over long-distance lines. Leased data circuits connecting terminals and the centralised computer over the telephone network (which were functionally equivalent to the internal transmission channels of a computer) effectively expanded the computer to include the telephone system. Before the two technologies could be merged and the capacity of telecommunications increased, three differences in the design goals had to be overcome.[14]

First, whereas computers were designed to transmit data, telephone systems were designed to transmit voice. The switching and multiplexing functions within a computer were designed to process signals coded in digital form. The telephone system handled signals in analogue form, which varied according to the infinite number of amplitudes of the human voice. Different switching and multiplexing technologies were required in handling analogue and digital messages. While a typical telephone call continued for minutes, computers often used telecommunication circuits for short bursts of a few seconds or less. In the 1970s, the average call set-up time on a public switched network was ten to fifteen seconds – a considerable lapse in time for computer use. Moreover, the capacity of the voice network for the transmission of data was also limited because the analogue system could not furnish full duplex operation, i.e. transmit in both directions simultaneously. Because of the limitations imposed by the two-wire portions of the analogue network and the need for echo suppressors, a delay occurred – imperceptible to the human ear – when conversation was reversed. This connection delay prevented efficient data transmission between high-speed computers. Pulse Code Modulation, the technique for converting voice signals into digital form, emerged in the 1960s and formed the basis of integrated networks capable of carrying voice, data and image messages.

Second, data transmission required extreme accuracy to enable the receiving terminal to be able to distinguish between two states (on and off) for each bit of digital information. Distortion in digital signals could be eliminated during transmission so that an exact replica of the message was received at the destination. By contrast an exact replica of the human voice in analogue form could not be reproduced. Analogue transmission can be transmitted with some degree of error because the human ear can tolerate distortion. Analogue systems can be amplified but not regenerated. Therefore, when used for data transmission analogue techniques increase error rates, and require costly corrective measures.

Third, computer systems were designed to cope with system failure for short periods of time. By contrast, the total breakdown in the telephone system would completely eliminate the service to the subscriber. However, with the development of large-scale timesharing and distributed computer networks, used extensively for processing transactions in banks, computers have also acquired a similar need to avoid total system failure.

Institutional change

By the 1970s, corporate demands for improved communications were felt in every country and culminated in worldwide pressures to restructure the monopolistic national telecommunications sectors. Under the traditional arrangement, PTTs provided a homogeneous service, while a few long-standing private telecommunications equipment suppliers provided standardised switching, transmission and terminal equipment used in public and leased-line networks. In Britain, for example, the Post Office procured most of its equipment from three suppliers: GEC, Plessey and STC. The PTTs set exacting standards for equipment attached to the network (justified to maintain system integrity) and suppliers were obliged to sell equipment to the monopoly carrier, not directly to end-users. Regulations prohibited users from attaching equipment to the network, ranging from telephone instruments and PBXs to sophisticated computers, that was not owned or supplied by PTT monopolies.

This traditional monopoly structure was slow to accommodate three pressures for change. First, large corporate users required transmission circuits capable of transmitting data traffic between computer terminals. Efficient data transmission (connecting scattered remote terminals to a centralised computer data base and timesharing of computers among numerous users) could not be adequately satisfied by a network designed for voice communications. By the 1980s, data communication requirements ranged from messages transmitted in short bursts to those requiring continuous interconnection; and from services requiring a small proportion of the voice channel to the communication of design information requiring large bandwidth capacity. PTTs managed to accommodate business user demands by leasing dedicated lines to data transmission users, or by creating separate analogue public data networks. However, because early public data networks were unreliable, many corporations relied on leased-line data networks.

Data transmission over public and leased-line networks was improved by the creation of packet-switching techniques, invented by the U.S. Department of Defense. Traditional voice telephone networks were based on circuit-switched transmission: a line was allocated to a single subscriber and kept open for the duration of the call. By contrast, packet-switching techniques break up the message into packets of information: computers are used to arrange and store groups of digitised data (packets) for transmission at high speeds over the fastest or cheapest path in a computer-controlled telecommunications network. Packets sent individually over various circuits are rearranged to furnish an exact replica of the message at the receiving terminal. While utilisable for voice and data transmission, packet switching is a particularly efficient means of data communication owing to its capacity to transmit large volumes of data at low cost, with few errors and with brief connection times. With the appropriate software (computer instructions and protocols), packet switched networks can be programmed to furnish connections between non-standardised computer terminals. For PTTs, the introduction of separate public and leased-line data networks were temporary measures, while the much slower process of upgrading entire telephone networks for digital transmission was underway.

Second, the merging of data processing and telecommunications equipment called into question the traditional regulatory assumption that control over an end-to-end service should be placed in the hands of a single supplier. Corporations wanted the freedom to decide which terminals, electronic PBXs, and computing equipment they attached to private leased-line networks. A wide variety of terminals was being installed in the user premises. For example, terminals for verifying credit cards were different from those for handling airline reservation systems, or for high-speed facsimile transmission. Each application required its own customised terminal equipment with the requisite speed, capacity, and flexibility of operation.[15]

Third, business users, equipment suppliers and potential suppliers of information services argued that the use of computers and development of computer services should not be subject to monopoly control. The computer generated demands for information services which were entirely different from the conventional voice telephone message. Once converted into digital form, information can be processed and transmitted (at various bit rates) as a number of 'value-added services' in the form of data, text and video messages. Value-added services utilise computers and software to add value to basic telecommunications circuits leased from local or long-distance carriers: examples include computer processing of data transmitted from remote locations, market data base storage facilities, electronic data interchange, electronic mail, videotext, videoconferencing and electronic fund transfers. Value-added services are bundled into applications tailored to the requirements of specific firms and industries (such as finance or motor vehicles), or particular functions such as part orders, credit card authorisation, Computer Aided Design or Computer Aided Manufacture communications. Although with spare capacity on public networks PTTs want to supply value-added services, they have largely been unsuccessful in providing the range and customisation of services required by business users.

In each of these three closed telecommunications markets, large users sought greater choice and flexibility over the telecommunication facilities they required to develop digital information and communication systems. Business users campaigned for the provision of leased-lines at cost price and alternative low cost forms of transmission (such as microwave radio and satellite communications),[16] together with the liberalisation of terminal equipment and value-added services markets. In the United States, Europe and Japan, a conflict of interests emerged between, on the one hand, an innovating sphere of large corporate users and computer manufacturers who wanted the telecommunications sector opened up to competition and, on the other hand, the established interests of the PTTs and traditional equipment suppliers who defended the monopoly.

Business users and electronic manufacturers were successful in their objective to open up segments of telecommunications markets to competition. Liberalisation began in the United States in 1956 when private users were allowed to establish microwave radio transmission networks. Private microwave networks developed rapidly amongst American corporate users. By 1982, 1,000 private microwave networks had been established using 266,000 route miles of facilities and 15,000 relay stations. This regulatory change was followed by the liberalisation of terminal equipment in 1968 and the decision to allow competition in data transmission in 1971. In 1972 competitive entry was permitted in satellite transmission, and in 1976 competing common carriers were allowed interconnection to AT&T's public network. Although the policy liberalisation in terminal equipment and value-added services was replicated in every major country by the late 1980s, prior to the 1990s only Japan and Britain introduced competition into the provision of basic transmission. Choice over a range of technologies enabled corporate users to accomplish the integration of data processing and communications under private management.

Public versus private information systems

In response to corporate user pressures for change, by the late 1970s national governments and PTTs initiated massive programmes of fixed capital investment to upgrade national telephone networks for digital transmission. Public networks are being modernised to accommodate the growth in business data traffic: in the late 1980s, although voice telephony still accounted for more than 90 per cent of PTT revenues, a growth rate of 20 per cent a year suggests a parity between voice and data traffic volumes by the year 2000.[17] The convergence of information processing and telecommunications in the domain of national telecommunications has occurred in two phases. First, it began in the United States during the 1960s when a computerised system called Stored Programme Control (SPC) was introduced to control the public telephone exchange.[18] Second, since the mid-1980s many countries have begun the process of converting the entire analogue telephone system to a fully digital communications network.

The economy, speed and reliability of digital switching and transmission led to the replacement of discrete public analogue voice, data and telex networks by higher-capacity digital public networks. The future of national telecommunications depends on the Integrated Services Digital Network (ISDN): a service linking telephone and computer messages. ISDN is a concept which was devised by engineers within telecommunications administrations to establish standardised technical access to digital services over voice telephone networks. ISDN transmits a range of voice, data and image messages in digital form over a single integrated transmission path.[19] The implementation of ISDN has been driven by the need to utilise sunk capital in telephone switches and twisted-pair wires to conserve existing plant and equipment while attracting corporate telecommunications traffic back onto the public infrastructure. The same lines used for voice transmission can be upgraded to transmit computer data, facsimile images, limited motion video, and to furnish network management features such as call forwarding, automated billing and access to data bases. ISDN installs software in telephone terminals. With the intelligence required to store and manipulate information, such terminals can store messages, offer paging services and communicate with computer terminals. With intelligence placed inside the ISDN, the public network is effectively transformed into a large-scale value-added service.

The introduction of ISDN has been hampered by delays in establishing standards and the need for large investments in digital telephone exchanges required in the digital routing of end-to-end ISDN messages.[20] Indeed, recent improvements in signal compression, multiplexing techniques and packet-switching of voice traffic, which largely accomplish what the ISDN was originally designed to achieve, raise questions about whether or not the ISDN standard was over-engineered.[21] Every major public telecommunications operator has initiated plans to build ISDN networks by the second decade of the twenty-first century. For example, France Télécom and Deutsche Telekom plan to interconnect a narrowband ISDN infrastructure with a broadband optical fibre transmission network, offering high-capacity switching and transmission of television programmes, videoconferencing and interactive CAD/CAM applications. Fibre optic networks which convert electrical impulses into laser beams of light make it possible to transmit millions of telephone calls simultaneously along minute and regular pure glass fibres. These beams carry signals in digital form, and there is no difficulty in reconverting light signals to electrical impulses for the purposes of switching and reconversion to sound.[22] Broadband ISDN networks will be linked by high-capacity switches to provide voice, data and image communications services on a nationwide basis.

While national analogue networks were being slowly modernised, a more rapid integration of data processing and telecommunications technologies was accomplished privately within the corporate domain. Whereas public networks have planning lead times of five to ten years, followed by operational life spans of thirty years for the largest fixed capital investments, computer equipment used in business communications can be introduced rapidly and has a typical life span of only three to five years. The opening up of terminal equipment and value-added services markets to competition facilitated the rapid development of a wider range of cheaper digital telecommunications equipment owned and controlled by corporations. Prices of telecommunications equipment and services declined by 3.5 per cent a year during the 1970s and 1980s. Computer and electronics companies led the way in designing, supplying and operating private network technologies. For example, in the late 1980s, there were 22,000 computer networks based on IBM's Systems Network Architecture proprietary standard, in comparison with only 600 networks using public Open Systems Integration standards.

With the geographical dispersal of multi-unit corporate activities, and the use of computerised data processing to coordinate and control far-flung operations, there was a sharp rise in telecommunications costs during the 1970s and 1980s. In 1976, a survey of

400 New York Stock Exchange firms revealed that telecommunications costs accounted for the third largest overhead cost after personnel and interest expenses.[23] According to one estimate telecommunications costs in the mid-1980s were seldom less than 20 per cent of total overheads in company budgets.[24] While some companies purchased computing and communications services from specialised suppliers, many large corporations established in-house telecommunications and data processing departments, employing skilled technicians and managers whose job was to operate the separate networks while minimising costs. Once data processing and telecommunications services were provided in-house they often resulted in excess capacity which could be sold to customers for a fee.[25]

During the 1970s, many corporations throughout the world operated a mix of public and private leased-line transmission networks. Separate analogue networks carried voice, data and video communications. However, the capacity of disparate transmission networks was often under-utilised because certain information services could not be transported over the various transmission networks. For example, data transmission networks were often incapable of transmitting high volumes of CAD information for interactive communication. Moreover, networks were prone to congestion because data traffic carried through a limited number of nodes soon became saturated. From the mid-1980s, the construction and operation of corporate integrated digital networks – small-scale versions of the public ISDN – were built to transcend inefficiencies associated with operating separate voice, data and video networks. Digital PBXs with the capacity to transmit integrated voice and data messages to computer terminals over the same transmission path lowered transmission costs. Using the advanced software of the PBX, the transmission capacity of private networks could be controlled to match variations in the volume and flow of traffic.

Integrated digital networks are being constructed to connect worldwide corporate operations. By 1984 there were more than 1,000 worldwide corporate communications systems used to control widely dispersed corporate empires.[26] For example, Texas Instruments, a diversified electronics company, had fifty major plants in nineteen countries and operated a satellite-based system to integrate 8,000 enquiry terminals for worldwide production planning, finance, cost accounting, marketing, personnel management and electronic mail. In 1987, there were estimated to be 8,000 private networks of all sizes in the United States, including 3,000 firms with large private networks.[27] In Japan, for example, the number of these systems increased from 40 in 1974 to 121 in 1979, and to 372 in 1983.[28] While transnational voice traffic was increasing at a rate of 5–15 per cent annually in the late 1970s, transnational data communication mainly operated by large business users was increasing at a rate of 30 per cent a year.[29] Annual expenditures of the largest transnational telecommunication users ranged from $20 million to $1 billion; the average lying between $50 million and $100 million. In 1984, American Express was spending in excess of $500 million annually on telecommunications to support its global activities.

Conclusion

In the period of mass production, information transmitted by telegraphic and telephonic means over corporate networks could be supplied more rapidly than it could be processed. From the 1950s, mass production was gradually transformed by the introduction of computers into the firm. This revolution in production technology multiplied the capacity and speed of data processing. To match the increased velocity of electronic data processing the telephone system had to be modernised to carry large volumes of data in digital form. Demands for advanced systems of telecommunications capable of transmitting data swelled as firms began to incorporate data processing facilities throughout globally dispersed operations. In the 1960s, 1970s and 1980s, under pressure from corporate users and computer manufacturers, parts of national telecommunications were exposed to competition. Slow progress in the application of computing to the telephone system forced corporations into developing their own corporate digital networks using a range of equipment and services supplied by the newly liberalised telecommunications markets.

Notes

1. The history of technology includes many examples, notably the machine-tool industry, of changes in one component of an interdependent system creating an inducement for technical changes elsewhere in the system. N. Rosenberg (1976), pp108–125, *Perspectives on Technology*, Cambridge University Press, Cambridge.
2. In the early nineteenth century, for example, infrastructures inherited

from the previous industrial period – including stage coach, canal and inland waterways, blocked the penetration of cheap goods mass produced by large-scale industry in Europe into foreign markets, and hindered the formation of national markets in Western Europe and the United States. E. Mandel, p51 (1975), *Late Capitalism*, Penguin, Harmondsworth.

3. A.D. Chandler, p21 (1962), *Strategy and Structure: Chapters in the History of the Industrial Enterprise*, MIT Press, Cambridge, Mass.

4. In Britain the railway boom from the late 1830s, together with the growing use made of the telegraph by the press, stimulated the expansion of private telegraphs owned, operated and controlled by railway companies.

5. R.L. Thompson, p204 (1947), *Wiring a Continent: The History of the Telegraph in the United States*, Princeton University Press, Princeton.

6. J.M. Herring and G.C. Cross (1936), *Telecommunications: Economics and Regulation*, McGraw-Hill, New York.

7. Ibid. The most important development was the automatic multiplex telegraph invented in 1915 by Western Union and the Western Electric Company which permitted the transmission of eight messages simultaneously over a single wire, four in each direction at high-speed. This and other improvements such as the keyboard printer and telegraph carrier system so increased the capacity of telegraph plant that by the 1930s it was capable of handling much more than the volume of traffic carried. 'The installation of multiplex apparatus on the main lines of the Western Union at an outlay of about $6,000,000 saved the company an expenditure of many times that amount for wire plant which would have been required to handle the increased traffic.'

8. S.H. Aronson, p29 (1977), 'Bell's Electrical Toy: What's the Use? The Sociology of Early Telephone Usage', in *The Social Impact of the Telephone* (ed.) I. de Sola Pool, MIT Press, Cambridge, Mass.

9. K. Marx, p530 (1973), *Grundrisse: Foundations of the Critique of Political Economy*, Penguin, Harmondsworth.

10. D. Schiller (1982a), 'Business Users and the Telecommunications Network', pp84–96 *Journal of Communication*, Autumn 1982.

11. J.M. Blair, pp144–145 (1972), *Economic Concentration: Structure, Behaviour and Public Policy*, Harcourt Brace Jovanovich, New York.

12. Blair, op. cit.

13. C. Antonelli (1987), 'The Emergence of the Network Firm', in *New Information Technology and Industrial Change: the Italian Case* (ed.) C. Antonelli, Kluwer Academic Publishers, Dordrecht.

14. G.W. Brock, pp267–269 (1981), *The Telecommunications Industry*, Harvard University Press, Cambridge, Mass. L.L. Johnson (1978), 'Boundaries to Monopoly and Regulation in Modern Telecommunications', pp127–155, in *Communications for Tomorrow: Policy Perspectives for the 1980s* (ed.) G.O. Robinson, Praeger Publishers, New York.

15. One of the most important items of terminal equipment was the modem – the means by which digital computer messages are converted into analogue signals for transmission over the telephone network.

16. Terrestrial microwave radio – a product of military research during

World War Two – furnished communication over long-distances using radio relay towers at twenty to thirty mile intervals to provide line of sight operations necessary in the microwave portion of the radio spectrum. Although microwave transmission offered a cheap alternative to wired coaxial cable over low-density routes of traffic, it was more expensive where high volumes of traffic were handled. Satellite transmission operated thousands of telephone calls over distances of thousands of miles, as long as receiving earth stations were within the line of sight of the satellite. While satellites offered lower unit costs in the transmission of messages than microwave or coaxial cable, satellite communication suffered from inaccuracy induced by overlapping, crowding and interference on all frequency bands in geo-stationary orbit.

17. J.C. Arnbak, p2 (1988), 'Telematics – aims and characteristics of a new technology'. Contribution to the international symposium, 'Telematics – Transportation and Spatial Development', 14–15 April 1988, The Netherlands Congress Centre, The Hague.

18. The telephone exchange consists of a control function, which monitors calls, identifies the caller and establishes connections, and the contact system, which establishes the physical link in the system. Electro-mechanical Strowger, Rotary and Crossbar exchanges established mechanical links between two metal pieces to make a contact. The system was controlled by analogue signals transmitted over analogue circuits. Digital switching substituted a computer for the electrical system. There are two main types of digital switches. Space division switching uses computers for the control function while utilising mechanical contacts between subscribers for the duration of the call, using reed relays and analogue signals. Time division switching uses computers for both the control function and for converting analogue signals based on pulse code modulation into digital form. Space division switching techniques have multiplied exchange capacity – a single switch can make 50,000 simultaneous logical connections – required to support higher volumes of traffic.

19. In Europe and the United States, information transmitted over narrowband-ISDN (using twisted-pair wires) can carry three separate channels, all using digital transmission: two 64 kbps B channels plus a 16 kbps D channel used for CSS 7 signalling (known as 2B + D). There are two types of ISDN services: basic access services for small business and domestic use over a single line for domestic customers; and primary access services for large corporations involving the bundling of a number of access lines together to offer higher bandwidth capacity (in Europe it is a 30 B channels + D service).

20. Open Systems Integration (OSI) reference model – a scheme developed by the International Standards Organisation (ISO), which is working in cooperation with national standards bodies, computer manufacturers and user groups – provides a normal standardisation procedure for integrating telecommunications and computing. ISDN is based on the seven layer OSI model. The bottom three layers of physical transmission refer to the function of telecommunications within the

seven layers of protocols. Operation of the transport mechanism (layer four) controls the transmission plant and equipment, and determines the ways in which value-added services are delivered to the end-user. The top five to seven layers which deliver specific value-added service applications to end-users refer to the field of data processing.

21. The answer depends on the extent of future demand for ISDN services. For a background discussion of issues concerning ISDN see N. Garnham (1987), 'Integrated Services Digital Network (ISDN) Research, A Background Paper', paper prepared for Programme for Information and Communication Technologies meeting 27 May 1987.

22. Fibre optics are applicable to those aspects of business communications requiring high bandwidths of capacity such as high-speed data transfers, exchanging manufacturing designs, or videoconferencing. Broadband networks based on high-speed fibre optic transmission for computer applications or high-definition television have a transmission capacity of between 150 megabits per second and several gigabits per second.

23. Schiller, p88 (1982a), op. cit.

24. G. McKendrick (1985), 'The Impact of New Trends in Telecommunications Services on Users', *Second Special Session on Telecommunications Policy*, OECD, 18–20 November 1985.

25. For example, Istel, the information technology firm, which was originally set up as a subsidiary serving the Rover Group with computer aided manufacturing systems, was divested in 1987. This broadened Istel's customer base, allowing it to serve financial services, manufacturing and travel industries, in addition to the Rover group.

26. United Nations Economic and Social Council, Commission on Transnational Corporations, 'The Role of Transnational Corporations in Transborder Data Flows', 18–27 April 1984, E/C10/1984/14, cited in D. Schiller and R.-L. Fregoso, p201 (1991), 'A private view of the digital world', pp195–208, *Telecommunications Policy*, June 1991.

27. J. Lusa (1987), 'Private Networks Proliferate Following Divestiture', *Communications Systems Worldwide*, November 1987.

28. K.P. Sauvant, p90 (1986), *International Transactions in Services: The Politics of Transborder Data Flows*, Westview Press, Boulder. The increase in transnational voice and data communications is also reflected in the growth in international leased-lines used by corporations: in OECD countries, the number of international voice circuits grew from nearly 9,000 in 1976 to 15,000 in 1981, while international data circuits increased from 3,000 in 1976 to almost 6,000 in 1981.

29. C. Antonelli and H. Ergas (n.d.), 'Computer Communications, The Costs of Coordination and Multinational Enterprise', mimeograph.

5 Case studies: corporate information systems

Since the onset of intensified corporate restructuring and global competition in the early 1970s, technological progress in physical activities has no longer been the main route to economic efficiency. Firms now depend on the use of cheaper flows of information transmitted through computers to generate improvements in productivity. No longer a general condition of production – like the telephone, electricity or road infrastructures – used collectively for business and public consumption, digital telecommunications technologies have become a 'particular condition of production', a source of competitiveness and profitability for individual firms.[1] Information carried over digital communications systems is used by corporations to shorten product development times, speed up production processes, minimise capital tied up as stock, and achieve a closer coordination of supply and demand. Digital technologies are used to coordinate the nervous system of the modern corporation: supporting corporate command and control centres, digital lines of communication provide almost instantaneous control of the information-intensive systems of flexible production.

This chapter examines the construction and operation of digital information systems under corporate control. Although the focus here is on case studies of corporate networks in Britain, empirical research shows that corporate telecommunications users in OECD industrialised countries have introduced similar technological and organisational changes in their systems of communication.[2] As we will see in Part III, since Britain has the largest number of private corporate networks and value-added services in Europe, the detailed case studies of a cross-section of British corporate users in the manufacturing and banking sectors of the economy provide a clear illustration of the ways in which corporations have been the pacemakers of change in the demand for digital telecommunications technologies. Corporate networks are composed of leased-line long-distance and international circuits linking geographically scattered plants, offices, and sites. The fixed capital invested in corporate networks – including private automated branch exchanges (PABXs), computer terminals, modems, and local area networks (LANS) – is either privately owned or, in the case of certain items of equipment such as transmission circuits, leased on a semi-permanent basis from national carriers. Telecommunication with the outside world is effected by interconnecting corporate PABXs with public exchanges. Public data networks and digital transmission capacity are used for certain forms of intra-corporate communications, such as communications with small offices and sites in remote locations where low traffic volumes do not justify the installation of leased circuits.

1. Information systems in retail banking

In comparison to assembly and flow-line production, a higher proportion of the production process in retail banking is accounted for by information activities involving the storage, manipulation, transmission and retrieval of data. In retail banks the production process is undertaken in branch offices and the product is a financial transaction between bank and customer.[3] Financial products sold over the network, such as instantaneous cash withdrawals (ATM systems) or electronic payment (EFT/POS), are consumed the moment they are produced.

Telecommunication networks in banks carry large volumes of customer information flowing from dispersed branches to centralised computers. The central computer supplies financial data to the terminals in bank branches, such as information required to perform standardised credit withdrawal transactions from automatic teller machines. Large retail banks have established worldwide telecommunications networks linking branches and subsidiaries. Commerzbank in Germany, for example, has installed a global network of leased lines linking its own branches with four subsidiaries, thirteen operative agencies, and sixteen representative offices, located in the important financial centres in Europe, the United States and the Far East. Information processed at one branch can be processed and reproduced at little or no marginal cost and communicated to all the other branches on the network. Money can be shunted between branches in different countries to exploit variations in exchange rates and profit opportunities. For example, a system of twenty-four-hour trading shifts the management of a bank's portfolio around the world from one branch to the next according to changes in time-zones.

In the 1970s, the major retail banks in Britain established separate analogue voice, data and video networks. In 1974 Barclays Bank installed separate analogue data and voice networks for in-house telecommunications.[4] The Bank's annual expenditures on telecommunications plant, equipment and operating costs amounted to approximately £100 million: £10 million of which was spent on leased circuits. The analogue data network was composed of long-distance leased circuits connecting 8,000 terminals in 2,400 of the bank's branches. It was interconnected via BT's public switched data network to international banking services operated in conjunction with other banks such as BACS, an EDI network which enabled people's salaries to be paid electronically into their bank accounts, and the SWIFT system for international interbank transfers.

Barclays' private telephone network was organised to serve the bank's regional areas. In 1987, long-distance circuits connected twenty-seven regional offices of the bank, which provided intra-corporate local telephony to 300 branches: local areas within a radius of fifty miles of each regional branch accounted for 80 per cent of the total intra-corporate voice traffic within the bank. Each of the regional offices was equipped with private PABX facilities to furnish private local telephone connections using leased-circuits with major branches of the bank. Most of the bank's smaller branches operated PBXs for switching messages to extensions within buildings and providing interconnections to the public telephone network.

These new demands for improved telecommunications stemmed from a shift in the production process of retail banks from manual punch-card information processing to electronic data processing. Substantial increases in data processing capacity required higher-capacity data communications bandwidth. This was achieved in Barclays Bank by installing a dedicated analogue network linking remote job entry terminals with centralised computers. After financial transactions had been recorded in the branch computers, data was transmitted to two centralised computers and batch-processed overnight. Records of transactions were processed and stored in files organised according to individual customer accounts.

In the late 1980s, retail banks sought to reduce the costs incurred in processing and transmitting growing volumes of information by building integrated digital networks. Digital transmission and switching techniques helped to tighten corporate control of the network by preventing traffic congestion and minimising the risks of a failure in the system.

For example, before 1985, Bank of America in the United States operated numerous analogue voice networks and seventy-six separate data networks.[5] In 1989, voice communications accounted for 70 per cent of the total traffic carried over the Bank of America's network, while data accounted for 30 per cent of total telecommunications costs. The bank's network control centre was unable to monitor all the different networks, and many of the different networks were unable to support new applications including a network of ATM machines, network management and money transfer systems. An integrated digital network carried the growing volume of traffic in data transmitted from point-of-sale terminals, and enabled the introduction of a branch computerised automation system. Using digital circuits, two backbone networks linking 130 locations were responsible for controlling traffic from the bank's 900 branches. In the mid-1980s, Bank of America was prevented from integrating the two voice and data digital networks because network management and control technologies capable of operating the bank's numerous networks were not available. Consequently, network management and control was established in two separate centres for voice and data transmission. Network control was placed in the hands of the bank's system engineering headquarters, while control of network maintenance tasks was handed over to AT&T. The network control centre developed a computerised inventory of the capacity and efficiency of every transmission link in the network. The bank estimated that improvements in capacity utilisation resulting from management of the networks as a single system would yield reductions of between 30 and 50 per cent over a period of five years in the average costs of messages transmitted.

Between 1987 and 1989, Barclays Bank adopted a similar strategy. It replaced its analogue networks with a separate private digital data network costing £35.5 million and separate voice network costing £3.7 million. By 1990, the traffic load handling capacity of the digital data system was 500 times greater than the old analogue network. In 1988, the bank spent approximately £350 million on new information technology equipment. Improvements in network capacity and cheaper information handling enabled the bank to conduct a growing volume of data transactions. Barclays had an ATM network in 2,400 branches, which was part of a larger

ATM network connected to 4,000 ATM machines shared with three retail banks. Between 1991 and 1992, the bank planned to install private circuits linking metropolitan branches with large corporate customers.

Barclays Bank converged the two digital networks to form a single system called Barclays Integrated Network System (BINS), capable of high-speed packet-switching of information services. The backbone of BINS consisted of 2 megabits-per-second leased circuits supplied by BT, linking major sites in London, Poole, Gloucester, Knutsford and Manchester. The digital system provided the additional capacity required to process, settle transactions and transmit large volumes of voice, data and video information services between branches. Eliminating the need for terminals dedicated to specific applications, a number of value-added services were offered over the network including ATM cash withdrawal services, credit authorisation cheque clearing, and EFT/POS.

In the late 1980s, a second phase of automation changed the production process in retail banking from batch processing to on-line, real time systems of data processing. Under batch-processing, customer files were organised on an account basis rather than a customer basis. The task of drawing together information about customers for marketing purposes was time consuming. The on-line, real time banking system, on the other hand, connected counselling workstations in bank branches, which enabled staff to retrieve and analyse details of customer records almost instantaneously. Branches were linked to central computers and changes in accounts recorded instantly. Computerised records retrieved on computer screens replaced handwritten and computer records of ledgers, customer accounts and financial reports. Instead of reading handwritten notes or lengthy computer printouts, branch managers could make quick decisions by inspecting standard reports, about such matters as overdrawn accounts and loan arrears, using desk-top workstations. In Britain, the four major retail banks integrated records of money and financial transactions with customers in centralised computers.[6] Using relational data base techniques, the computer interrogated different sets of customer records and made cross-references between different files of information. Staff released from counter duty operated workstations to respond instantly to enquiries and deal face-to-face with customers. Using desk-top terminals and video screens bank staff sold a variety of financial services (credit contracts, assurance, home mortgages, or advice on portfolio investments). Computerised data about customers, recorded when selling one service, were used to market – or 'cross-sell' – additional flexible services to satisfy particular market segments: distinguished by age, salary, type of residence, family circumstances, and other aspects of lifestyle.

In 1989 Barclays Bank installed an on-line computer system of high-capacity intelligent workstations.[7] General-purpose terminals were introduced in the bank's 2,400 branches. These workstations supported a new cheque and credit clearing system consisting of more than 1,500 terminals, capable of processing up to forty cheques per minute. All data from the intelligent terminals were transmitted to Barclays Bank's Central Accounting System for automatic account update. In each branch clusters of terminals were interconnected to a branch controller – a minicomputer – linked to the two computing centres via the digital data network. A 'Global Banking System' for customer accounts was created by interconnecting branches to its worldwide network.

All of the retail banks in Britain have built excess capacity into digital networks to accommodate further growth in the volume of data traffic associated with the substitution of on-line, real time automated banking systems for routine paper-based information processing and communication activities. Banks have constructed 100 per cent redundant transmission and centralised computing capacity in order to protect on-line banking systems from the risk of transmission failure. By the mid-1980s, the business of banking became so totally dependent on digital networks that a failure in the network would paralyse corporate activities. To avoid the delays in connection times and congestion in traffic experienced during peak calling periods over the public packet-switched data networks, Barclays Bank installed duplicate leased-line circuits supplied by Mercury, Britain's competing long-distance carrier, which provided redundant capacity along the routes of the backbone digital network.

2. Information systems in textiles and clothing

In contrast to assembly processes where a variety of intermediate products enter the production process and are assembled at different stages, in large-scale textile and clothing production huge quantities of homogeneous raw materials and garments are transformed into finished items after flowing through the various stages of spinning, weaving, dyeing and cutting. Flow-line production processes in textiles and clothing plants rely on accurate information from corporate headquarters concerning the management of supplies, scheduling of production runs and destination of finished products.[8] Information flows along a triangular network from marketing, sales outlets, headquarters to production plants. Manufacturing plants have little autonomy and depend on information concerning orders and production schedules transmitted from the head office. In textiles and clothing production, a great deal of information is absorbed in monitoring and controlling physical activities before and after production; in relation to the supply of inputs, and sale and distribution of finished products.

Modifications in the product made in the final stages of production require relatively few exchanges of information. For example, the main products of Levi Strauss, the clothing company, are mass produced jeans. Sophisticated information networks linking marketing organisations to Levi's production plants have not been installed because there are few design changes in this standardised clothing product. In the production of fashion clothing, by contrast, frequent design alterations (which accommodate new tastes and seasonal alterations in styles, colours and materials) depend on computer-aided flexible production processes. Consequently, in the production and development of a range of fashion items which are tailored to the requirements of constantly shifting markets, large volumes of processed information are transmitted between design centres, marketing organisations and production plants. Rapid changes in the product mix affect supplies and stocks of inter-mediate products and production cycles. Digital telecommunications networks have also transformed corporate planning: probabilistic planning of production in anticipation of demand has been superseded by real-time planning using constantly up-dated information about rapid selling stocks to organise production runs of clothing. Enabling a close match between production output and fluctuations in demand, these networks have also contributed to reductions in the size of inventories.

In the early 1970s, Britain's large textiles and clothing companies invested in separate analogue voice and data networks. Courtaulds, the multidivisional textiles and clothing manufacturer (which diversified in the post-war years into chemicals, paints and woodpulp), created a private analogue nationwide voice network linked to electromechanical PABX switches in the company's main sites in Coventry, Spondon, Felling, Manchester and London.[9] The rest of the company's operations in Britain were connected to this hub network by leased-line circuits.

Whereas the development of the voice network was centrally coordinated, data networks evolved under the decentralised direction of autonomous corporate divisions. Each corporate division installed non-standardised computerised data processing and data transmission networks. Approximately thirty specialised data networks were installed, each dedicated to computer applications suited to different lines of business. This lack of coordination in the development of the early data networks was inefficient and costly, since it resulted in incompatible computer equipment and network protocols, duplication of leased-line circuits, and prevented the introduction of new applications (such as electronic mail, access to the public packet-switched data network or viewdata) on a corporate-wide basis.

In 1984, the Courtaulds management therefore initiated a strategic plan to expand the use of information technology in the operating divisions. An information technology forum was created which reported directly to the board of directors. With the formation of Courtaulds Information Service in 1986, Courtaulds merged previously separate telecommunications and data processing departments in order to furnish single integrated solutions for the company's information and communication requirements. The corporate plan was based on a centralised information strategy to create an integrated corporate telecommunications system able to carry a variety of applications at low cost.

In the 1970s, two punch-card data processing bureaus located in Coventry and Spondon were gradually replaced by electronic processing applications for recording corporate information, such as payroll and financial accounts. Although the development of information technology within various corporate divisions evolved in a decentralised way, there was a need for corporate-wide data communications between remote sites and divisional headquarters. In 1985, Courtaulds Information Service put forward a plan to modernise the voice network to form a backbone digital network for integrated voice, data, facsimile, telex and videoconferencing transmission. The integrated digital network was designed to reduce the costs of information processing and communication, while improving centralised lines of communication providing rapid and accurate information to dispersed manufacturing plants and marketing organisations. While Courtaulds information network requirements could have been satisfied by a widely available public digital network, the slow development of ISDN in Britain forced the company to build a private network. In doing so, the company selected plant and equipment from a range of digital PABXs and used low cost leased circuits made available after the liberalisation of telecommunications in Britain in the early 1980s.

In 1988, approximately 100 of Courtaulds' sites in Britain were connected to the company's private digital voice and data networks. A fixed capital expenditure of £2.25 million was made to convert the analogue speech and data networks into digital transmission systems. On the one hand, a backbone digital voice network was built using long-distance leased circuits (with a transmission capacity of 2 megabits-per-second) supplied by British Telecom, connecting the company's main business operations in London, Coventry, Derby, Manchester, Bradford and Newcastle. Courtaulds' dispersed plants and offices were linked to this hub network using 64 kilobits-per-second leased-lines. On the other hand, a company-wide digital data network was built in 1988 using 64 kilobits-per-second circuits connecting six existing Hewlett Packard minicomputers in Spondon, Grimsby and Coventry. Originally this data network was created to meet the data communications requirements of one corporate group, the fibres division. Although it used the same transmission capacity as the voice network, the data network was connected to packet-switch exchanges located in London, Coventry, Derby, Manchester, Grimsby and Newcastle. Radiating from this hub data network were leased-line circuits connected to local plants and offices. Operated from a single location in Coventry, transmission faults were automatically reported to the control centre, and the capacity of the digital transmission network was automatically adjusted to accommodate changes in the volume of traffic flowing between headquarters, plants and marketing units, and new computer applications were introduced on a corporate-wide basis.

Textiles, the most highly integrated of Courtaulds' divisions, consisted of a chain of interrelated flow processes in textile spinning and weaving, through labour intensive clothing manufacture, to the distribution of the finished products to retailing outlets. With few external connections with other corporate divisions, the private network supported data processing activities in 207 of Courtaulds' textile and clothing plants and marketing organisations. Three important network services were introduced to support the coordination and control of manufacturing plants and marketing offices in Courtaulds' textiles division.

First, IBM's Managed Network Service provided an application called Production Planning Control System over an SNA proprietary computing and data network. Courtaulds invested £1.5 million in plant, equipment and software required to operate the data network in the company's clothing plants.[10] The Courtaulds Clothing group, a part of the textiles division, consisted of forty companies specialised in the production of a range of garments for multiple retailing shops, such as Marks and Spencer and British Home Stores. In 1988, twenty-eight of Courtaulds' clothing factories had personal computers using the production planning system which were linked to a centralised computer that monitored the progress of every piece of material and garment flowing in and out of each plant in interrelated supply chains.

Supplying production managers in each plant with accurate and reliable data, this value-added service contributed to improvements in the coordination of inputs and reductions in goods tied up as inventories, reduced waste, and cut production times. It was designed to keep track of individual orders by identifying the style, colour and size of garment. Production managers used the information to calculate how many plastic bags and hangers were needed for each order. Having monitored the progress of raw materials and garments through various physical processes, the system checked whether supplies arrived on time, and whether the quantity and quality matched the original order. Using multi-dimensional spreadsheets, the system created a model of the whole production cycle, measuring the extent to which costs were reduced by efforts to speed up the various stages of production.

The Production Planning Control System was used to eliminate bottlenecks which disrupted the flow-line processes of vertically integrated textiles plants. The automation of physical production activities was more advanced in textiles plants, especially in the areas of spinning and weaving, where long production runs of standardised products – in the form of reels of cloth – enabled high-speeds of throughput. There was, however, a limit to the degree of automation of physical activities in clothing plants, where production was labour intensive. Although computerised cutting and automated handling systems had been installed, the product (various garments) could not be standardised to the same extent as the output of textiles plants and the fabrics used were often too delicate to be handled by automated machinery. The production planning system was designed to increase the speed with which semi-finished items flowed through the clothing stages of the production process. Disruptions in production caused by interruptions in the supply of raw materials could be quickly overcome by switching to alternative production plants. By 1988, Courtaulds' subsidiary, the Broughton company, the first firm to adopt the production planning system, had quadrupled the number of styles produced, reduced the amount of sub-standard merchandise to 1 per cent, and cut its raw material stocks by 30 per cent. Following the introduction of the information system the number of orders supplied within five days of the agreed delivery date increased from a third in 1986 to three-quarters in 1988.

Second, Tradanet, an electronic data interchange (EDI) application operated by a third party supplier called Information Network Services (jointly owned by GEIS and ICL), provided a communication service linking Courtaulds' clothing plants with its major retail customer, Marks and Spencer. Instantaneously recording orders and invoices, and transmitting notifications of deliveries, this EDI network substituted paperless trading for manual systems of ordering and invoicing. Because of the vertically integrated structure of textiles and clothing in Courtaulds, the EDI network was used to coordinate the distribution of outputs rather than supply of inputs. Marks and Spencer used Tradanet to issue orders to enable clothing suppliers to plan production schedules, rather than supply information to alter the product mix to accommodate fluctuations in demand.

Third, Courtaulds introduced a graphics application supplied by the software company, Silicon Graphics, to transmit design information from personal computers in retail shops to the company's textiles CAD operations. Using the new communication service to transmit orders for sophisticated styles in smaller quantities, supplied more rapidly and frequently, retailers no longer had to place large orders for standardised items of clothing. Access to computer terminals located in major department stores, such as Littlewoods, allowed customers to select styles, colours and make minor product alterations. A more interactive relationship between customer demand and product design was established, with designers responding to initiatives generated by customers. The system aimed to be responsive to changing customer demand by reducing the lead times from design creation to first availability of the product, and by speeding up the replenishment of runs of existing products. Pre-production costs were reduced because computer aided photographic designs eliminated costs incurred in sampling – samples of garments to order cost around £500 in materials, labour and overheads to produce.

Instead of having buyers travel to textile design offices, design alterations were communicated over Courtaulds digital data network to the manufacturing plants, both within Britain and in the Far East. The coordination of complex flows of traffic between connected plants and design offices was controlled from the network management and control centre in Coventry. Rather than using the public network for transmission, store and forward transmission over 2 megabits-per-second leased circuits were installed to deposit design files and reports sent by retailers in the mailboxes in Courtaulds' design offices. By 1989, according to company estimates, the design application had reduced product lead times from thirteen to six weeks – that is to say, clothing operations could design, produce and distribute an entirely new range of garments in a six-week cycle. Eventually the design application will be combined with the Production Planning Control System and Tradanet to form a single integrated information system with a central point of control handling a circuit of information beginning with customers, flowing through design and production plants, and ending with the garment being delivered to the retailer.

3. Information systems in motor vehicles

In the mass production of motor vehicles, the great variety of intermediate products which enter the assembly process must be delivered on time while capital tied up in stocks is kept to a minimum.[11] A large volume of information is processed and transmitted in supplying inputs, delivering the final product, and in coordinating the direct production process. A triangular information network operated by a head office is used as a command and control centre from which to orchestrate a close relationship between vertically integrated stages of motor vehicle production and distribution. Flows of information transmitted to the headquarters and passed on to plants as production orders consist of data about marketing situations and forecasts, inventory levels of goods on-hand for sale, transport logistics, current orders and invoices.

The principles of the mass production in the motor vehicle industry were pioneered by the Ford Motor Company. Until the 1970s, Ford's mass production plants developed special purpose machinery and mechanised tooling equipment for each model of car. Once set-up the machinery could not be easily switched to another model. Large volumes of standardised cars were produced in long production runs. Since the 1970s, the application of electronics to control physical processes in these large-scale plants transformed the technology of mass production by introducing the flexibility to produce a variety of models for segmented markets. A number of computer automated general-purpose machines were installed in production plants (such as Computer Numerically Controlled Tools and Flexible Manufacturing Systems), and in office work, engineering and product design (such as Computer Aided Engineering (CAE) and CAD). General-purpose computerised machines facilitate the flexible production of differentiated products tailored for particular markets while minimising the set-up costs entailed in changing over to the production of a new model. In the late 1980s, many motor vehicle manufacturers reorganised their information and communication technologies to form single digital networks which used design information in all stages of the production process. Most notably, General Motors created a network of CAD/ CAE/CAM/CIM (Computer Aided Manufacture/Computer Integrated Manufacture), named the 'C4 strategy', which linked the physical and information processes of design, manufacture and marketing into a single information-intensive system.[12]

In the motor vehicle industry, information networks linking marketing organisations to the production process are used to achieve a close match between output and market demand. Marketing information is used to make minor modifications in standardised models, colour and accessories, and to achieve a close match between output and changes in consumer demand. Yet in motor vehicle production it is information generated in the creation of new models which places the heaviest demands on telecommunications capacity. The capacity of information networks required in exchanging design and engineering data during product development increases proportionately with the number of interdependent design and engineering units connected to the network, and the spatial distance separating each of them.

After the Second World War, Ford expanded its worldwide operations and adopted a multidivisional structure divided into separate geographical regions. In the Ford of Europe region of this new structure, information concerning the assembly plants and marketing units flowed to the European headquarters in Brentwood, Britain – the divisional command and control centre.[13] In the late 1980s, Ford of Europe operated separate voice, data and video-conferencing networks linking 130 locations dispersed throughout Europe, including circuits linking six assembly plants, and marketing, dealers, component and material suppliers in sixteen European countries. Ford operated a single analogue voice network installed in 1964 based on electromechanical PBXs. By the mid-1980s, the private voice network had approximately 1,000 leased-lines, connecting thirty-four European locations. Two separate analogue data networks were installed in 1974 to support the transmission of corporate and engineering data processed by centralised computers. A videoconferencing network was installed in 1984. The European head office was joined by an international leased-line voice network to the parent company's Dearborn head-quarters in the United States. By 1988, fixed capital investments in analogue plant and equipment amounted to $104 million.

In 1987, Ford of Europe began the construction of a private ISDN network, called Fordnet, to carry growing volumes of voice, data and videoconferencing services between its European operations. The company estimated that the improved reliability, transmission speed and network management of Fordnet would yield cost reductions of $2 million per year.[14] While Ford retained in-house control of the European network, a single private supplier, Siemens, provided Ford with a 'one-stop-shopping service'. On behalf of Ford, Siemens negotiated with the PTOs in the countries where Fordnet had connections, and was responsible for installing Ford's leased-lines, terminal equipment, multiplexors, gateways between networks, and PABXs. Operating at full capacity, in 1991 the network could carry voice, data and graphics messages between 14,000 digital telephones, 3,000 analogue telephones, and 2,000 CAD/CAM terminals.[15] By the end of 1992, the 2,000 CAD terminals were expected to exchange approximately 14,000 engineering drawings per day. Initial fixed costs of plant and equipment in Fordnet were estimated to be $90 million, with variable costs of $47 million per year.

Rather than choosing to upgrade existing analogue networks, an entirely new integrated network was constructed using 64 kilobits-per-second and 2 megabits-per-second circuits. By 1993 the company aimed to have connections with every one of Ford's European plants and offices and major suppliers.

Integrating voice, data and videoconferencing over a single transmission path Ford secured higher levels of capacity utilisation and lower information and communications costs. Prior to the introduction of the private network about 22 per cent of the company's international calls failed to connect, and of those that did connect 11 per cent were furnished over poor quality lines. By the mid-1980s intra-corporate telecommunication traffic volumes had increased significantly in Ford of Europe: while voice communication still accounted for 90 per cent of the traffic carried over the private analogue networks, the company estimated that with the formation of an integrated digital network, growing volumes of CAD/CAM information would increase the proportion of data traffic to 50 per cent of the total. The construction of the integrated network supplied the bandwidth capacity needed to transmit data, particularly CAD/CAM applications.

Ford was reluctant to utilise public network facilities because of the difficulties in coordinating fragmented national networks operated and owned by sixteen separate European PTOs. The private ISDN capabilities of Fordnet were extended only to principal suppliers and dealers. Ford's private ISDN-based network was built to be technologically compatible with public ISDN infrastructures as they develop in European countries. Ford will extend public ISDN connections to smaller customers and suppliers that cannot afford private leased circuits or dedicated access to Fordnet's private facilities. Fordnet was designed to transcend the problems of traffic congestion and transmission failures. This was achieved by locating network control in the Brentwood head office and building sufficient excess capacity to route traffic through alternative paths over Fordnet's numerous long-distance and international leased-lines. While digital leased-lines were widely available in Britain and Germany by the mid-1980s, Ford's southern European operations in Portugal and Spain (where national telecommunications resources were less developed) were confined to analogue lines. But most of the company's plants and offices connected to Fordnet's standardised and integrated digital network elsewhere in Europe had access to computer applications such as EDI, electronic mail, and videotext.

Fordnet was a key link in the chain of Ford's worldwide network established and coordinated by the Ford group's centralised headquarters in Detroit. The construction of Ford of Europe's network between design centres was part of the overall group's plan of the late 1980s to develop a new version of world car engineering, and revitalise the principles behind the unsuccessful world car concept of the 1970s. By integrating Ford's global activities the original strategy made superficial variations on a single model – for example the Ford Escort – to meet the demands of many national markets while cutting production costs. It failed for two reasons: first, the design and engineering components of European and North American cars had evolved so independently that they could not easily be standardised to yield productivity improvements; and, second, fluctuating demand for cars in Europe and the United States prevented attempts to consolidate the market around a standard, transnational design for a car.

The 1980s renewed version of the world car strategy, by contrast, aimed to draw upon Ford's worldwide design and engineering operations to accelerate the development and production of entirely new models of cars for the world's major regional markets. It symbolised Ford's attempt to counter the threat of rapid product innovation from Japanese competition. By the late 1980s, Japanese car producers had reduced the design and development time entailed in getting a new model from a concept on paper to the final customer. In 1989, for example, European and American producers spent an average of sixty-two months on product development compared to only forty-three months for their Japanese counterparts.

Whereas Ford's multidivisional regions previously operated autonomously, under the new system of worldwide engineering each region was designated a 'centre of excellence' which specialised in the design and engineering of particular models of cars.[16] Regional design centres specialised in product innovation from concept inception, through design, engineering and manufacture in order to customise products for market destinations. For example, Ford of Europe was given entire responsibility for designing new compact/upper medium sized cars such as the model code-named CDW 27, and producing differentiated versions of the model to suit the requirements of both the European and North American markets. Since the basic engineering tasks were undertaken by a single region, the company aimed to reduce design and engineering costs, cut product development times, and minimise the duplication of effort in design work undertaken by various regions. The design centres focused on common product development, component commonality, and worldwide sourcing flexibility.

To support this new strategy of simultaneous engineering across corporate divisions the Ford group constructed a $77 million global digital network of computers uniting the company's 20,000 engineers and designers in the regional divisions in Europe, North and South America, Australia and the Far East.[17] With telecommunications links to the regional design centres, a single product planning organisation was established in the United States to coordinate worldwide product development. The global network was interconnected to the company's other two major networks in the United States and in Europe. Five nodes in the global network will be located in the company's Dearborn headquarters, the European head office, and offices in Japan, Australia and Brazil. Fibre optic transmission will be installed to connect the Dearborn headquarters with Europe and Japan, and the five nodes shall be connected by international leased-lines using a mix of 56 kilobits-per-second circuits, and fibre optics and satellite transmission.[18]

Ford of Europe's integrated network was one of Europe's first transborder digital networks. In 1991, the design and engineering centres in Germany, Britain and the United States, used public packet-switched data and voice networks for much of their transborder communications between thirty-five minicomputers and 700 terminals in the three regions. The computer systems located in the design centres in Britain and Germany were subsequently connected by a $55 million private integrated network; the core of Fordnet – consisting of 2 megabits-per-second circuits linking two design centres in Britain and two equivalent centres in Germany, to form four network nodes. Each node operated electronic PABX equipment, a packet-switching exchange, cross-connect equipment and network management technologies. Centrally operated from Brentwood in Britain, by 1990 the core network supported real-time, interactive telecommunication between the European CAD/CAM offices in Britain and Germany.

Linked into this core network, Ford designers and engineers in Germany and Britain had access to centralised design data bases for several applications, such as CAD/CAM, Design Verification Planning Tools, used to illustrate car-model plans, and Crash Analysis Systems, to simulate the effects of accidents. Before the core network was installed, computer files were transmitted from localised CAD/CAM activities via LANS and batch processed by centralised computers in the two separate locations. The core network between Germany and Britain supported real-time transmission capacity of up to thirty single-megabyte CAD/CAM drawings at a rate of one megabyte every 150 seconds. This enabled the rapid transmission of files and made it possible for designers to exchange ideas on computer screens in real time. Eventually the 2 megabits-per-second circuits will be replaced by fibre optic circuits and optical exchanges with a capacity to switch voice, data and video images at 140 megabits-per-second.

Yet in 1992 Ford of Europe announced a change in strategy; it decided to concentrate European R&D activities in two sites at Dunton, Essex, in Britain, and at Merkenich, near Cologne, in Germany, in place of the previous four locations in Britain and two in Germany.[19] This marks a shift away from the emphasis on connecting geographically scattered design and engineering plants by telephone and videoconferencing. To gain the full advantages of simultaneous engineering Ford of Europe will bring members of particular R&D teams together in single locations. Yet in contrast to Japanese manufacturers like Toyota that do all their basic design and engineering in close spatial proximity in their country of origin, Ford's European design team will continue to use the global communications network to share skills and solutions among teams in different countries.[20]

Although the structure of Fordnet was primarily shaped by the information and communication requirements of design and engineering activities, information networks were also established with suppliers and customers. By 1989, EDI networks connected Ford's assembly plants with so-called 'development suppliers' which had their own engineering and design capabilities, and were closely involved in Ford's global product development. Digital communication with suppliers helped to schedule production output with changes in demand, and minimise the volume of buffer stocks and goods on hand for sale. Ford developed electronic interfaces which enabled preferred suppliers to communicate with a standard order-receiving mainframe computer. While development suppliers exchanged designs for components electronically with Ford, they were prevented from having access to the core design network in order to maintain the tight security required in the development of new models. Information was transmitted over the public voice and data networks from Ford's 385 main dealerships which supplied a further 642 retail dealers.

4. Information systems in electronics

This section examines the development of information systems in GEC, the electrical and electronics conglomerate formed by the British government in 1968 to encourage rationalisation by merging small companies. GEC was created by an amalgamation of many firms producing specialised products in small batches to order, notably machine tools, defence and space industries. The company diversified into a range of industries including consumer electronics (radios and televisions), domestic appliances (cookers, washing machines, etc.), nuclear and coal-fired power and telecommunications. GEC adopted a decentralised management structure, with the head office monitoring the profit and loss accounts of the company's subsidiaries. In consequence, the activities controlled by GEC operated as if they were 120 autonomous companies. Since productive activities were not organised to serve mass markets, GEC's companies secured business by tendering for contracts.

In contrast to mass production corporations, the conglomerate organisational form became widespread in the 1960s in parts of industries with specialised markets and limited growth prospects.[21] Whereas mass production firms grew in size by internal expansion of existing lines of business, the conglomerate corporation expanded by acquiring existing firms, rather than investing in its own plant and labour, and often did so in unrelated lines of business. Corporations embarked on strategies of unrelated acquisition and diversification when it became evident that their own industries showed few prospects of continued growth. The acquiring firm tended to purchase small firms in those industries producing specialised products for individual orders such as machine tools, ocean shipping, defence and space sectors.

The organisational structure of the conglomerate reflects its strategy for growth. Operating units have more autonomy than the divisions of traditional multidivisional corporations. A typical conglomerate has no centralised corporate head office specialised in purchasing, sales, research and development, advertising and production. The general office in conglomerate corporations is usually dedicated to financial and legal procedures, and the formulation of strategic investment decisions. The managers of conglomerates are specialists in making direct acquisitions of profitable new business activities. As a result, the conglomerate firm is organised to make investments in new industries and new markets, and retreat from existing lines of business when markets contract.

In 1987, GEC's subsidiaries were located in 167 major sites, consisting of 229 production plants and offices, and 280 smaller branch offices and sales outlets dispersed throughout Britain. Prior to the creation of the integrated digital network, GEC's subsidiaries purchased their own long-distance leased-lines from BT and Mercury.[22] Analogue circuits were installed to reduce the costs of calls made between GEC's sites. Not guided by a centralised plan for telecommunications, the various decisions to install leased-lines made by operating companies cohered into a mosaic of fragmented sub-networks. Leased-lines were only installed in those cases where operating units were in regular contact. The sub-networks within GEC supported communications between the communities of interest which tied together parts of otherwise unrelated productive activities, including the Marconi companies, GEC Computer Services, GEC Power Engineering and GEC Avery. Under this arrangement, leased-lines connecting all of GEC's dispersed sites could not be cost justified, and there was considerable duplication in circuitry along high-density routes where bandwidth capacity could have been shared.

In 1987 GEC conducted a cost–benefit analysis which showed that telecommunications operating costs could be reduced by diverting 74 per cent of intra-corporate traffic over a single standardised and integrated digital network. Between 1988 and 1990 a private integrated digital network called GNet was constructed linking many of GEC's dispersed sites. Like the other case studies in this chapter, GEC created a private ISDN several years before the widespread introduction of the public ISDN network. Furnishing voice, data, telex and videoconferencing services over a single transmission path, the large capacity of GEC's £10 million digital network was operated at lower costs – without needless duplication of circuitry – than disparate analogue and digital networks. In 1987, GEC made an average of 28 million voice and facsimile calls each year: 11 million of this total was diverted over GNet. The 5,000 long-distance 64 kilobits-per-second and 2 megabits-per-second circuits used in GNet were leased in bulk from BT and Mercury. The network incorporated the company's previously separate 425 data networks. For the company as a whole, bulk purchasing was cheaper than the previous arrangement of numerous contracts for a few leased-lines made between telecommunications operators and individual subsidiaries. And in comparison to public switched voice tariffs, users of GNet secured cost reductions of 15 to 20 per cent.

Network management and control of GNet was undertaken from Chelmsford by GEC Communications, one of the company's subsidiaries which specialised in computer systems. Consisting of 2 megabits-per-second circuits joining nineteen network nodes throughout Britain, the network management centre operated the layered structure of GNet: the first layer connected the major network nodes in London, Chelmsford, Rugby, Stafford, and Manchester to form the backbone transmission capacity for voice messages, a data network and electronic mail; the second layer connected dispersed sites to the nearest major node with 64 kilobits-per-second circuits; and the third layer consisted of redundant transmission along the routes of the backbone network to provide excess capacity in the event of a transmission failure or congestion in the network.

The motive behind the creation of a corporate-wide network was the need to tighten the communications links between GEC's diversified productive activities. By improving its internal lines of communication GEC aimed to overcome the two organisational weaknesses attributed to conglomerate organisations.[23] First, the information flowing between the conglomerate head office and the subsidiaries was kept to a minimum. Consequently, when it came to efforts to improve divisional operating performance, the conglomerate was less effective in monitoring and evaluating divisions than other multidivisional corporations. Second, since their formation, conglomerate firms did not develop the centralised research and development resources required in the systematic and rapid innovation of complex process and product technologies.

In an attempt to solve these organisational deficiencies, GNet linked scientists and engineers in the company's 120 subsidiaries.[24] With access to a centrally controlled digital network, teams of scientists and engineers could improve product and process development by sharing knowledge and avoiding duplication in research and development. In order to shorten product lead times, GEC pulled together the technologically innovative strengths of the group's research and development and engineering activities. This strategy was a response to intensified competition in the 1980s when poor communications between GEC's autonomous units resulted in few examples of common approaches and shared solutions to product development work. The previous arrangement of decentralised research and development activities was effective as long as there were few technological reasons to bind the division together. From the late 1970s, however, with the convergence of electronics and telecommunications, and application of electronics to various products and processes, a more coherent and unified approach to product development was required. The majority of GEC's operating units had become engaged in the development of generic technologies, converging previously separate technological disciplines, such as microelectronics, factory automation, and software engineering. The pressure to consolidate technological resources, plant and workers resulted from the international competitive pressure to cut product development times and amortise high research and development costs through sales in world markets.

In 1989, GNet linked together 10,000 computer terminals in the company and extended to GEC's 20,000 research and development staff, allowing them to exchange technical ideas and develop common product development procedures. Connected to a central-ised computer data base, engineers and designers were able to access technical and management data and share standard computerised designs for common engineering components. A technology information pool was formed to encourage divisions to learn from each other. The pool included half the company's scientists and engineers who received information communicated over the digital network, by post or through face-to-face meetings. The pool covered eight technical areas: embracing CAD, quality control, systems engineering and printed circuit technology. The concept of sharing information contrasted with the traditional corporate culture in which contact with other units was random and where there was no formal procedure for bringing the units together. Rapid telecom-munications links between design, engineering and production reduced the time taken for a product to complete its lifecycle from specification and design, through production planning and prototype manufacture, to automatic testing and maintenance.

Conclusion

The development of information and communications systems within the firm occurred in two stages. First, during the 1970s, companies established discrete voice, data and telex networks. Data processing facilities within the firm were linked by data transmission circuits. However, economies of scale in the operation of separate networks were difficult to obtain because traffic volumes were not sufficient to bring reduced transmission costs. Second, during the 1980s, companies constructed and operated private digital networks which integrated voice, data and video messages. Carrying large volumes of integrated services over a single transmission path, digital networks obtained economies of scale and scope by improving capacity utilisation. Using network management and control software, the transmission capacity of a single network was controlled to match changes in business requirements for communications. Value-added services carried over digital networks were supplied in-house or outsourced to companies such as IBM for specific applications.

New technological and economic developments in the 1990s may, however, reverse the growth in private corporate networks. Common carriers are offering new global communications services which substitute for corporate networks. On the one hand, common carriers, such as AT&T and British Telecom (BT), aim to replace leased-line private networks with software-defined 'virtual private networks' (VPN) and ISDN services. Sharing excess capacity built into digital transmission and switching systems, these new products capture substantial economies of scale, scope and system through the provision of all the integrated services currently carried over private networks at lower costs. For example, BT offers a VPN product, operating with AT&T's software-defined switches, called Flexible Access Services to financial users in the City of London. US Sprint Communications and Cable and Wireless have built a global VPN linking the United States, Britain and Hong Kong. Moreover, the formation of national ISDNs from the mid-1990s, and the early take-up of ISDN services in France, indicate that this public integrated service may also replace private networks.

On the other hand, corporate control of communications services carried over private networks can be relinquished to third party value-added service providers such as IBM, Electronic Data Systems (EDS), General Electric Information Services (GEIS), or AT&T-Istel.[25] These companies are offering a service called facilities management.[26] This phenomenon of 'outsourcing' entails the purchase of computing and communications plant and equipment installed in corporations, and the hire of in-house telecommunications staff responsible for operating and monitoring traffic on the corporate network. Corporate users seeking to outsource private digital networks will be furnished with voice, data and video services, combined with network management and control facilities. Eastman Kodak corporation's decision to outsource its digital communications facilities to IBM and Digital Equipment Corporation (DEC) in 1989, and Unilever's decision to outsource its voice and data facilities to EDS are indications that large users will divest their investments in digital information systems. Kodak estimated cost savings in computing of between 40 and 50 per cent. In 1990 the facilities management market in the United States was estimated to be worth \$29 billion.[27]

Retail banks, such as Barclays and France's Banque Nationale de Paris (BNP), perceive corporate network equipment and operations to be too strategic to outsource completely. While BNP has signed a contract to use France Télécom's public packet-switched Transpac data network, BNP retains the control to reconfigure the network structure.[28] BNP is using network management and control technologies, supplied jointly by France Télécom and AT&T, to monitor and modify the bank's national and international networks as a single entity and from a single point of control. The American Bank, Merrill Lynch and Company, was dissatisfied with IBM's and MCI's ability to manage the bank's voice and data network. In 1990, the bank decided to place network management in the hands of an in-house subsidiary, Teleport Communications Corporation. In manufacturing sectors, by contrast, the strategy of outsourcing may be adopted more readily. Unlike the banks, the product of manufacturing companies is not directly dependent on a privately controlled corporate network. By the mid-1980s, for example, Courtaulds had already outsourced specific network applications in order to gain from the reductions in costs offered by facilities management companies like IBM and GEIS. The shortage of skilled telecommunications managers and technicians is another factor encouraging manufacturing companies to seek outsourcing, VPN or ISDN solutions.

What is occurring is the basis for a shift back to monopoly or oligopoly in the provision of corporate telecommunications services. In their attempts to cater for the global communications needs of widely dispersed companies like Ford of Europe, common carriers face competition from other national operators and from international providers of information services. Common carriers and data communications companies are forming alliances, mergers and joint ventures to provide 'one-stop-shopping' services which substitute global communication services managed from one location for the traditional pattern of leased-line services provided over fragmented national networks.

In conclusion, then, this chapter provides case study material referring to the use of telecommunications in major corporations across different manufacturing and service sectors to illustrate the argument that a transformation in the mass production economy called for a revolution in the means of telecommunications.[29] Whereas the mechanisation of physical conditions predominated before the 1970s, in the current phase of corporate restructuring it is the mechanisation of information and communications systems which dominates the nature of technological progress in production. Yet before integrated systems of information and communication could be installed in the production process, increases in the capacity and speed of computerised data processing called for equivalent improvements in telecommunications transmission.

In this respect my theoretical explanation differs from the work conducted for the OECD by Bar and Borrus (1987). These authors sought to explain changes in modern telecommunications infrastructures from the micro-level perspective of the individual firm, focusing on the ways in which different national telecommunications regimes constrained or conferred economic advantages on individual corporations. Invoking the problem of methodological individualism, Bar and Borrus's explanation proceeds in one direction: the parts – the individual actions and choices made by corporations – explain developments in the digital telecommunications infrastructure as a whole. Emphasising a demand-pull explanation of changes in telecommunications, they argue that the shape of the emerging digital infrastructure is a product of a chain of individual corporate decisions and the policies of national governments.

On the contrary, from the perspective of the economy as a whole, I have argued that a transformation in the technology of the system of mass production stimulated a set of demand-side pressures for the integration of systems of information processing and telecommunications within corporations. Yet the outcome of such demands for change depends on supply-side conditions. From this different level of theoretical abstraction, I will argue that the technological, economic and institutional transformation of national telecommunications infrastructures is being determined by a combination of political and economic forces: (i) the various possibilities for organising national networks depends on the balance of political and economic power in particular countries; and, (ii) the economics of large fixed capital investments in digital technologies is conditioning the future technological and organisational paths of development in the telecommunications sector.

Thus the new requirements for improved corporate telecommunications, which as we will see were voiced by firms and industries throughout the world, could not be accomplished without a modernised and worldwide digital telecommunications infrastructure. The traditional institutional arrangement, founded upon national telephone monopolies and designed to accommodate incremental change in communication technologies designed for analogue transmission, had to be restructured to respond to this dynamic period of radical technological change and proliferating business user demands. The outcomes of such pressures were determined on the terrain of the nation state. In Part III, which examines the political and economic conditions behind the restructuring of traditional telephone technology and organisation, the corporation enters the scene as a collective political actor exerting its demands for modern telecommunications by influencing the outcome of supply-side developments.

Notes

1. Particular conditions of production are placed under private control because such equipment raises productivity and contributes directly to the profitability of individual firms. See K. Marx, p531 (1973), *Grundrisse: Foundations of the Critique of Political Economy*, Penguin, Harmondsworth.
2. The empirical research for this chapter originated as part of an OECD-BRIE Telecommunications User Group Project. The information draws primarily on a series of interviews, workshops and presentations with telecommunications and data processing managers in four corporations: Barclays Bank, Courtaulds, Ford of Europe and GEC. The final case study material was published as 'Information Networks and Competitive Advantage: Comparative Reviews of Telecommunications Policies and Usage in Europe', report presented at the final seminar in Paris, 19–20 October 1989.
3. This definition of transaction activities is made by B. Wieland (1989), 'From good connections to public access: Telecommunications use and telecommunications policy in West Germany', report to final seminar on Information networks and business strategies, OECD, Paris, 19–20 October 1989.
4. The interviews for this case study included S. McLean (1988), interview

by A. Davies and K. Morgan, Barclays Bank, May 1988, Knutsford; and J. Sweeney (1988 & 1989), interviews by A. Davies, Barclays Bank, May 1988 & January 1989, Knutsford.

5. F. Bar (1989a), 'Bank of America', OECD/BRIE telecoms user group project.

6. A. Cane (1988), 'Countdown to user-friendly banking', *Financial Times*, 11 November 1988; and P. Rawstorne (1988), 'Profits in the files', *Financial Times*, 8 March 1988.

7. J. Bird (1988), 'Interest grows in empty banks', *Sunday Times*, 20 November 1988.

8. C. Antonelli, p19 (1987), 'The Emergence of the Network Firm', in *New Information Technology and Industrial Change: The Italian Case* (ed.) C. Antonelli, Kluwer Academic Publishers, Dordrecht.

9. The interviews for this case study included: M. McNulty (1988 & 1989), interviews by A. Davies, Courtaulds, April 1988 & January 1989, Coventry; N. Reynolds (1989), interview by A. Davies, Courtaulds, January 1989, Coventry; and M. Fisher (1989), interview by A. Davies, Courtaulds Textiles Division, September 1989, London.

10. A. Rawsthorn (1988), 'A system to cut out inefficiency'. *Financial Times*, 18 November 1988.

11. C. Antonelli, p19, op. cit.

12. F. Bar (1989b), 'General Motors', Case Study, OECD/BRIE telecom user-group project.

13. The interviews for this case study included: D. Freeburn (1988 & 1989), interviews by A. Davies, Ford of Europe, May 1988 and January 1989, Brentwood.

14. W. Dixon (1992), 'Ford's Strategic Multinational Network', pp80–84, *Telecommunications*, 1992.

15. D. Hayes (1991), 'The ISDN Crosses New Borders', *CommunicationsWeek International*, 10 June 1991.

16. C. Leadbeater, and K. Done (1989), 'Ford eager to acquire "major enterprise"', *Financial Times*, 1 May 1989.

17. K. Done (1989), 'Gearing up for the race of the 1990s', *Financial Times*, 25 January 1989.

18. *CommunicationsWeek International*, 'Ford Expands Network', 18 June 1990.

19. K. Done (1992), 'From design studio to new car showroom', *Financial Times*, 11 May 1992.

20. W.H. Fike (president Ford of Europe) (1992), 'Ford's fully-integrated operations across the EC', letter, *Financial Times*, 5 March 1992.

21. For a discussion of the origins and strategies of the conglomerate form see A.D. Chandler, pp480–482 (1977), *The Visible Hand: The Managerial Revolution in American Business*, Harvard University Press, Cambridge, Mass.

22. The interviews for this case study included: P. Blackledge (1989), interview by A. Davies, GPT, September 1989, Coventry; P. Briggs (1989), interview by A. Davies, GEC, August 1989, Coventry: and A. Durkin (1988), interview by A. Davies, N. Garnham and K. Morgan, GEC, April 1988, Coventry.

23. Chandler, pp481–482 (1977), op. cit.
24. P. Marsh (1987), 'GEC to link subsidiaries in computer network' and 'Meeting of the minds on GEC's glasnost', *Financial Times*, 14 August 1987.
25. J.L. Schenker (1991), 'Searching for a Single Solution', *CommunicationsWeek International*, 13 May 1991.
26. Carriers offering to build and manage global corporate networks include private vendors such as IBM, Digital Equipment Corporation (DEC), Electronic Data Systems Corporation, General Electric Information Services, and Cable and Wireless; and new outsourcing consortiums of Public Telecommunication Operators, such as the Pathfinder services, offered by British Telecom, Japan's Nippon Telegraph and Telephone Corporation, and Germany's Telekom.
27. M. Laws (1990), 'Private Nets are Turning to Third Parties', *CommunicationsWeek International*, 1 October 1990.
28. R. Poe (1991), 'Banks don't Count on Outsourcing', *CommunicationsWeek International*, 13 May 1991.
29. Although the empirical basis of this chapter focused on Britain, the case study material generated by the OECD/BRIE (1989) research indicates that, despite their different organisational structures, companies in every country in the world adopted similar technological strategies towards the integration of information processing and telecommunications.

Part III

The second technological divide: digital telecommunications

6 Restructuring the national monopolies

By the late 1970s the national monopoly model of telephone organisation was in crisis. The driving force behind the demands to overturn monopolised telecommunications markets came from private multinational corporations. In every country large corporate users, computer equipment suppliers and providers of information services pressed for liberalisation of national telecommunications. This 'electronic alliance' of corporate users and data processing suppliers demanded advanced low-cost digital transmission, no restrictions on the attachment of terminal equipment to telecommunications circuits, and competitive supply of value-added information services.[1] Such pressures were resisted by a traditional coalition of interests consisting of Postal, Telegraph and Telephone agencies (PTTs), the cartel of telecommunications equipment suppliers and employees. Under the leadership of national PTTs, these traditional interests aimed to protect the existing monopoly arrangement. This political contest raised the question of whether or not national telecommunications infrastructures should be controlled by the state to promote social equity and support national economic strategies, or take the form of private competition to enhance the flexibility and control of multinational corporations.

The crisis ushered in the second technological divide. The relative strength of different political and economic interests in each country, rather than technological and economic forces, has determined the various ways in which the national monopolies have been restructured. Two contrasting paths of organisational restructuring were followed: whereas on mainland Europe, the state monopoly structure has been retained, in the United States, Britain and Japan, the preferred organisational change was private competition. In these liberalising countries the defence of the state monopoly interests was undermined when national governments withdrew their political support of the traditional arrangement.

1. State monopolies: the Continent of Europe

On the Continent of Europe, PTTs, domestic equipment manufacturers and employees largely succeeded in defending the traditional monopoly arrangement. In the 1970s, the demands of corporate users never included the privatisation of national monopolies and liberalisation of transmission.[2] By the late 1980s, large corporate users and computer equipment manufacturers did secure the liberalisation of equipment attached to user premises and value-added information services. With the exception of Britain, the electronic alliance was weak in Europe in comparison to the power vested in the traditional 'postal–industrial complex'.[3] Since the seventeenth century, the legal monopoly held by the state-owned postal authorities was used to prevent competition from private mails. In the 1880s the state postal authorities used their legal power to protect capital sunk in telegraph plant and equipment from the premature devaluation associated with incursions from private telephone interests. In possession of this legal monopoly and with the support of national governments, European PTTs in the 1980s chose to amortise existing analogue investments while slowly upgrading the telephone system for digital communications. The main justification for retaining state ownership was the need to promote national social and economic goals, while maximising the advantages of economies of scale, scope and system attributed to a centrally controlled network.

The compromise between monopoly and competition

Nevertheless the demands of the electronic alliance did gain support in Europe after the British Telecommunications Act of 1981 which liberalised terminal equipment, gave users more control over private leased-line circuits, and permitted the resale of leased circuits with value added. Britain became a more attractive location for business users seeking to establish international communications across the Atlantic. This in turn reinforced the multinational corporate leverage against monopolised terminal and services markets across the rest of Europe.[4] Liberalisation promoted the rapid development of value-added services and terminal apparatus used in corporate networks in the United States and Britain. Modernisation in Britain engendered an impetus to introduce liberalising policies to stimulate innovation in services and equipment available to business users in other European markets.

Changes in national telecommunications policies in Europe have been influenced by European Commission (EC) directives established in the 1987 Green Paper to liberalise telecommunications equipment and services.[5] The EC objectives oblige national telecom operators to permit private suppliers to provide value-added services and basic data communications (from 1993) in competition with the state monopoly. In 1989, member states agreed a new directive on telecommunications services and a framework directive on open network provision: the former opened up value-added services – such as electronic mail – to competition, and the latter established criteria for allowing non-discriminatory access to leased-lines. The Commission has attempted to distinguish between telecommunications issues addressed at the European level (namely the creation of a single market in services and equipment) and national debates concerning the ownership and organisation of the telecommunications operator. Article 222 of the Treaty of Rome places the question of property ownership under national authority – which depends on the political philosophy of a nation with regard to public and private ownership.[6]

In accordance with EC directives, member states have granted concessions – known as partial liberalisation – allowing private competition in the two market segments: terminal equipment and value-added information services. By 1990, every European PTO allowed business users to connect private circuits to the public network and charged leased circuits on a flat-rate basis. In 1991, following the recommendations of the Duopoly Review, Britain became the only European country to permit private companies to lease circuits in bulk from common carriers and resell excess capacity to the public at discount prices. This policy has been disallowed elsewhere in Europe to prevent large traffic volumes and revenues from being diverted over private rather than public networks.

In the mid-1970s, the inefficiency of PTTs and protected telecommunications suppliers was highlighted by the world economic recession. European governments sought ways of minimising the drain on state expenditures entailed in upgrading the system to digital transmission, while improving the productivity of PTTs and their capability of innovating in the field of digital telecommunications. In the 1970s and 1980s, the imperative of digitising national telecommunications systems required escalating fixed capital investments: by 1987, for example, it was estimated that investment in national telecommunications would have to increase by 5 per cent per annum to modernise the system.[7] Every European country recognised the strategic role of telecommunications infrastructures in promoting renewed national economic performance. By the early 1990s, many European countries separated postal and telecommunications authorities, placing the latter in the hands of state-owned public corporations, known as Public Telecommunications Operators (PTOs). Under this policy, PTOs were no longer responsible for carrying what was often the financial burden of the postal service's deficits.

One policy which aims to improve the efficiency of PTOs has been to encourage private investment in national networks. For example, on 1 January 1990, the Dutch PTT was transformed from a government agency into a private holding company, Royal PTT Nederland NV, controlling postal (PTT-Post) and telecommunications (PTT-Telecom) subsidiaries. PTT-Telecom has remained owned by the state, but following Britain and Japan, the shares may eventually be floated. The centralised managerial hierarchy of PTT-Telecom has been replaced by more decentralised management to promote efficiency, cut costs and develop new markets. With greater management autonomy and financial responsibility in setting and pursuing commercial goals, decentralised units organised into regional operations aim to respond more quickly to customer demands. Information flowing from the decentralised units will inform strategic management decisions.[8] But the early phase of restructuring did not yield the improvements in productivity and increases in turnover needed to cover massive investment programmes and pay the government an annual dividend. A capital expenditure increase of 25 per cent in 1989 alone forced PTT-Telecom to raise money from the capital markets in early 1990.[9]

During the 1970s and 1980s, nationalistic procurement policies linking PTTs and favoured equipment suppliers were undermined by heightened international competition in public telecommunications equipment markets – especially public switching, the largest single item of fixed capital in the network. For most of the twentieth century, domestic markets were large enough to recover the costs of building national telephone networks. However, protected and guaranteed public telecommunications markets promoted inefficiency: in the early 1980s European PTTs paid between 60 and 100 per cent more than the price of equipment in the United States.[10] The pressure to reshuffle traditional relationships with equipment suppliers was associated with the high research and development costs incurred in upgrading analogue exchanges for the digital ISDN infrastructure (particularly in the area of software).[11] In spite of the intensified competition and process of economic concentration in the equipment industry, PTTs continued to procure equipment from remaining long-standing domestic suppliers. Yet the cost of developing new digital switching technology has forced national operators like France Télécom to buy equipment from foreign manufacturers in addition to Alcatel, the dominant local supplier. In Germany, the PTT has retained its traditional suppliers of transmission and switching, Siemens and SEL (a foreign-owned subsidiary of Alcatel), only purchasing foreign equipment in fringe areas such as intelligent payphones.

Reorganising the state monopoly: the FRG and France

Now we turn to investigate these changes in more detail focusing on two countries: the Federal Republic of Germany and France. In Germany the legal monopoly held by the Deutsche Bundespost (DBP) has been guaranteed by Article 87 of the Basic Law (the Constitution). The Telecommunications Installation Act – which originated in the Telegraphy Law (1892) of the German Reich – gave the DBP the exclusive right to monopolise the operation of the national telecommunications network. According to this law, the DBP must be administered as a Federal institution. Because changes in the Basic Law can only be effected by a two-thirds majority in the Federal parliament, the monopoly status of the DBP remained largely unchallenged until 1992.

During the 1970s, the DBP exercised direct control over the supply of customer premises equipment through its monopoly over equipment approval attached to the national network. Public utilities were granted the right to construct their own networks but these could not be interconnected to the national network. Usage-sensitive pricing of leased-lines was introduced in 1981 to discourage the development of corporate private networks, prevent the provision of value-added services over leased-lines, and inhibit leased-lines from reducing the volume of traffic carried on the public network. The DBP attempted to respond quickly to business user requirements for advanced value-added services: the majority of the 4,000 value-added services available in the FRG in 1986 were furnished over the public videotext service.

Because the network was rapidly upgraded and modernised, the DBP was able to deflect political pressure coming from the large user–computer-supplier alliance which was so active in the United States, Britain and Japan.[12] After the computer industry's attempt (led by Nixdorf and IBM) to dismantle the DBP's control over the terminal equipment market in the late 1970s, this source of political pressure was less prominent. The DBP accommodated the needs of IBM and Nixdorf by including these suppliers in the select club of equipment manufacturers. The only representative of large user interests, Deutsche Telekom eV formed in 1979, was small and relatively disorganised compared to user groups in the United States and Britain.

Under the new Telecommunications Law, ratified on 1 July 1989, the DBP was split into three parts: telecommunications (renamed Telekom), postal services and the postal bank. Each part was transformed from a government administration into a public corporation. The Ministry of Posts favoured an organisational reform which retained the state monopoly of the telecommunications network and 90 per cent of the services (voice telephony), while fully liberalising other telecommunications services and terminal equipment. The removal of political control in day-to-day decision-making was designed to give Telekom the freedom it required to make commercial investments. Regulatory and political administrative procedures were separated from telecommunications operations and exercised by the Ministry for Posts and Telecommunications. Since Telekom did not face competition in basic telephone service, incentive pay schemes were introduced to improve the efficiency and dynamism of the monopoly operator.

A three-tier system of telecommunications services was created: monopoly voice services, mandatory services (facsimile, telex and telegrams) available on demand across the country, and fully competitive value-added services. The monopoly of the national telecommunications network was designed to retain the technical integrity of a standardised system while preventing cream-skimming by competitors along high-volume, profitable routes.[13] The profits generated by the basic monopoly voice services will be used for reinvestment in the infrastructure and to provide mandatory services. But since the digitisation of the network blurs the distinction between integrated voice and non-voice services, the boundaries between basic voice, mandatory and competitive value-added services may be difficult to define, allowing Telekom to expand the definition of monopoly and mandatory services leaving only a small competitive segment.[14] Moreover, there is no regulation preventing Telekom from subsidising mandatory services from its monopoly profits. In the competitive services market, private suppliers of value-added services and users of leased-lines are permitted to interconnect with the public network. Telekom is allowed to lease its own lines to furnish value-added services in competition with private companies.

The financial strain of German unification has, however, raised the question of the privatisation of Telekom. The burden of an investment programme of DM5.5 million and the installation of 550,000 new connections in 1991 in eastern Germany placed a strain on Telekom's ability to finance further expansions in capacity.[15] In 1992, leaders of the opposition Social Democrat Party (SPD) considered abandoning their traditional resistance to the sale of state assets and accepting the government's proposal approved by Chancellor Helmut Kohl of privatising telecommunications. In the government's view, permission to allow the national operator to raise money in capital markets to fund investment and expansion outside Germany would transform Telekom into a more effective international competitor. Yet by the end of 1992, the proposed privatisation was held up by political interests representing the postal–industrial complex, including the trade unions and opposition SPD. The ruling coalition government failed to persuade parliament, particularly the Bundesrat (upper house) dominated by the SPD opposition, to amend the Federal constitution which lays down that telecommunications 'shall be conducted as matters of direct federal administration'.[16]

Adhering to its distinctive 'strong state' and dirigiste tradition of enlightened bureaucratic intervention in the economy, France has also retained the state monopoly structure of telecommunications. What distinguishes France from other industrialised states, is the extent to which it has pursued political goals by actively supporting national telecommunications interests vis-à-vis the transnational interests of the electronic alliance.

State intervention in French telecommunications was extended in scope under the governments serving President Giscard d'Estaing (1974–1981) which initiated the huge task of modernising the backward French telephone network. From 1975 to 1980, under the direction of the Direction Générale des Télécommunications (DGT), the French PTT agency, the state invested FFr140 billion in the telephone network. During the 1970s, the world's first fully digital exchange, the E 10 system, was introduced into the French telephone network. The influential Nora–Minc report published in 1978, which was commissioned by the French government, recommended the continuation of the state-led model of modernisation. Recognising the growing internationalisation of telecommunications, the report referred specifically to the dangers facing domestic interests in information technology posed by the threat of foreign control by American companies like IBM.[17]

The Nora–Minc recommendations prompted the DGT into supplying mass markets with value-added services. On 22 November 1978, Raymond Barre's centre-right government initiated the 'Plan Télématique', a videotext pilot project near Paris, forming the first stage of a future common carrier network for the value-added services regarded as the core of the revolution in telematics – a neologism coined by Nora and Minc to signify the growing convergence of computers and telecommunications. In pursuing these goals, 'the DGT was concerned to both safeguard its "common carrier" monopoly status and, even more ambitiously, to ensure thereby its future control of the promising new value-added services as well' (Humphreys 1990: 216). During 1979 to 1980, the DGT's technical experiments in the Télétel videotext service began in the suburbs of Paris and Brittany. Embarking on an expensive supply-side strategy, the DGT guaranteed the success of its telematics programme by supplying terminals, called Minitel, to customers free of charge. But to some extent departing from the traditional PTT-centred policy of service provision, the DGT permitted service providers to connect freely to the host computers of their choice. However, since the DGT retained control of the network, the supply of telematic terminals, and equipment standards, this 'model of cooperation with private commercial actors could be seen as an ingenious way of adapting the telecommunications monopoly to the exigencies of the new, expanding and more competitive industry structure while pre-empting any really radical change' (Humphreys 1990: 218).

Inspired by the recommendations of the Nora–Minc report, the French Socialists, in government from 1981 to 1986 under François Mitterrand's presidency, gave telecommunications a pivotal role in the highly *étatist* plan of the 'filière éléctronique', to promote the merger of the data processing and telecommunications sectors. This national programme of economic concentration substituted the direct coordination by the state for the market mechanism. It sought to transform the French information technology sector into a world-class competitor capable of catching up with the leading American and Japanese firms. In March 1986, however, with the election of a conservative coalition government of Gaullists and Liberal Conservatives under the premiership of Jacques Chirac, a radically new proposal to adopt liberal telecommunications policies promised to mark a distinct break with the previous state-led programme of modernisation. Gérard Longuet, the Liberal Conservative minister appointed in charge of the DGT, argued that telecommunications policy in France had to emulate the model of liberalisation in the United States, Britain and Japan. A new telecommunications law was drafted, to be enacted in late 1987, recommending the transformation of DGT into a private company under state ownership, which could operate with greater commercial and financial autonomy.

While these political changes were taking place, powerful international corporate users in France were demanding access to a range of price-competitive and innovative value-added services. In contrast to the United States and Britain, where such services had grown rapidly under newly liberalised regulatory regimes, in France value-added services remained under the control of the DGT. Despite the DGT's prescient recognition of the future market potential of telematics, by the mid-1980s France was lagging behind liberalised countries like Britain in the race to attract international investment in new information services. Consequently, just prior to the electoral defeat of the conservative government in 1988, Longuet opened up the DGT's monopoly of value-added services to private competition.

Yet attempts by Chirac's conservative government to depart from traditional nationalistic telecommunications policies and embark on a programme of liberalisation and privatisation were resisted by the trade unions and the powerful corps of telecommunications engineers. From 1988, after the premature end to the period of conservative rule, the reform of telecommunications was gradual rather than radical. Subsequent efforts to achieve a compromise between monopoly and competition did not, however, avoid further conflicts and protests from the postal–industrial complex. Following the recommendations of an independent report – commissioned by the French socialist government – by Huber Prévot (former head of the national planning agency), in January 1991 the postal and telecommunications arms of the PTT were split into separate bodies. The French CGT trade union federation tried unsuccessfully to prevent the separation of the 435,000 postal and telecommunications employees into independent bodies. The DGT was renamed France Télécom and a separate office was established for regulating competitive telecommunications services. France Télécom was transformed from a government department into a semi-independent state-owned and monopoly provider of public voice services.

Since 1991 the Finance Ministry can no longer use telecommunications revenues to fund the state budget. Subsequently there have been few political restrictions on France Télécom's finances with the one exception that the French government sets a maximum level of borrowing for public enterprises. Value-added services and mobile communications have been opened up to competition. Although terminal equipment was liberalised in 1986, France Télécom continued to exercise direct control in the form of restrictive type approval procedures. These organisational changes gave France Télécom the financial and commercial autonomy needed to compete in world markets, while continuing to modernise and expand the public infrastructure.

In summary, then, in these European countries the traditional organisational scheme of a state monopoly was retained because the postal–industrial interests were supported by the nation state in resisting the liberalisation of the telecommunications infrastructure. Yet in order to promote innovation in terminal equipment and value-added services every EC country has liberalised these markets. Maintaining a monopoly of the telecommunications infrastructure and basic voice and telex services, these national telecommunications administrations have continued to follow a familiar path of development: centralised control of nationwide telecommunications infrastructures.

2. Breaking up the private monopoly: the United States

In 1983 the privately owned national telecommunications system in the United States was dominated by a single monopoly, AT&T: a vertically integrated network operator, supplying a complete range of telecommunications services. Through its twenty-two wholly owned and two partly owned local Bell operating companies, AT&T supplied approximately 85 per cent of the local exchange service. Through its long-lines department, AT&T supplied approximately 90 per cent of all domestic and international long-distance services. An AT&T subsidiary, Western Electric, was the largest producer of telephone equipment, providing virtually all the manufacturing and procurement of telecommunications supplies of the Bell System. Bell Laboratories, jointly owned by Western Electric and AT&T, generated all the new technology in the American telecommunications system.

In 1983, with assets of $150 billion, AT&T was the world's largest corporation: AT&T and its subsidiaries generated $69.4 billion in revenues, employed almost a million employees, and operated a network of 87 million access lines. Yet it was in the United States that the process of worldwide telecommunications deregulation was initiated and gathered momentum. After 1956 the FCC gradually deregulated the parts of telecommunications demanded by users and new suppliers: long-distance point-to-point and switched services, terminal equipment and leased-lines with value-added. On 1 January 1984, AT&T divested its local Bell operating companies. The traditional state-regulated private monopoly was broken up into a single vertically integrated long-distance and international AT&T operator interconnected to seven independent Regional Bell Operating Companies (RBOCs).

Since no single corporation could mobilise equivalent or greater power than AT&T, only the collective interests of the business users and electronic equipment manufacturers, unified by corporate requirements for control and choice over a range of digital communications technologies and services, were more powerful than AT&T.[18] The collision between AT&T and this private coalition resulted in a war of position: opposing interests struggled to exert greater control over the modernisation of national telecommunications. The removal of regulatory controls and the break up of the private monopoly depended, however, on the gradual conversion of Federal and state institutions to the interests of the electronic alliance. By the early 1980s, American telecommunications policy accepted the view that the efficiency of the telecommunications system depended on competition rather than the economies of scale, scope and system attributed to a single supplier.

Deregulation

With the Kingsbury Commitment of 1913, AT&T was permitted to retain a private monopoly subject to Federal and state regulations. The previous policy in favour of competition was replaced by reliance on a single integrated monopoly to promote an efficient telephone service. The Communications Act of 1934 created the Federal Communications Commission (FCC) whose purpose was 'to make available, so far as possible, to all people of the United States a rapid, efficient nationwide, and worldwide wire and radio communication service with adequate facilities at reasonable charges'.[19]

There were three main justifications for state-regulation.[20] First, that only a single firm could provide a voice service to a geographical area with efficiency, since economies of scale in local and long-distance transmission resulted in declining costs with increases in traffic volumes and subscriber access.[21] Second, a rapid nationwide service could be promoted by allowing monopoly carriers to average their costs in setting rates to customers. Under state regulation, profits from high-volume routes could cross-subsidise unprofitable services to sparsely populated, rural areas. Common carriers were allowed to price individual services according to their discretion, subject to the overall constraint that profits should not exceed a 'fair and equitable' return on their investment. Third, common carriers should furnish a technically integrated end-to-end service, including transmission, switching and terminals. Technical integrity could only be guaranteed if competition in the supply of equipment attached to the network was disallowed.

The policy of competition first substituted for Federal regulation in small segments of telecommunications markets but gradually spread to all parts of the Bell System used in furnishing business communications: long-distance transmission, terminal equipment and value-added information services.

Deregulation of long-distance transmission began in 1959 with the 'Above 890 Decision'. Potential business users and microwave equipment manufacturers pressed the FCC to authorise private point-to-point networks. The FCC permitted users to establish in-house private microwave systems using microwave frequencies above 890 megahertz. Microwave systems provided efficient transmission of telephone, data and video messages without requiring right-of-way privileges, and afforded cheaper long-distance communications and greater centralised control over dispersed, multi-unit corpora-tions. By the mid-1960s, the cost of using AT&T's single channel leased-lines on high-volume routes was five or six times higher than the cost of service using advanced alternative technologies. In 1969 the FCC approved the request of Microwave Communications Incorporated (MCI) for common-carrier status. MCI proposed to build a microwave system between St Louis and Chicago to furnish voice, data transmission, and facsimile over private lines in competition with AT&T. Under the policy 'Specialised Common Carrier', announced in May 1971, the FCC converted the MCI experiment in competition into a national policy. Applicants were permitted to construct private-line services, over single routes, in competition with AT&T.

In July 1976, specialised common carriers received full inter-connection rights to the Bell local exchange system. AT&T's expensive 1969 private-line rates encouraged a large number of companies to establish nationwide private networks between major cities linked to AT&T's network for local services. For example, to satisfy the growing demand for computerised data communications, the University Computing Corporation established Datran, an all digital microwave network. Once specialised common carriers had invested in the technology to furnish long-distance private-line services, using the same plant and capacity they could also offer switched dial-up services which bypassed AT&T's public switched network. MCI filed a tariff, and in January 1975 began marketing a new switched dial-up service charged by the minute, called Execunet. In the late 1970s MCI, Southern Pacific Communications, and other specialised carriers also began offering long-distance switched services.

Liberalisation of terminal attachments began with the 'Hush-a-phone' precedent of 1956, allowing the attachment of a device to the telephone instrument which enabled private conversations in crowded offices. The Carterphone decision of 1969 permitted the connection of a two-way mobile radio system providing telephony to oil wells located at a distance from local exchange operations to the Bell System. Potential equipment suppliers and business user organisations (including the National Retail Merchants Association and American Petroleum Institute) protested to the FCC that foreign attachments must be determined by private users. They wanted regulation to accept the principle that computer com-munications equipment should be an unregulated activity. With the

Carterphone decision, the regulatory tie between common carriers and traditional equipment suppliers was broken. An interconnect industry soon developed to supply business users with a variety of specialised terminal equipment ranging from telephone instruments to sophisticated electronic PABXs.

The regulatory rules established in 1971 as a result of the FCC's First Computer Inquiry created an arbitrary line between data processing and communications. Control of data processing was not subjected to Federal regulation. During the proceedings, the emerging business-user–equipment-producer alliance, whose interests were represented by the American Bankers Association, insisted that the use of computers 'is not, and should under no circumstances be deemed subject to regulation . . . whether or not involving the use of communication facilities and services'.[22] Companies from different sides of the regulatory boundary interpreted the dividing line in their own interests. On the telecommunications side, AT&T provided products combining computing and communications facilities, such as a digital PBX system which performed data processing functions, and treated them as regulated services. On the data processing side, companies like IBM and Xerox offered merged computer and communications systems as unregulated services, such as digital information networks combining satellite technology with computerised switching, multiplexing, and terminal equipment.

Under the final decision of April 1980, emerging out of the Second Computer Inquiry (1976–1980), only 'basic' voice transmission remained regulated. Private companies were permitted to offer 'enhanced' value-added services by leasing circuits from the common carriers, attaching computers, software and specialised equipment to private networks, and reselling data processing and data communications to business customers. In justifying the decision, the FCC maintained that value-added carriers provided new services and new ways of satisfying existing requirements for data communications previously unmet by common or specialised carriers. Terminal equipment was fully deregulated in 1982. AT&T was permitted to provide merged computer communications equipment and services through a separate subsidiary, AT&T Information Systems. The artificial distinction between basic and enhanced services was recognised by the Third Computer Inquiry which began in 1985.

During the period of deregulation, AT&T defended its monopoly against new competition in two ways. First, by introducing various anti-competitive practices. Selective price reductions (such as TELPAK tariffs) and new service offerings such as WATS (Wide Area Telephone Services) and WADS (Wide Area Data Service), were designed to eliminate incentives encouraging large-volume subscribers from using rival systems. AT&T imposed restrictive interconnection procedures on the attachment of terminals to the telecommunications network. And while the agreement to interconnect independent telephone companies had been accepted during the anti-trust pressure which culminated in the Kingsbury Commitment of 1913, in the 1960s and 1970s AT&T repeatedly used its control over local exchange operations to discourage rival companies from establishing long-line operations.[23] Because a long-distance service would be useless without some method of connecting to end-users, AT&T attempted to prevent competition in long-distance lines by prohibiting local-service interconnections. As late as 1978 AT&T refused to provide a local service to the Execunet switched network, until the courts finally ordered AT&T to furnish local exchange interconnections.

Second, in the legal proceedings which led to deregulation, AT&T, allied with the traditional common carriers (Western Union and the independent telephone companies), invoked the principles of common carrier regulation to defend the monopoly arrangement from competitive incursions. However. in each case the FCC accepted the arguments made by the electronic alliance that the introduction of competition stimulated technological change in the telecommunications system, helping to satisfy new business communications markets and realise latent but unsatisfied demand for existing services.

The traditional telecommunications interests contested the opening up of long-distance transmission to competition in private point-to-point and switched services on the grounds that alternative services undermined the provision of a universal cross-subsidised service.[24] For example, during the review which led to the 'Above 890 Decision' the traditional common carriers argued that if large private users were encouraged to leave the common system, which was organised to serve all users, the system would be left with small users who could not afford to build private systems.[25] As a result of bypass, rates would increase as volume declined, sending medium-sized users off the common system.[26] In justifying the new policy, the FCC maintained that the common carriers would not lose much traffic because the costs of constructing a private system were too high to attract more than a few system builders. Similarly MCI's application to build a microwave system was opposed by the common carriers (AT&T and independent companies), who argued that MCI's service would cream-skim AT&T's high-density traffic, and result in a duplication of plant. Ignoring AT&T's cream-skimming argument, the commission argued that MCI's proposed system was too small to adversely affect AT&T's revenues. The FCC argued that new carriers would develop new services and expand the size of the total communications market.

AT&T's argument for excluding Carterphone and other foreign attachments to the telecommunications system was based on the assertion that total integrated control was needed to prevent improper equipment from causing malfunctions in the network. In permitting the Carterphone device, the FCC ruled that the Carterphone system posed no threat to technical integrity and satisfied unmet demand.

Divestiture

AT&T's political response to deregulation and attempts to preserve the monopoly were shaped by its immense political resources.[27] For sixty years since the Vail compromise, AT&T assumed quasi-governmental functions and acquired a distinctive corporate culture based on regulatory cooperation. The Bell System had an extensive lobbying network at the Federal level and considerable political resources in the local operating companies, both of which were coordinated by a single hierarchy. The pro-competitive policies attacked AT&T's special status. Under the centralised leadership of John de Butts, AT&T rejected a compromise and fought to defend the traditional monopoly.

In 1976 AT&T attempted to use its financial power and size to force the Consumer Communications Reform Act – the so-called 'Bell Bill' – through Congress. In the second quarter of 1976 AT&T spent $1 billion on lobbying alone in support of the campaign. The company's chairman, John de Butts, threatened to raise AT&T's rates if Congress did not pass the Bill. The refusal of AT&T's leadership to seek a compromise on competition galvanised oppositional forces. Even AT&T's employees, represented by the Communications Workers of America, found the Bill extreme and refrained from endorsing it. Competing common carriers formed the Ad Hoc Committee for Competitive Telecommunications. Existing organisations – such as the Computer and Business Manufacturers' Association – became more active after the defeat of the Bill. And finally, liberals in Congress pressed for a more fundamental restructuring. Yet between 1978 and 1982, Congress remained deadlocked over the question of AT&T's appropriate organisational form: the Democrats were opposed to big business and Republicans were against structural reform. Indeed Reagan's Republican administration was actively opposed to the break up of AT&T: it established a working group which advocated the importance of integrated telecommunications in support of national defence.[28]

The first attempts to break up the Bell monopoly originated in the FCC investigation of AT&T in the 1930s. The Justice Department filed a Sherman Act anti-trust suit against AT&T's vertical integration with Western Electric. During the suit which led to the consent decree of 1956, AT&T enlisted the support of the Defense Department which emphasised the importance of a vertically integrated communications system of R&D, manufacturing and service operation in times of military emergency. Although the consent decree barred AT&T from entering unregulated lines of business, such as data processing facilities, the monopoly was allowed to retain ownership of Western Electric. The steps which led to AT&T's divestiture began with the Federal anti-trust case, *United States* v. *American Telephone and Telegraph*, filed in 1974, and went to trial in 1980. To prevent AT&T's abuse of monopoly power, the Justice Department asked the court to promote competition by divesting AT&T of Western Electric and all the local Bell operating companies.

Under the new leadership of Charles L. Brown, AT&T abandoned its campaign against competition. Congress had already approved a number of radical pro-competitive policies in public utility industries and seemed likely to defeat political opposition from AT&T. Unlike the traditionalists in AT&T, Brown reached an accommodation with pro-competitive policy-makers in the FCC, the Justice Department, and Congress. Judge Harold Greene threatened to order vertical divestiture of AT&T. AT&T's management wanted to protect the firm's vertical integration in order to compete effectively in the provision of global corporate communications with companies like IBM and Xerox.[29] AT&T's manufacturing arm, Western Electric, which supported most of Bell Lab's development work, was responsible for generating innovative terminal apparatus and data processing and electronic switching equipment. Brown's accommodation with the Justice Department was contrived to avoid the spinning off of Western Electric.

On 8 January 1982, AT&T and the Federal government jointly announced a settlement to the anti-trust case. The subsequent court approval of the settlement, known as the Modification of Final Judgment, of 5 August 1983, ordered the divestiture to take place on 1 January 1984. The Bell System would divest the twenty-two local operating companies, forming seven regional Bell operating companies (RBOCs).[30] While AT&T gained control of the intrastate traffic previously in the hands of local operating companies, the RBOCs were restricted to furnishing exchange access and exchange services encompassing only local 'natural monopoly' services. The RBOCs were required to furnish all long-distance interexchange carriers with interconnection on an equal basis to local exchange operations. The RBOCs later formed a joint venture, called Bellcore, to provide centralised research and development, and support services for the local operators.

The Department of Defense objected that the break up of AT&T and abandonment of centralised control over national telecommunications threatened to undermine national security interests. The settlement did, however, provide a solution to these objections. The national security provision in the Modification of Final Judgment stated:

Notwithstanding the separation of ownership, the BOCs may support and share the costs of a centralised organisation for the provision of engineering, administrative and other services which can most efficiently be provided on a centralised basis. The BOCs shall provide, through a centralised organisation, a single point of contact for coordination of BOCs to meet the requirements of national security and emergency preparedness.[31]

AT&T remained a vertically integrated operation composed of long-lines, Western Electric and Bell Labs. AT&T controlled intrastate long-lines and customer premises equipment embedded in the twenty-two local Bell operating companies. The Justice Department modified the 1956 consent decree: AT&T was no longer restricted to the provision of regulated telecommunications services. Severed from regulated local operations, AT&T was allowed to compete in the unregulated field of computer equipment, data processing and transmission, and global business information services.

Often wrongly attributed to the Reagan administration, the adoption of pro-liberal policies had by the late 1970s gained widespread support amongst Democrats, and policy-makers in the FCC, the Justice Department and Congress. This new liberal agenda coalesced with the demands corporate users and new equipment producers had been making since the 1950s. Large users had access to competing long-distance services at lower costs and a range of computerised terminal equipment. The form of divestiture also benefited AT&T: it no longer faced regulatory and anti-trust measures, and was able to concentrate on generating new information services in the highly profitable long-distance market. Subsequently, the shape and future development of American long-distance and international telecommunications and data processing systems has been determined by competing private interests: AT&T, rival common carriers, data processing and information services suppliers and large business users.

3. Privatising state monopolies: Britain and Japan

In contrast to mainland Europe, Britain and Japan followed the lead in telecommunications liberalisation taken by the United States. In both countries, the presence of a large body of multinational corporate users and American-owned computer equipment manufacturers strengthened the power of the electronic alliance. The political influence of the postal–industrial complex in Britain and Japan was weakened by the poor record of productivity and efficiency of their PTTs. It was, however, radical changes in government policy in Britain and Japan which led to the withdrawal of state support for the traditional monopoly arrangement. In order to introduce competition into long-distance telecommunications transmission, the telecommunications arms of state-owned British and Japanese PTTs were separated and privatised. Instead of separating local and long-distance operations to prevent the abuse of monopoly power, regulatory bodies were created to monitor and direct the activities of privatised monopolies.

Privatisation and liberalisation in Britain

Prior to 1981, the Post Office, a public corporation since 1969, was in possession of a legal monopoly of the British telecommunications service and assumed the role of a regulatory agency. For example, the Post Office determined what terminal equipment could be attached to the network without provision for external review or appeal. The process of deregulation lasting nearly three decades in the United States was compressed into a period of five years in Britain.

Pressure for institutional change came from two sets of interests: corporate users and a neo-liberal state. First, the original push for liberalisation surfaced in the 1970s. Large business users wanted access to advanced equipment and services at lower prices, and new domestic and foreign computer manufacturers and suppliers of information services, notably IBM, wanted to supply these markets. In comparison to the Federal Republic of Germany and France, the structure of the business user population in Britain was biased towards large multi-plant firms, often under American ownership.[32] This powerful coalition of multinational corporate users wanted the liberalisation of provisions for the use of advanced services obtained in the United States replicated in Britain. User organisations like the Telecommunications Managers Association (TMA) and the International Telecommunications Users Group (INTUG), claimed that the monopoly structure was inefficient, that the prices of telecommunications leased circuits and services were too high, and that major business users were forced by cost-averaging to cross-subsidise other subscribers. Large users argued that only competition could reduce prices in line with costs.

In 1976 the Labour government commissioned an investigation into the Post Office, published in 1977 as the Carter Report, which described the poor productivity and efficiency of the Post Office and cast doubt on its ability to satisfy the requirements of corporate users. The report recommended liberalisation in the supply of certain equipment including PABXs. It pointed to the end of an era of rigid standardisation 'in which the customer was told precisely what he would be allowed to have'. By the mid-1970s there was a generation of business users whose 'increasingly sophisticated understanding of telecommunications (particularly in the field of data communications)' could not be 'satisfactorily met by an organisation which has its thinking still firmly rooted in the requirement to provide an entirely standard and basic telephone service'.[33]

Second, in comparison to countries on mainland Europe, the British state failed to resist American multinational corporate pressures to end the monopoly provision of telecommunications. Close economic ties between the United States and Britain were reflected in investment in telecommunications links between the two countries.[34] In 1979 Britain was the recipient of 12 per cent of all US direct foreign investment, and, in turn, Britain accounted for 18 per cent of total direct foreign investment in the United States.

The prospective Thatcher government gave its commitment to abolish the monopoly of terminal equipment in 1978. A radical programme of liberalisation and privatisation in the telecommunications sector was introduced by the Thatcher government between 1979 and 1984. Under the Thatcher government the Department of Industry (DoI) set about investigating how to implement liberal policies in national telecommunications. But a new institutional structure was difficult to devise because, not surprisingly, the Post Office refused to cooperate in the provision of technical expertise which would contribute to the abolition of its own legal monopoly. The DoI therefore set about mobilising an expert body of opinion from outside the Post Office including liberal economists, former civil servants and large business users. In 1980 the DoI commissioned a report from Microelectronics Design Associates on the feasibility of a rival carrier in telecommunications transmission.[35] The report which became widely influential concluded that a rival common carrier was technically and politically viable. The report emphasised that the high costs and poor efficiency of the Post Office's telecommunications services threatened to undermine the reputation of the City of London as a global centre for international banking and rapid communications.

In addition to corporate pressure for an improved service, the decision to liberalise telecommunications was guided by a combination of political factors: a pressure to alleviate the government fiscal crisis by reducing the size of the public sector borrowing requirement (PSBR); a general antipathy to powerful public sector trade unions; and an ideological faith in the view that improvements in the efficiency of domestic equipment manufacturers and services could be achieved through the disciplines of the market.[36] The bureaucratic inefficiencies reported in the Carter Report thus made the Post Office a prime target for this radical liberal government.

In September 1979, it was announced that the mail and telecommunications sides of the Post Office were to be separated in order to isolate the costs and subsidies associated with each activity. Liberalisation of transmission was recommended by the Beesley Report, published in April 1981.[37] In 1981, the government announced that it had received a proposal from the Mercury

Consortium, led by Cable and Wireless – an international communications carrier with extensive telecommunications links to Britain's former colonies – to build a fibre optic long-distance and international network for business users in competition with the Post Office. Government support for the proposal was provoked by the poor service the Post Office was providing to the City.[38]

Liberalisation was pushed forward by the British Telecommunications Act 1981 which transferred state telecommunications operations to a newly established public corporation named British Telecom (BT). While Mercury was licensed to compete with BT in all components of telecommunications transmission in February 1982, it avoided competing in the local loop, concentrating instead on developing digital long-distance and private leased circuits for the highly profitable business traffic. The terminal equipment market was liberalised in two phases: in November 1981 telephones and modems were exposed to competition, and the PABX market was finally liberalised in July 1983.

In April 1982, a general licence was announced permitting any private company to establish itself as a value-added network service operator using BT and Mercury circuits, providing that these services were additional to the basic network service. However, a regulatory problem emerged in Britain, as it did elsewhere in the world, over how to distinguish between value-added services (which are in addition to basic voice) and the transmission of information over networks. A value-added service was defined as a computer network which furnished an additional service such as information processing or storage. Value-added providers were prevented from reselling spare capacity to other users. In 1984 BT and IBM jointly proposed to introduce a managed data network (MDN), code-named Jove, adopting IBM's proprietary SNA standard for the connection of data processing facilities to dispersed sites in large corporations. While this MDN was a specialised value-added service, it also fitted into the regulatory category of basic transmission. The government vetoed this project on the grounds that it threatened to create a joint BT–IBM monopoly in value-added services. On 25 February 1987, after heavy lobbying from IBM, the government announced a new general licence for value-added services. Altering the government's earlier decision the new licence permitted unrestricted resale of the transmission of computer data, including MDNs, while allowing BT and Mercury to retain the duopoly over voice telephony.

In his statement to parliament, the then Secretary of State for Industry, Patrick Jenkin, justified BT's privatisation in terms of the policy of opening up the telecommunications sector to competition to promote lower prices, improve efficiency and offer higher quality services. The main reason for changing BT's ownership structure was, however, connected to the monetarist policy of reducing state spending, which had grown rapidly while the economy and government revenues declined.[39] The desire to maximise the revenue from the sale of BT's shares explains why the option of breaking up BT – a solution petitioned by corporate lobbyists in 1983 – was dismissed by the government.[40] Despite opposition from the postal–industrial coalition – which included rural users (who feared that uneconomic services would be axed), the Post Office Engineering Union, Labour Party opposition, together with traditional telecommunications equipment manufacturers like GEC who feared that BT could squeeze them out of the equipment market – the Bill was pushed through parliament.

Under the 1984 Telecommunications Act, British Telecom was transformed from a state-owned monopoly into a limited company operating under licence, with 49 per cent of the shares owned by the state. British Telecom's licence contained a provision which placed national telecommunications facilities in the hands of government during times of national emergency. The decision to retain a large integrated local and long-distance monopoly meant that Mercury had to be artificially protected from competition to allow the infant telecommunications industry to become established. The duopoly of telecommunications transmission was to remain intact until this policy came under review in 1990. Private corporations were permitted to build networks for their own use, but regulatory restrictions prohibited companies from freely interconnecting private networks with the public system and other private networks. Resale of private issued circuits was prohibited until 1989. Competition was introduced in local exchange operations by licensing two cellular radio consortia.

Whereas the American policy employed a structural remedy to reduce anti-competitive behaviour, British policy created a regulatory remedy. The new competitive structure of telecommunications in Britain was regulated by the Office of Telecommunications (Oftel) under the Director General of Telecommunications (DGT) who reported directly to the Secretary of State for Industry. This change removed telecommunications policy from direct parliamentary control. According to Section 3 of the Telecommunications Act, Oftel was charged with the responsibility of reconciling the conflicting goals of universal service, which was written into BT's licence, and the promotion of efficiency and competition in Britain. Regulatory choices between conflicting goals involved political decisions. Oftel, however, did not possess the status and political power to carry out its political role and discipline BT.

Privatisation and re-regulation in Japan

The policy of privatisation was also introduced in Japan. Under the traditional arrangement, Nippon Telegraph and Telephone (NTT) was Japan's state communications monopoly controlled by the Ministry of Posts and Telecommunications (MPT). International leased circuits were operated by a state-regulated company, KDD, which held a monopoly over international communications.

Pressure for liberalisation of the Japanese private-line and equipment markets came from large business users who complained about NTT's high charges, particularly on long-distance routes. NTT was slow to provide data transmission linking the computers used by Japanese firms.[41] Domestic manufacturers, such as Fujitsu, a leading electronics supplier, and American firms, demanded that NTT's highly profitable markets – including an annual revenue growth of 14 per cent in data communications and leased circuits – be opened up to competition.[42] Competition in the provision of terminal equipment and value-added services was supported by MITI (the Ministry of International Trade and Industry responsible for the expansion of the private sector of Japanese industry), and encouraged by large American companies and the United States government.

From 1970, MPT gradually relaxed monopoly restrictions on telecommunications in order to accommodate the requirements of large business users and speed up the convergence of data processing and computers. Terminal equipment was liberalised in 1957, and again in 1970, about the same time as the Carterphone decision in the United States. A revised Telecommunications Law in 1971 allowed business users to connect the public network to leased-lines. Under the new Business Communications Law of 1982, MPT liberalised the value-added services market, which permitted Japanese and foreign corporations to establish internal value-added networks, and they were later able to compete in a fully liberalised market. However, entry into the value-added market was subject to MPT control in the form of registration requirements. This interventionist role allowed MPT to structure the market to benefit Japanese firms, including a policy of developing specific services for small business users.

There was also inter-ministry rivalry. MPT allied with NTT and the cartel of major electronics manufacturers wanted to retain the state monopoly. MPT later favoured the new deregulatory measures after recognising that competition would expand the size and regulatory role of the ministry. MITI, which had administrative control over electronics and computing industries, was in favour of privatisation in the hope that bringing NTT into the private market would place the telecommunications monopoly under MITI's jurisdiction. MPT defined the rules in the draft law which resulted in the privatisation of NTT. Support for privatisation came from business users and equipment manufacturers, including major American computer firms like IBM,[43] and more importantly from the ruling Liberal Democratic Party. This ministerial rivalry influenced the future course of regulation. For example, by the mid-1980s MITI successfully opened up earlier restrictions limiting foreign involvement in value-added services. American information providers joined forces with Japanese companies and entered the market, for example, General Electric Information Services created a joint venture with the electronics manufacturer NEC.

On 1 April 1985, Nippon Denshin Denwa Kabushiki Kaisha Law was enacted and NTT was transformed into a private company. The form of liberalisation and NTT's structure was raised by the Second Ad Hoc Commission on Administrative reform in 1981. NTT management and its trade union, Zendentsu, supported by opposition parties, were opposed to the break up of NTT into local and long-distance companies. Although the Commission's recommendation to divest NTT along the lines of the break up of AT&T was ignored, proposals to privatise the company – which closely followed developments in Britain – were implemented. For a period of five years, ownership of the new NTT was to remain in government hands, but the state would then gradually cede ownership of the monopoly, while always retaining at least one-third of the shares. In practice, however, NTT was privatised in February 1987 when NTT shares were listed and floated.

The NTT law created two carriers: Type I common carriers

licensed to build and operate long-distance telecommunications systems; and Type II value-added service carriers using leased circuits to furnish information services over the telecommunications network. NTT was allowed to compete in the Japanese market for value-added services, and permitted to set its rates to offer low-cost services in competition with new long-distance common carrier entrants on high density voice and data routes. Several groups, such as Daini Denden (the 'second NTT') soon established communications systems in competition with NTT between the two main business centres of Tokyo and Osaka, which carried approximately 25 per cent of total Japanese telecommunications traffic in 1985. Unlike BT which has introduced additional suppliers – such as Ericsson and Northern Telecom – beyond its traditional transmission and switching equipment manufacturers, NTT retained close links with its domestic circle of manufacturers including NEC, Fujitsu and Hitachi.

Privatising the monopoly: a failure in organisation

The first two sections of this chapter described two clearly defined organisational forms: the institutional changes introduced on mainland Europe retained the state-owned monopoly structure of telecommunications, and the separation of AT&T from regulated local exchange services provided a basis for competition in long-distance communications. In contrast the policy of privatisation introduced in Britain and Japan has left unfinished the job of devising an appropriate organisational structure. There have been subsequent political pressures to break up private monopolies into regulated local services and competitive long-distance lines.

In Japan NTT's control of local and long-distance operations came under pressure from officials in MPT. In 1989, the ministry published an interim report from the Telecommunications council, an advisory body which recommended breaking up NTT. The report maintained that NTT was bureaucratic, over-centralised and too large to be managed as a single entity, and unable to allow fair competition in the telecommunications market. The report argued that despite reductions in NTT's workforce from 304,000 in 1986 to 277,000 in 1987, the ratio of labour costs to total expenditures was rising.[44] NTT was accused of being slow to furnish the three new common carriers in the long-distance market with interconnections to NTT's local exchange operations – analogous to the accusations of specialised common carriers in the United States that AT&T refused to provide adequate local-service access. The report recommended dividing NTT into a single long-distance company interworked with eleven local exchange operators to stimulate competition. However, the division of NTT required a new telecommunications law. In 1991 NTT was granted a partial reprieve from government plans to break up the monopoly into separate parts. The existing institutional form will be maintained until 1996, after which it will be reviewed.

The question of whether or not BT should be restructured in order to promote competition has not been officially considered by government or the regulator. In contrast to MPT, Oftel does not possess the ministerial power to recommend divestiture. However, following complaints about the interconnection fees which BT charges its competitors for use of the local network, in July 1991 Oftel suggested that BT might in future place local and long-distance operations in separate subsidiaries to promote competition. The subsidiaries would deal with each other on an arm's length basis and be required to furnish the same terms and conditions to competitors. This also raised the question of a radical restructuring of BT: splitting the company into local and long-distance subsidiaries, and divesting it of these subsidiaries, as happened to AT&T. There would then be no doubt as to whether BT was abusing its dominant position by restrictive interconnections to local exchanges or by cross-subsidising competitive long-distance services using revenues generated by monopolistic local operations.

Conclusion

It was politics rather than technological and economic imperatives which determined the different paths of restructuring of national telephone monopolies. The shape of the diverse organisational schemes depended on the outcome of a political contest between traditional nationally based monopoly interests and an alliance of multinational corporations. Differences in the political forms of restructuring were, however, underpinned by material changes in mass production: they were driven by corporate requirements for digital systems of information processing and communication. However, in countries on mainland Europe, like France and Germany, multinational corporations and computer equipment producers did not possess sufficient power to dismantle the traditional state-controlled monopoly. In the United States, Britain and Japan, the abolition of the state telecommunications monopoly was a product of the strength of the user–electronic-equipment alliance in these countries.

Essentially two different ways of reorganising national telecommunications systems were adopted. On most of mainland Europe, the state retained control over the development of converged data processing and telecommunications systems. By adhering to the established practice of the state-led modernisation of telecommunications, these countries aim to build national infrastructures to promote national economic development, while retaining a commitment to public service obligations through the provision of a cross-subsidised universal service. In the United States, Britain and Japan, on the other hand, the convergence of information processing and telecommunications is being decided by competition between private common carriers and multinational computer companies. The traditional regulatory goal of promoting a high-quality universal service has been abandoned. Under the coercion of international competition, privatised common carriers have been reorganised to provide specialised information and communication services, charged at low rates, for the profitable market of business users. Where a policy of competition was not accompanied by a separation of local monopoly exchange services from competitive long-distance operations there have been further political struggles over how to reshape privatised monopolies.

The assumption that the most efficient organisational arrangement of national telecommunications is a single monopoly can no longer be taken for granted. New policies introduced throughout the world indicate the potential for decentralising the organisational structure of national telecommunications. First, every country in the industrialised world has liberalised the provision of value-added services and customer terminal equipment. The provision of telecommunications transmission and switching of voice telephony has been separated from the delivery of non-voice services to the customer. Second, the divestiture of AT&T in the United States demonstrates that the trend towards large-scale integrated national monopoly structure can be reversed. Local or regional geographical monopolies under independent control can be separated from the provision of long-distance and international telecommunications. Third, as Japan has shown, domestic telecommunications can be separated from international operations.

Notes

1. This analysis of a conflict between the electronic coalition and PTT interests has been developed by D. Schiller (1982a), 'Business Users and the Telecommunications Network', pp84–96, *Journal of Communication*, Autumn 1982; and D. Schiller (1982b), *Telematics and Government*, Ablex Publishing Corporation, Norwood.
2. G. McKendrick (1989), Executive Director of INTUG, interview by A. Davies, 16 August 1989.
3. E.M. Noam (1987), 'The Public Telecommunications Network: A Concept in Transition', pp30–47, *Journal of Communication*, Winter, 1987.
4. Schiller, pp118–121 (1982b), op. cit.
5. Commission of the European Communities (1987), 'Towards a Dynamic European Economy', Green Paper on the Development of the Common Market for Telecommunications Services and Equipment, COM (87), 290, final, Brussels, 30 June 1987.
6. However, the Commission has the power to intervene in national arrangements by the use of Article 90 of the Treaty to issue directives aimed at breaking up unjustified public monopolies. Because of the institutional diversity in European telecommunications administrations, Dr H. Ungerer of Directorate-General XIII (Telecommunications, Information Industries and Innovation) of the Commission has clarified that 'it is preferable that each country tries to solve the issue of innovation dynamism with regard to competition on its own base'. H. Ungerer (1987), p86, Oral evidence, 23 July 1987, Select Committee on the European Communities, *European Community Telecommunications Policy*, with evidence, HMSO, London.
7. G.J. Mulgan, p140 (1991), *Communications and Control*, Polity Press, Cambridge.
8. W. Dik (1990), 'Royal PTT Netherlands: Strategy for the Future' pp10–13, in *1992: Single Market Communications Review* (ed.) H. Chaloner, Vol. 2, Issue 3, October 1990; and P. Van Hoogstraten (1992), PTT-Telecom, interview by A. Davies, 4 September 1992.
9. L. Raun (1989), 'Holland's telecoms agency rings in the New Year changes', *Financial Times*, 30 December 1989.
10. G. Dang Nguyen, p98 (1985), 'Telecommunications: A Challenge to the Old Order', in *Europe and the New Technologies* (ed.) M. Sharp, Frances Pinter, London.
11. In order to secure the economies of scale achieved by rival American and Japanese producers, individual European public switching manufacturers had to capture an estimated 8 per cent share of the world market to reap an adequate return on development programmes and the annual upgrading of products. Unlike Japan and the United States, there were eighteen national markets in Europe, none of which was sufficient in size to recoup the costs of developing digital switches. It is estimated that European suppliers invested $7 billion in the development of their digital switching exchanges, in comparison to figures of only $3 billion for the United States and $2 billion for Japan.

During the 1980s, a wave of mergers and joint ventures led to the consolidation of the fragmented European public switching industry. See D. Gilhooly (1987), 'The Politics of Switching', *Telecommunications*, 1987.

12. This discussion of Germany draws from S.K. Schmidt (1991), 'Taking the Long Road to Liberalization', pp209–222, *Telecommunications Policy*, June 1991.

13. The concept of cream-skimming refers to the effects associated with the construction of alternative transmission facilities in addition to the public network which allow competitors to skim the cream of the traffic over profitable telecommunications routes, while leaving the unprofitable traffic – the skimmed milk – to the monopolist.

14. D. Goodhart and H. Dixon (1989), 'Fortress Rhine lowers the drawbridge', *Financial Times*, 30 June 1989.

15. C. Parkes (1992b), 'Eye-catching but with little for sale', *Financial Times*, 11 August 1992.

16. C. Parkes (1992a), 'German telecoms earmarked for sale', *Financial Times*, 7 February 1992.

17. S. Nora and A. Minc (1980) (French edn 1978), *The Computerisation of Society: A Report to the President of France*, MIT Press, Cambridge, Mass.

18. M. Derthick and P.J. Quirk (1985), *The Politics of Deregulation*, The Brookings Institution, Washington D.C., and Schiller, p61 (1982b), op. cit.

19. Communications Act of 1934, 73rd Congress, 2nd Session, S. 3285, ch. 652, 48 Stat. 1064, 1934.

20. L.L. Johnson (1978), 'Boundaries to Monopoly and Regulation in Modern Telecommunications', pp127–155 in *Communications for Tomorrow: Policy Perspectives for the 1980s* (ed.) G.O. Robinson, Praeger Publishers, New York. See also H.M. Trebing (1969) p307, 'Common Carrier Regulation – The Silent Crisis', pp299–329, *Communications: Part 1, Law and Contemporary Problems*, Vol. 34.

21. The only competitive part of the industry was between Bell and Western Union for private-line services which consisted of two sub-markets for business users: private telegraph lines, used mainly by newspaper wire services; and private telephone lines for large businesses.

22. 'In the Matter of ... the Interdependence of Computer and Communication Services and Facilities'. Docket 16979, March 4, 1968, p19, cited in Schiller, p91 (1982a), op. cit. Evidence submitted by all sectors of American industry – including for example, the American Newspapers Association, and the National Association of Manufacturers – demonstrated that integrated computer communications equipment and services had diffused widely throughout the economy.

23. G.W. Brock, p199 (1981), *The Telecommunications Industry: The Dynamics of Market Structure*, Harvard University Press, Cambridge, Mass.

24. The conventional view that the long-distance service cross-subsidised

local services is challenged by Melody. In practice the subsidy may have flowed from local to long-distance services. Since local exchange plant was technically upgraded to furnish long-distance transmission, the latter service should bear the cost. See W.H. Melody (1989), 'Efficiency and Social Policy in Telecommunications: Lessons from the U.S. Experience', pp657–688, *Journal of Economic Issues*, Vol. XXIII, No. 3.

25. F.W. Henck and B. Strassburg, p84 (1988), *A Slippery Slope: The Long Road to the Breakup of the Bell System*, Greenwood Press, New York.
26. Large users and new carriers could bypass the public network by bulk leasing private circuits from common carriers, which were charged at lower prices than equivalent parts of the public network, and reselling excess capacity at prices which undercut regulatory rates. Because the rates charged for leased circuits did not reflect the public network costs of switching, planning and investment in spare capacity to cover peak loads, bypass users could resell capacity at lower rates.
27. Derthick and Quirk, p179 (1985), op. cit.
28. R.B. Horowitz, p240 (1989), *The Irony of Regulatory Reform: The Deregulation of American Telecommunications*, Oxford University Press, Oxford.
29. P. Temin, p349 (1987), *The Fall of the Bell System: A Study in Prices and Politics*, Cambridge University Press, Cambridge.
30. While differing in the size of geographic service area, the RBOCs are approximately the same size (equivalent to a medium-sized European PTT like NV PTT) according to a number of indicators: for example, in 1984 the number of employees in each RBOC ranged from 99,100 at BellSouth to 74,700 at SouthWestern Bell; the number of access lines ranged from BellAtlantic's 14.6 million to SouthWestern Bell's 10.5 million. A.A. Gilroy, p6 (1984), 'The American Telephone and Telegraph Company Divestiture: Background, Provisions, and Restructuring', Report No. 84–58 E, Congressional Research Service, 11 April 1984.
31. U.S. District Court, District of Columbia, Modification of Final Judgment, *United States* v. *Western Electric Inc. & American Telephone and Telegraph Co.*, Civil Action No. 82-01982, 24 August 1982, Section 1B. Cited in Horowitz, p242 (1989), op. cit.
32. K. Morgan (1987), 'Breaching the Monopoly: Telecommunications and the State in Britain', University of Sussex, *Working Paper Series on Government-Industry Relations*, No. 7.
33. *Report of the Post Office Review Committee*, p43, Chairman Mr C.F. Carter, presented to parliament by the Secretary of State for Industry, July 1977.
34. Schiller, p118 (1982b), op. cit.
35. Morgan, p8, op. cit.
36. J. Hills, p89 (1986), *Deregulating Telecoms: Competition and Control in the United States, Japan and Britain*, Frances Pinter, London.
37. M.E. Beesley (1981), *Liberalisation of the Use of the British Telecommunications Network: Report to the Secretary of State*, HMSO, London.
38. Hills, p93, op. cit.

39. *The Future of Telecommunications in Britain*, p1, presented to parliament by the Secretary of State for Industry, July 1982: 'Unless something is done radically to change the capital structure and ownership of BT and to provide a direct spur to efficiency, higher investment would mean still higher charges for the customer'.
40. N. Garnham (1985), 'Telecommunications Policy in the United Kingdom', pp7–29, *Media, Culture and Society*, Vol. 7.
41. G. de Jonquieres (1985), 'Deregulation, Japanese-style', *Financial Times*, 29 March 1985.
42. Hills, p139, op. cit.
43. Industrial views represented to the committee included the Equipment Manufacturers Association, Communications Industry Association, and Keidanren, which represented the interests of over 800 companies, including powerful companies like Toyota and Nippon Steel, and about ten foreign companies, including IBM and Philips.
44. S. Wagstyl (1989), 'NTT under fire as critics seek to ring the changes', *Financial Times*, 10 October 1989.

7 Restructuring the regional systems

Regional monopolies in Denmark and Finland avoided nationalisation during the first technological divide, but did not escape worldwide pressures for restructuring in the age of digital telecommunications. Corresponding to the pattern of change elsewhere in the industrialised world, so an epochal shift in the mass production process from electromechanical to electronic technologies was the transforming force behind corporate demands for data communications services and computerised terminal equipment in Denmark and Finland. In these Nordic countries, however, such pressures were felt within quite different political circumstances: the multinational interests of the electronic alliance had less impact on domestic regulatory changes, and the existence of a state controlled postal–industrial complex commanded little influence over Danish and Finnish telecommunications. Consequently, the modernisation of the regional systems has been undertaken without embracing either the model of privatisation introduced in Britain and Japan, or reverting to the traditional policy of a centralised national monopoly retained in France and Germany. Rather, the Danish and Finnish states have pursued their own distinctive paths of transformation.

In terms of the ideal-typical forms of organisation – national monopoly, decentralised cooperation and private competition – Denmark has shifted towards the monopoly end of the spectrum, placing semi-autonomous regional and long-distance operators under the centralised control and ownership of a holding company, in competition with foreign carriers and service providers. Introducing this hybrid mix of cooperation and consolidation, the Danish telecommunications sector has been reorganised to capture the advantages of centralised management obtained by national monopoly organisations, while retaining the decentralised small firm structure of independent regional, long-distance, and newly formed nationwide data and mobile service companies. In Finland, by contrast, the restructuring of telecommunications has moved towards greater competition between two domestically owned carriers controlling local and long-distance telecommunications: an association of forty-nine independent regional companies, and a state-owned long-distance and international operator. The following two sections on Denmark and Finland aim to explain how these countries resisted nationalisation after the first technological divide, and why – despite inheriting similar traditional organisational schemes – the two countries have followed contrasting paths of restructuring since the 1980s.

1. Cooperation and consolidation: Denmark

The special organisation of Danish telecommunications during the twentieth century originates in the Telegraphs and Telephones Act of 1897.[1] Under the Act, the General Directorate of Posts and Telegraphs (P&T) was granted a monopoly of all telecommunications: the P&T controlled interregional and international telephone and telegraph networks, and granted concessions permitting private companies to operate regional services within geographical areas. In comparison to Finland, where for particular historical reasons the early telephone developed entirely under private rather than state ownership, with its legal monopoly the Danish state had greater power to influence the size and ownership structure of the regional companies.

The tradition of cooperation

In the 1940s and 1950s, various Danish governments intervened in the structure of the telephone industry by amalgamating the eleven regional companies into four regional monopolies to search for economies of scale in the operation of standardised and automated regional exchanges. These four regional companies were placed under different forms of ownership. Two limited liability companies were granted concessions: the Copenhagen Telephone Company Ltd (KTAS) under the Telephone Concessions Act of 30 June 1919 and the Jutland Telephone Company Ltd (JTAS) under the Act of 13 March 1922. The Funen Telephone Company (FT) was owned and operated by the municipality of Funen. The state-owned and controlled South Jutland Telephone Company (TS), was formed in 1920 after this region of Denmark was ceded from Germany.[2] Each monopoly held a concession to provide a telephone service in specified geographical areas. The Telephone Concessions Act of 1919, which contained a redemption clause allowing the state to purchase private shares in the regional companies at a fixed price, was invoked in 1939 and 1942 to confer majority state ownership of the two regional companies, KTAS and JTAS.[3] But this change in ownership did little to alter the autonomy and control held by the regional monopolies.

Rules governing the details of cooperation and preventing destructive competition between private and state authorities were not formally established until the telephone agreement of 1950. Referred to as 'the Concordat', the agreement shaped the organisational and technological form of the Danish telecommunications sector during the second half of the twentieth century.[4]

Organisationally, the regional telephone companies operated all equipment related to regional telephone traffic, and the national P&T controlled equipment, including lines and exchanges, for interregional and international traffic. Regional companies were responsible for collecting revenue and billing customers for all telephone messages. The P&T was refunded revenue collected for interregional and international telephone traffic, and revenues for local calls were retained by the regional companies. Telex, telegraph and, in the 1970s, data services, were transmitted over the telephone transmission network, and controlled and marketed by P&T.

Technologically, Danish telecommunications consisted of two distinct networks combined into the traditional hierarchical structure: regional operations were interconnected to the P&T's triangular network – the long-distance network linking the triangle of Copenhagen, Århus and Kolding, with an additional link between Kolding and Åbenraa. Agreements about standards, tariffs and operating procedures were decided by the Directors' Committee of the five authorities. The creation of the Directors' Committee provided an institutional mechanism for the resolution of disputes and maintenance of trust whose operation was satisfactory to all parties concerned. Such cooperation facilitated the transition to automatic electromechanical exchanges in the 1950s, and the introduction of Subscriber Trunk Dialling in the 1960s and 1970s.

In contrast to the bureaucratic management style of traditional European PTT monopolies, there was considerable dynamism internal to the Danish regional model in the form of managerial competition. Regional authorities vied with each other to provide the lowest rates and most advanced services tailored to the requirements of customers in their geographical areas.[5] Each company was distinguishable by its management style. For example, despite the close cooperation between the KTAS and JTAS regional companies (they shared a single numbering scheme, and controlled a single network in terms of planning and operation), both companies competed to increase efficiency and improve services.[6] The press was an instrument used by the public to stimulate critical judgement of the performance of the concessionary companies and state authorities. In this way, the incentive to be the best operator judged by the public interest substituted for the market mechanism as a stimulus to innovation and efficiency.

While the cooperative arrangement furnished an efficient telephone system for Denmark as a whole, paradoxically the Danish state persisted in trying to transform the telecommunications sector into a government agency modelled on the European PTT organisation. Attempts to nationalise the industry failed for two reasons: the state was unable to finance the takeover of all the private assets; and this form of organisational change was resisted by the trade unions representing employees in the companies, and politicians – especially from Jutland – defending the independent control and ownership of the regional telephones. Informed by an intensive study (Styregruppen for Teleundersoegelsen) of 1978, a final attempt to nationalise the telecommunications sector was made in 1980. Experience of this last unsuccessful attempt at nationalisation convinced subsequent Danish coalition governments in the 1980s that a new regulatory framework should be established, retaining the independence of existing private companies and the state authority.

The road to consolidation

Pressures to modernise the Danish telecommunications sector came from two sources: large corporate users and foreign competition. First, from the late 1960s Denmark had experienced the common pressure of corporate demands for modern data transmission services and terminal equipment to support computer communications. Since the cooperative agreement of 1950 only dealt with telephony, new technological and organisational problems arose as a result of the implementation of data communication services. Under the 1950 agreement, the development of the data services was retarded by the monopoly held by the five authorities, which prohibited the hiring out of switched or leased lines to third parties, and placed telephone, telex and data modem equipment (excluding low-speed modems) under monopoly supply. Despite early attempts by the regional companies to establish data communications for corporate customers, the market for data services was placed under the P&T monopoly, alongside the telex service which also utilised the telephone network for transmission. The only exception was JTAS which set up packet and circuit switched data networks.

On 1 June 1986, restrictions on leased-line non-voice services were removed, allowing providers of value-added services to use a mix of public and private networks without restrictions and offer basic data services, including the connection of computer terminals to modems and packet switching networks. IBM, for example, offered a data transmission service, and banking and insurance companies provided debit-card services over leased-line networks, previously confined to the state monopoly. Largely in response to previous European Commission (EC) decisions, the Danish data communications services market was fully liberalised and restrictions on permanent leased-lines were removed on 31 December 1992. Liberalisation of terminal equipment on 1 June 1989, conforming to the EC Directive of the previous year, transformed the Danish telecommunications equipment industry.[7]

The second pressure was the growing international competition in the Danish telecommunications equipment and services markets from foreign equipment suppliers, carriers and service providers, including Siemens, AT&T, BT, and US Sprint. By 1992, foreign companies were already offering data communications services – such as network management and 'one-stop-shopping' global services for corporate users – inside Denmark. Regulatory reform in the United States, Britain and Japan in the early 1980s and EC Directives fostering the liberalisation of services, permitted newly privatised and liberalised carriers and suppliers to offer equipment and services for large users in previously closed, monopolistic markets of foreign PTTs. The Danish government was particularly concerned about the ability of the small-scale, decentralised Danish telecommunications sector to compete successfully against large foreign suppliers.[8]

While every European country has been subjected to these two universal pressures to dismantle the monopoly walls surrounding national telecommunications, the particular form of the reorganisation of the Danish telecommunications sector is a product of nationally specific political changes. The election of a conservative–liberal coalition government in September 1982 ended the post-war domination of Danish politics by coalition governments controlled by the Social Democratic Party. In 1982 the country was suffering from huge balance of payments and budget deficits. Under prime minister Poul Schülter, the coalition government sought to restore the country's finances by adopting a new political agenda. Because Denmark had the highest taxation levels in Europe, attempts to lower taxes depended upon the opening up of new sources of revenues, particularly in the field of telecommunications. Inspired by the liberalism of the Thatcher government in Britain, the Danish government believed the sale of the P&T shares would help alleviate the problem of a growing national debt, and the introduction of liberalisation would limit the power of the Danish telecommunications monopolies.[9]

The operation, ownership and regulation of the Danish telecommunications sector was transformed in two stages. The first stage was initiated by the Telecommunications Act of 22 May 1986 which simplified the regulation and operation of the Danish regional system.[10] With the exception of more routine regulations such as licences for radio operators and cable television companies which were undertaken by the newly formed Telecommunications Inspectorate, the Ministry of Communications was responsible for regulation and granting concessions. In the discussions which led to the drafting of the Act, the Telecommunications Council continued to represent the interests of residential and Danish business users (including foreign-owned corporations with Danish plants) and employees of the five companies represented by the trade union, Dansk Tele Forbund. In each of the regions, the interests of local users were addressed by Subscribers' Committees. Under the umbrella of this corporatist framework, the two stages of restructuring were reached by consensus, since the whole spectrum of interests in Danish telecommunications was consulted in the process of reform.

The 1986 Act established a new division of responsibilities among the five companies, but did nothing to alter the control of the Danish telecommunications by regional and state monopolies. Prior to December 1986, when JTAS and KTAS received their new concessions, the regional companies had no incentive to develop and market interregional voice, data and mobile services, because all interregional revenues were returned to the P&T.[11] This anomaly was rectified by the 1986 Act when all customer-related functions for interregional obligations (except maritime, radio and television services), plus 1,800 of the employees of the state operator responsible for non-voice services, were taken over by the regional companies. Limited only by the requirement to refund the cost of carriage for using the state-owned long-distance transmission network, the four regional companies subsequently had an incentive to expand the market for interregional services in search of larger revenues. The state operator received all the revenues for international calls, and continued to own and operate the long-distance and international networks. This organisational change was motivated by the search for economies of scope obtained by integrating and lowering the costs of the marketing and sales functions of new regional and long-distance services.[12]

Until 1 January 1991, therefore, the organisation of the Danish regional telecommunications system consisted of a mixture of private and public and state ownership: four regional monopolies, and the interregional and international state owned carrier, ST. The state owned 51 per cent of the private shares in JTAS, 54 per cent in KTAS, and 100 per cent of TS. Funen Telephone company was still organised as a cooperative society owned by the municipalities of the county of Funen.

The consolidated regional system

The next stage of restructuring began in 1990 with the announcement that the regional concessions would not be extended beyond the concessionary period ending 1 March 1992. On 22 June 1990, the Danish government entered a political agreement with the opposition party, the Social Democrats, to change the organisation of telecommunications in Denmark.[13] Both political parties agreed that the provisions of the agreement should apply for a five-year period until the expiry of the concessionary period ending 1 March 1997.

Two organisational solutions were considered. First, mirroring what will be introduced in Finland in 1994, two parallel competing companies could have been formed, based on competition between the existing Jutland and Copenhagen authorities – the largest regional companies in terms of numbers of employees and subscriber lines. Under this proposal, each company would have controlled duplicate regional, interregional and international lines. It was rejected because of strong opposition from the telephone companies of Funen and South Jutland. Second, the preferred solution was a single holding company, based on a continuation of the monopoly of regional and interregional services held jointly by the five companies, separated from competitive international services.

The terms of the political agreement were brought into effect during the autumn of 1990 when the Danish Folketing (parliament) passed the Telecommunications Act of 14 November 1990. Four new limited companies were created: a holding company, called Tele Danmark Ltd; ST, renamed Telecom Denmark Ltd; the Funen Telephone Ltd; and Telecom Jutland South. On 1 January 1991, the new holding company, Tele Danmark, became sole concession-holder for telephone, text and data services; permanent leased-lines; the existing mobile NMT (Nordic Mobile Telecommunications) service; satellite services; and conveyance through the telecommunications network of radio and television programmes. In November 1990 the Folketing also passed the Act on Public Mobile communications which licensed Tele Danmark and a second operator, Dansk Mobil Telefon to provide new joint-European Groupe Speciale Mobile (GSM) mobile telephone services. The separation of regulation from the operation of the telecommunications system was designed to prevent the General Directorate and the political interests from influencing business decisions, allowing the market to be the incentive for Tele Danmark's efficiency. Ownership of the five regional companies was transferred to the holding company. Under the supervision of Tele Danmark, the companies subsequently operated as semi-autonomous subsidiaries. Although the share capital in Tele Danmark, amounting to 1,310 million Krone, initially remained majority owned by the state with 94 per cent of the shares, the Act provides for the sale of a further 43 per cent of the shares to private shareholders.

While the Danish political parties agreed that the traditional regional system was well adapted to static conditions of monopoly and incremental technological change, there was a consensus that the traditional organisation could not meet the call for 'flexibility and adaptation' required by a dynamic phase of radical technological change and new competition.[14] With the prospect of new technological, market and regulatory changes in the 1990s, Danish telecommunications had to be radically changed: first, this was due to the introduction of an increasingly liberalised domestic market, resulting from EC directives and the introduction of new technology; second, the restructuring was necessary because 'these changed conditions call for a competent and dynamic overall organisation, capable of supporting research and product development and of furthering the cooperation with both Danish and international enterprises'; and, third, in the competitive race to adapt to the new dynamic phase, organisational change was enforced by the privatisation and liberalisation policies of other countries.[15] The agreement's main purpose was to strengthen the competitiveness of the Danish telecommunications sector in response to the entry of foreign privatised and liberalised carriers inside the national market.[16]

In combination, such changes called for decision-making capability which the Directors' Committee of the five companies could not guarantee. Without the creation of the holding company structure and centralised planning, decisions about the introduction of new nationwide telecommunications services (such as the mobile GSM network) would have been left in the hands of the Directors' Committee, which gave each individual managing director the right of veto and power to prevent the committee from taking collective action. To complicate matters further, the Directors' Committee was composed of members representing rival interests in the supply of terminal equipment and data services. Thus the inability of the Directors' Committee to reach common decisions may have blocked the development of a range of competitive value-added and mobile services. While the Directors' Committee continues to exist under the holding company structure, in the event of a failure to reach agreement between the subsidiaries, the chairperson of the committee has been given the authority needed to carry through collective action.

Structural change was, therefore, seen as a precondition for improvements in the range and quality of services offered to Danish telecommunications users. Despite close cooperation between the five companies, before 1991 each company developed specialised technical solutions, resulting in a duplication of activities. Whereas under the traditional cooperative structure, a large user would have to contact several different companies to obtain voice, telex, data and mobile services throughout Denmark, the new consolidated organisation offers a single point of contact for nationwide services.[17]

In summary, then, the newly consolidated organisation was devised to preserve the autonomy of management in the decentralised, small-scale cooperative structure of the Danish telecommunications system, while making Tele Danmark responsible for centralised planning, subject to business priorities and market exigencies. In the words of the political agreement,

Tele Danmark should not uncritically interfere with the internal affairs of the individual telecom companies. This means that planned centralisation will not be carried out further than warranted by the purpose of the structural change. Tele Danmark's responsibility for the operation of subsidiaries will thus basically consist in setting up result targets for the telecom companies.[18]

With no more than forty employees, Tele Danmark's small head-quarters – which is responsible for corporate control and strategic management – has been established in Århus. Tele Danmark has become the key link in a corporatist chain of industrial organisation, cooperation and joint ventures, joining together equipment suppliers, operators and state-financed R&D to sustain the international competitiveness of the Danish telecommunications sector.

Until 1990, the structural separation between regional and long-distance services prevented the use of cross-subsidies to promote a universal service. But the concessionary companies were obliged to satisfy public service obligations, such as the provision of services on smaller islands. While Denmark as a whole had a reasonably uniform tariffing structure, a low-cost telephone service was furnished by the companies at prices which varied between regions.

With the creation of Tele Danmark, the new Danish regulatory regime aims to achieve a balance between the provision of a public service at reasonable prices, while offering low prices in highly competitive segments of national and international telecommunications markets. Although the efficiency of the Danish system resulted in low prices for residential and business customers, relatively high prices in profitable segments of the market, including leased-lines, long-distance and international services, could attract competition from foreign carriers. Consequently, the political agreement indicated that a precondition for lower prices was cost-oriented tariffs, especially for internationally competitive services such as leased-lines for large business users. On the other hand, new regulation sought to provide 'basic telephony in a low-priced, uniform and fair manner for the ordinary user in the monopolised field'.[19] Indeed, one of the regulatory tasks of the Ministry of Communications is to ensure a continued drop in consumer prices for telephone services, by setting limits on Tele Danmark's tariff increases.

2. Cooperation and competition: Finland

Although Finland's population is dispersed over a large geographical area, with 2,670,000 lines serving about 5 million inhabitants in 1987 (about 53 lines per 100 inhabitants), Finland was placed fifth in the world ranking of telephone density. Yet despite its efficient record, the Finnish regional model has been dismissed as an archaic system.[20] Like the Danish case, the existence of this decentralised organisation raises doubts about the inevitable march of technological progress towards the more efficient model of a large-scale, centralised bureaucracy, and establishes the possibility of a concrete alternative. Since the late 1980s Finland slowly departed from the principles of cooperation associated with the traditional regional system, embarking instead on a process of liberalisation fostering closer cooperation between the forty-nine private local telephone companies, while introducing the most competitive telecommunications system in the world.

The tradition of cooperation

Under Russian imperial rule, the Finnish authorities gained domestic control of local telephones by the policy of licensing as many private companies as possible.[21] After Finnish independence in 1917, this earlier policy left the legacy of a telecommunications sector dominated by private and state interests, and set the scene for an intense rivalry between two groups of private and state operators.

The completion of the first technological divide in Finland was delayed until 1935, when an early period of competition was brought to a close by the nationalisation of all long-distance telegraph, telex and telephone services. Subsequently, ownership and operation of the Finnish telecommunications network was in the hands of two groups. On the one hand, the state-owned Posts and Telecommunications (P&T) carrier – similar in management style to centralised PTT agencies – held a monopoly of telegraph, telex and long-distance and international telephony, and local services in some sparsely populated areas. On the other, a group of private local telephone companies, called telcos, had concessions to provide basic telephony within defined geographical areas.

In spite of the diverse types of company ownership – municipal, limited liability, economic associations and cooperatives – in practice the dominant ownership structure of the telco companies was the cooperative form. For example, although the Helsinki Telephone Company was an economic association, like the cooperative companies it was owned by subscribers. Customers requiring access to a telephone line either rented or purchased a share (approximately $1,000 US dollars in 1992) in a regional company. In 1991, for example, 80 per cent of subscribers (or one and a half million Finnish inhabitants) possessed shares in telco companies.[22] Consequently each company's stock of capital grew in proportion to increases in the number of the company's subscribers. Receiving no interest or dividends which might accrue on the capital contribution, the only motive for share ownership in a company was access to cheap services charged at monthly or usage rates. Since companies operated on a cost-price principle, with prices of services fixed not to show excess profits, improvements in efficiency were passed on to customers in the form of lower rates and new investments in networks.

Coordination of the activities of the telco group of local companies was achieved by mutual agreements and by their membership in the Association of Telephone Companies. Founded in 1921, the Association organised cooperation among the private local companies by harmonising commercial relations between the companies, coordinating equipment procurement, improving service quality, and standardising networks. The Danish experience of managerial competition between regional operations was also a feature of Finnish local operations.[23] Working according to the competitive principle of 'who is first, is best' – based on performance information such as employees per line published by the Association – managers of the telcos were stimulated into making improvements in efficiency and service.

While there was no centralised control of the Association, the Helsinki Telephone Company (HTC) commanded a leading position because it was the largest and most powerful telco. In 1992, for example, it was almost equal in size to the other forty-eight companies combined; its gross sales were almost six times bigger than the second largest company; and its earnings represented 40 per cent of the combined total of all the telco companies. Technological innovation in the group has been driven by the activities of HTC: it was the first company to convert to automated electromechanical exchanges, completed between 1922 and 1929; and more recently, the first to introduce digital Pulse Code Modulation transmission, fibre optic systems and mobile services.

From a peak of 850 companies in 1939, the local telcos were concentrated and centralised into forty-nine independent operators by 1992.[24] Regional companies which were too small to operate efficiently sought to obtain economies of scale through mergers with other telcos, or were bought out by the P&T. Between 1950 and 1962 – the high-point of the merger movement – 293 local companies were taken over by the telco group and 282 were purchased by the P&T. When the electromechanical phase in automation of the telco systems was completed in 1970, the pressure for economic concentration diminished until a new phase was unleashed in the 1980s by the digitisation of switching and transmission. The application of digital techniques depended on a high level of technical resources and skills, and large funds for investment in new technologies. In 1992, for example, according to a P&T estimate, extensive economies of scale in switching enabled one exchange with a capacity of 100,000 lines to offer a low-cost service in a wide area covered by several individual telcos with as few as 1,000 subscribers.[25] But in the view of the telco group, the digitisation of networks did not necessarily force the creation of larger local exchange systems to obtain economies of scale. A recent report to the World Bank shows that the conversion to digital switching has been accomplished more rapidly in smaller telcos, and the standard of service and efficiency achieved by the smaller telcos has been comparable to the larger ones.[26]

The interconnection of local and trunk networks under different forms of ownership was solved by cooperative agreements between the telcos and P&T. Several factors contributed to the success of this method of interconnection: the network structure was simple to operate with the telcos surrounding the P&T hub; no complicated access charges were applied; and the shares of interconnection expenditure among the various partners were simple to arrange. Local operators billed the subscriber for all charging impulses and returned the share for long-distance calls to the P&T.

Proposals to consolidate Finland's telecommunications companies into a single nationalised monopoly were dismissed by the Finnish parliament in 1931 and 1932. Nationalisation was resisted because the Association mobilised its powerful lobbying network to protect the interests of local companies, and during the world economic recession the state was unable to fund a costly takeover of numerous regional companies. A further attempt at nationalisation was made after the Second World War when the Communist Party received legal status and gained significant political support. In 1948 a Socialisation Committee put forward a proposal to nationalise the entire Finnish telecommunications infrastructure, but it was not introduced because by the late 1940s a changed political climate had diminished the influence of the Communists.

Technological and institutional transformation

In the late 1980s the Finnish telecommunications system was structurally adjusted to cope with a period of dynamic technological change and competition. In contrast to Denmark, where foreign competition provided one of the main incentives to transform the telecommunications sector, in Finland the driving force behind the transformation of the telecommunications industry has been domestic competition between the telco and P&T groups over the supply of data communication services demanded by large corporate customers. Not the product of consensus as it was in Denmark, the Finnish path of restructuring has been shaped by a contest between political coalitions supporting the diverging interests of the telcos and P&T.

From the late 1960s, Finnish telecommunications organisation passed through three phases of technological transformation: first, the upsurge in corporate demand for data communication services and terminal equipment since the late 1960s; second, the rapid growth in mobile voice services in the 1980s; and, third, the introduction of new optical fibre and digital technologies for long-distance voice telecommunications. Each technological change posed a challenge to the traditional institutional division of responsibilities.

During the three phases, the two sets of commercial interests, the telcos led by the Helsinki Telephone Company and large business users on one side, and the P&T and some of its large customers on the other, used all possible channels of political communication – politicians, media, publicity and lobbying – to influence the Ministry of Transport and Communications. Competitive success hinged on the terms and conditions of concessions and regulations established by the Ministry. The press was an instrument with whose aid political decisions about telecommunications received the critical commentary of public opinion. Political interests polarised between the conservative party which opposed nationalisation and favoured granting concessions, and the socialist parties which preferred a state-run service. Yet the choices of some individual politicians proved exceptions to this rule. The telcos, in particular, have developed close relations with local politicians, who have often been elected to positions on telco management boards.

Initiating the first phase of transformation, a dispute over the provision of leased-line data services began in 1969 when the Helsinki Telephone Company offered corporate users a data transmission service by modems. The Finnish long-distance monopoly came under additional pressure when MCI and US Sprint breached AT&T's monopoly on long-distance calls in the United States, unleashing a worldwide reappraisal of telecommunications regulation.[27] Large business customers complained about the high prices the P&T charged for its data services. The P&T claimed data services as part of the monopoly on telegraph services which included all kinds of transmission of written information. Refusing to be excluded from large potential markets, the telcos claimed data services as part of the local monopoly concessions because telephone lines were used for data transmission. Both groups offered data services before regulatory decisions regarding data transmission had been reached, knowing that the Ministry of Transport and Communications was unlikely to announce the closure of services connected to customers. In the early 1970s, the telco group won a legal dispute – known as the 'tele fight' – after the Finnish courts concluded that data transmission was not a telegraph within the meaning of the 1919 Telegraph Act.

The creation of Datatie Oy in 1985, a data communication service company jointly owned by the largest privately-owned telcos and some large users, initiated competition in the nationwide data services market. Datatie provided packet-switch data communications and value-added services, such as electronic data interchange, within and between the areas of about twenty telcos. Since existing legislation did not apply to long-distance data communication services, the telco group operated Datatie for two years without a concession. With an annual growth rate of 20 per cent, Datatie soon gained a large market share as a low-cost provider of data services. The P&T responded by building a parallel packet-switched network and by reducing its rates for leased data lines by as much as 50 per cent. Emulating developments in the United States at this time, the P&T began competing within the telcos' local concessionary areas, by connecting the private branch exchanges of large customers directly to its long-distance facilities, thus bypassing the local loop.[28] Consequently the two packet-switched networks operated side-by-side with no interconnection.

But the P&T's predatory behaviour forced the government to intervene with the passage of the 1987 Telecommunications Act.[29] The dispute over data services was solved by a compromise. Both groups were granted concessions to continue their services. Datatie received a concession allowing the telcos to offer packet-switched data services in their local areas. To counterbalance the erosion of P&T's revenues by the incursion of Datatie in the long-distance market, the state operator received a concession to establish a separate company offering its bypass services. Jointly owned by the P&T, banks, and a few of the P&T's large customers, Yritysverkot Oy (Business Networks) was established in 1988 to operate nationwide data services over P&T's leased-lines in competition with Datatie. Modelled on the existing regional telephone organisation, HTC operated a local packet-switched data network interconnected to the P&T's long-distance data network.

The 1987 Act marked a turning point towards advancing liberalisation, which soon spread to other parts of the telecommunications infrastructure. In December 1990, Datatie was granted a new concession allowing it to offer nationwide data services jointly with the telcos in competition with the P&T. Following the Telecommunications Act of 1992, data communications required no concession and were fully liberalised; permitting full competition and interconnection between nationwide data networks.

The introduction of mobile voice services initiated the second phase in the transformation of Finnish telecommunications. Traditional responsibility for mobile voice communications was divided between local services offered by the local operators, and nationwide services furnished by the P&T. By the 1980s, however, the volume of mobile traffic had grown to become one of the P&T's largest services, and telephone revenues began to shift from local to mobile networks. In 1992, for example, the Finnish part of the Nordic Mobile Telephone (NMT) system had as many as 300,000 subscribers.

In response to the dramatic growth in mobile services, the telco group entered the market in 1989 with a trunked mobile service called AutoNet. But P&T's mobile services faced a more significant competitive threat when the telco group and some large corporate users established a new nationwide company, called Radiolinja Oy. Arguing that it could offer a mobile service at lower prices than the P&T's service, Radiolinja applied for a licence to operate digital cellular services using GSM standards. In its defence, the P&T claimed that competition would lead to the unnecessary duplication of GSM facilities given the small size of the Finnish market. But after Datatie had set a precedent for competition in nationwide data services, the justification for the P&T's monopoly of mobile services could no longer be sustained. Radiolinja was granted a concession for the provision of cellular services in 1990. With two-thirds of the shares, large corporate users had majority ownership of Radiolinja. While Radiolinja was responsible for operating the nationwide mobile network, the telcos operated the portions of the network within their local areas.

The next target for liberalisation, long-distance voice telephony, started the third phase of transformation. Arguing for several years that the prices of P&T's long-distance calls were too high, the telco group together with a few large users – which were shareholders in Datatie and Radiolinja – founded a new company called Kaukoverkko Ysi, and applied for a licence for the operation of a long-distance telephone network and service. The commercial interests supporting Kaukoverkko claimed that it could construct a competing long-distance network covering the whole of Finland for as little as 300–500 million Finn Marks, while the turnover of long-distance telephone services was 1 billion Finn Marks.[30] Unlike Mercury Communications, which had to build an entirely new long-distance network when the British government created a duopoly, the telco group could make a relatively inexpensive upgrade of its long-distance optical fibre network, used jointly for mobile and data services.[31] Larger volumes of traffic generated by the addition of voice services would increase capacity utilisation of the network, while accelerating the turnover time of sunk capital. Moreover, the Association claimed that the service would be priced 50 per cent lower than the P&T's.

Admitting that its long-distance services were overpriced, the P&T claimed in its defence that the government used long-distance services as a means of collecting money for the treasury. In justifying its monopoly, the P&T argued that the efficiency of long-distance operations was improving since prices were decreasing by 15 to 20 per cent a year.[32] It pointed to the wasteful duplication and costs for the country as a whole incurred by investment in a second long-distance carrier. According to the P&T, the problem of monopoly was in local services where the total turnover was as much as 3 billion Finn Marks per year. Consequently, the P&T applied for a licence to compete with the telcos in local telephone services.

On 21 August 1992, the Council of State reached a compromise over long-distance competition. On 1 January 1994, Kaukoverkko Ysi will receive a concession to offer switched long-distance calls in competition with the P&T. The government also allowed the P&T to offer local services in competition with the telcos in all local areas, while permitting the telcos to offer services in the P&T's local areas. Rather than duplicate copper wires in the local loop, the P&T aims to compete in the local areas of telco companies by introducing a combination of fibre optic broadband transmission and mobile access for local subscribers, and by continuing its policy of purchasing telco companies (as illustrated by its bid to buy Turku's municipal system in 1992). In justifying the decision to permit full competition, the Ministry of Transport and Communications argued that despite the duplication of long-distance operations, competition stimulates improvements in efficiency and lower prices. According to the Ministry estimates, trunk competition will result in annual savings of 360 million Finn Marks for business customers and 90 million Finn Marks for residential subscribers.[33]

Since the decision on long-distance competition, the telco group has mobilised its lobbying power to liberalise international telephone traffic – the only remaining monopoly area. Given the need to furnish global services to multinational corporate customers, the telco group argues that domestic competition will be unfairly balanced in favour of the P&T until the monopoly grip of international traffic is broken.[34] By the end of 1992 there were incipient signs of the forthcoming liberalisation of international telecommunications after a number of limited licences for international links to neighbouring countries were granted to individual telco companies; such as HTC's concession to carry international traffic between Helsinki and Tallinn in Estonia.

Interconnection and competition

The institutional transformation of Finnish telecommunications could not be completed, however, without the creation of a new regulatory regime. Regulation of Finnish telecommunications has passed through two phases.[35] First, under the period of 'stability' prior to the 1987 Act, regulatory functions were controlled by the P&T. But since the P&T was an operator involved in the emerging competitive process, it was not well equipped to enforce regulation. Second, the 1987 Act started a period of 'experimentation and change' in regulation. In compliance with EC legislation, the Finnish government separated the regulatory and operational functions of its communications ministry. Indeed, the 1991 European Economic Area Agreement to facilitate the free movement of capital, people, goods and services between the European Free Trade Association (EFTA) and the EC includes an acceptance by EFTA members of most of the EC laws on telecommunications. With the intention of becoming part of the European Economic Area in 1993, Finland has shaped its regulatory regime to comply with EC directives.

Part of a wider policy offensive to improve the productivity of government departments, the 1990 Law on Posts and Telecommunications transformed the corporate form of the P&T from a government department into a state-owned public corporation, called Telecom Finland. Divested of most of its regulatory responsibilities, Telecom Finland was changed into a concessionary company but remained part of the P&T under the Ministry of Transport and Communications. A further amendment freed Telecom Finland from an obligation to furnish a universal service to all unserved customers in Finland. This change in corporate form was seen as the first step in a longer process to transform Telecom Finland into a limited liability company under private ownership. Although Telecom Finland still has to satisfy financial and service targets set by the ministry, after the 1990 Act it has operated on a commercial and profit-oriented basis, receiving its funding from customers or by borrowing, rather than the government.

Operating with new concessions issued by the highest regulatory authority, the Council of State, in 1993 there were two groups of concession holders: Telecom Finland dominated long-distance and international services and the telco group controlled over 70 per cent of local services. While there was considerable variation in local tariffs, under the terms of the concessions the telcos provided telephone services to all customers in their geographical areas 'on fair and equal terms'. As the regulator monitoring regional tariffs, the P&T did, however, set its own local prices around the average of telco tariffs, and heavily subsidised services in remote rural areas.

While still subject to concessionary public service obligations preventing the differentiation of prices for particular customers, companies are permitted to offer differentiated prices for a variety of services (voice, data and mobile). Nevertheless a significant shift away from the principle of universal service is indicated by the requirement that customers located more than a few hundred metres from the existing infrastructure will have to pay the full cost of line construction plus usage fee. Operators cannot offer one service at packaged discount prices using cross-subsidies from another technology or service. In November 1992, for example, Telecom Finland was ordered by the regulator to change its pricing policy of using revenues from its installed base of analogue cellular subscribers to cross-subsidise its GSM digital cellular service.[36]

From 1 January 1994, a new regulatory regime of 'full competition and interconnection' will begin, permitting competition in the provision of the local and long-distance components of the national telecommunications infrastructure. Under the Telecommunications Law, local operators must offer their customers equal access to the rival long-distance operators. Yet by forcing reductions in prices of leased-lines, long-distance and international telecommunications services for profitable business markets, the policy of full competition may exert a pressure to raise prices of local services for residential customers, making the regional averaging of tariffs and universal service provision hard to enforce. Indeed, Telecom Finland and several telcos have already introduced tariff structures which charge the full cost of telephone line construction when subscribers are located far from the existing infrastructure.

In comparison to the United States, Britain, Japan and Sweden – countries which have also introduced infrastructural competition – the Finnish competition policy is unique because in Finland there has never been a powerful incumbent national PTT monopoly to influence the course of technological and institutional change. On the contrary, the sector is structured into a duopoly of equally powerful telecommunications groups. Both interest groups claim that the efficiency and low prices obtained under the highly competitive Finnish telecommunications sector will discourage the establishment of new operators. There are, however, already indications that foreign and new domestic companies will enter the Finnish market, as they have done in Denmark. While not aiming to establish a third competing national operator, global carriers may seek cooperation or joint ventures with either Telecom Finland or the telco group. By 1992, for example, the telco group had an agreement to interconnect its national packet-switch network with US Sprint's global network, and in January 1993 it signed a distribution agreement with Unisource (a joint venture between PTT-Telecom, Swedish Telecom and Swiss Telecom) to manage the Finnish node offering access to Unistream services, such as 'managed bandwidth' for corporations.[37] In January 1993 two additional domestic operators received licences: Telivo, a subsidiary of the electricity company, was granted a licence for long-distance and international telecommunications traffic, limited to a maximum of 5 per cent of the total turnover of the two market segments; and the national railways also received a licence for interconnection with Hitrail, the company operating the international network of the European rail companies.

Conclusion

As a result of the different balance of political and economic power in the Danish and Finnish telecommunications sectors, the transition from a static cooperative arrangement to a period of dynamic competition and technological change has produced two new hybrid forms of regional organisation. Under Denmark's corporatist framework, the transition towards a more consolidated organisational form was achieved by a high degree of consultation among the range of interests in the sector; including operators, users, employees, and equipment manufacturers. The Danish state was able to exercise control over the shape of restructuring because it owned long-distance and international systems, and held majority ownership in the regional networks. Reflecting the peculiarities of its political past, the state's monopolistic hold over telecommunications in Finland was never so complete. The shape of the transformation of Finnish telecommunications was the product of a political and economic contest between two groups of state and private interests.

Technological change from analogue to digital telecommunications forced a considerable degree of economic concentration and centralisation of decision-making in the Nordic regional systems. But each country has attempted to retain the advantages of flexibility, local entrepreneurialism and dynamic innovation achieved by the traditional cooperative, decentralised organisation. In the face of foreign competition, Denmark, on the one hand, chose to consolidate its activities under a single state-owned company; emphasising the advantages of economies of scale, scope and system, and the disadvantages of duplication. While centralising strategic decision-making and creating nationwide companies for data and mobile services, Denmark has retained the decentralised, independent management structures of its regional operators. Denmark seeks to balance the provision of a public telephone service at equitable prices, while introducing competitive prices in profitable business markets. Acquiring the reputation of the 'radical of Europe', Finland, on the other hand, has adopted full competition and is likely to introduce cost-oriented tariffs for business and residential customers, making it harder to enforce universal service provision in thinly populated areas. Finnish regulation accepts the liberal policy rationale that the costs of duplication (namely the creation of parallel local and long-distance networks and services), are outweighed by the benefits of efficiency, cost reductions and new services which arise from competition.

Notes

1. See chapter 3. With only a few amendments (namely the Telecommunications Acts of 1919 and 1922), this Act was the legal foundation for the regulation and operation of telecommunications in Denmark until the most recent major amendment almost a century later on 22 May 1986. See Danish Ministry of Communications (1990b), 'Act to Regulate Certain Aspects of the Telecommunications Sector', p6, The Minister of Communications, Draft Proposal, September 17 1990.
2. There was a curious exception to this structure: a fifth authority, a local state-owned and operated company on the island of Møn, which was taken over by the Copenhagen telephone company in January 1987.
3. J.S. Anderson (1992), Deputy Permanent Secretary of Posts and Telegraphs, interview by A. Davies, 26 November 1992.
4. S.E. Jeppesen, K.B. Poulsen and F. Schneider (1987), 'The Status and Future Development of the Danish Telecommunications Sector', paper prepared for the FAST/COM 3-project: The Spectrum of Possible Future Market Configurations for Telecommunications.
5. F. Schkolknik (1992), Managing Director, KTAS, interview by A. Davies, 26 November 1992.
6. J. Lindegaard (1992), Managing Director, KTAS, interview by A. Davies, 3 December 1992.
7. Prior to this liberalising measure, several independent Danish suppliers, such as GN Telematic and Bang & Olufsen, supplied the regional companies with telephone sets, digital switches, and optical fibre transmission equipment. After liberalisation, a number of foreign companies, including Ericsson and Northern Telecom, entered the terminal equipment market in competition with established Danish

suppliers and new equipment suppliers formed by the regional companies, such as the private branch exchange supplier, Copenhagen Business Telephone Company. By 1992, this phase of competition had reduced the Danish equipment industry to one major supplier, Bang and Olufsen.

8. For example, BT and FT disrupted the earlier pattern of cooperation between international PTTs by investing in global service facilities, namely Managed Data Network Services (MDNS) and satellite communications, devised by Conference of European Postal and Telecommunications Administrations (CEPT), and operated by competing private consortia. When the British and French later withdrew support for the European MDNS, the Danish P&T decided to concentrate on strategic alliances rather than internationally agreed standards. B.S. Østergaard (1992), 'Is Small Still Beautiful? An Analysis of the Structural Changes in Denmark Leading to the Creation of the Tele Danmark Holding Company', chapter 8 in *Telecommunication: New Signposts and Old Roads* (eds) P. Slaa and F. Klaver, IOS Press, Amsterdam.
9. Ibid.
10. Danish Ministry of Communications (1986), 'The Issue of Installation and Operation of Certain Telecommunications Services Act', the Minister of Communications, No. 270, 22 May 1986.
11. Lindegaard, op. cit.
12. Jeppesen, et al., pp27–28, op. cit.
13. Danish Ministry of Communications (1990a), 'Political Agreement on the Telecommunications Structure', 22 June 1990, and 'Press Release', 23 June 1990, The Minister of Communications.
14. Ibid, p4; and J.A. Andersen (1992), 'New Regulatory Challenges Following the Restructuring of the Telecommunications Sector in Denmark', *Communications Policy Research, '92*.
15. 'Political Agreement' (1990) (see n13), pp1–2.
16. B.L. Petersen (1992), Tele Danmark, interview by A. Davies, 27 November 1992. Indeed, to support Tele Danmark's search for closer cooperation with foreign partners in the Nordic region, the Danish government postponed the sale of state shares (94 per cent in 1992) in the holding company.
17. The Board of Tele Danmark has already created three companies offering nationwide services: Tele Danmark Mobil offers nationwide NMT, GSM and paging services; a data services company; and an electronic data processing company which serves the internal needs of all the companies.
18. Danish Ministry of Communications (1990a), p7. op. cit.
19. Ibid, p16.
20. Professor S.J. Halme (1992), University of Technology, Helsinki, interview by A. Davies, 30 November 1992.
21. See chapter 3.
22. Association of Telephone Companies in Finland, p6 (1991), 'The Finnish Way, The Platform for Success: Private Enterprise in Public Telecommunications'.

23. P. Heikkinen (1992), Technical Director, The Association of Telephone Companies in Finland, interview by A. Davies, 30 November 1992.
24. World Bank Report (1992), 'The Study of Alternative Solutions for the Provision of Telecommunications Services in Developing Countries: Case Study Based on the Regulatory and Organisational Structures in Finland', p33, November 1992, Prepared by Telecon Ltd for Finnish International Development Agency, Ministry of Transport and Communications of Finland, and The World Bank.
25. Scale economies in switching technologies were pointed out by T. Virtanen (1992), Assistant Director, Telecom Finland, interview by A. Davies, 1 December 1992.
26. World Bank Report, p45, op. cit.
27. M. Kosonen, p5 (1992), 'Liberalisation of Telecommunication in Finland', 7th Conference European Communications Policy Research, Sorø Storko, Denmark, 21–23 October 1992.
28. Kosonen, p7, op. cit.
29. Under the 1987 Act, terminal equipment and value-added services were liberalised. Users were granted operating licences to use leased-lines to establish private corporate networks for their own use and for the use of a third party.
30. J. Karpakka, p9 (1992a), 'Telecommunications Liberalisation in Finland', mimeograph of The Association of Telephone Companies in Finland, 28 August 1992.
31. A. Evagora, (1992a), 'Finland Creates Telecoms Duopoly', CommunicationsWeek International, 5 October 1992.
32. Kosonen, p9, op. cit.
33. Karpakka, p9 (1992a), op. cit.
34. p10, ibid.
35. O. Mattila (1992), Telecommunications Administration Centre, interview by A. Davies, 1 December 1992.
36. A. Evagora (1992b), 'Telecom Finland Cited', CommunicationsWeek International, 23 November 1992.
37. J. Karpakka (1992c), Head of Department, Value Added Networks, Helsinki Telephone Company, interview by A. Davies, 3 February 1993.

8 Paths of modernisation

Although the restructuring of national telecommunications infrastructures has been shaped by political interests, the viability of each path of modernisation will be decided by economics. At the end of the first technological divide the large-scale, centralised national monopoly was held up as the best way of organising telecommunications. During the second divide there has been a preoccupation with markets. A liberal explanation of how telecommunications ought to be organised is put forward by the economist Alfred Kahn (1983). In his view, the exposure of the telecommunications industry to competition marks the end of the public utility concept in telecommunications. Kahn argues that only the free play of market forces can determine which part of telecommunications will remain a natural monopoly. Unregulated competition is the appropriate organisational structure for controlling rapid and unpredictable technological change in telecommunications. The benefits of dynamic technological change and risk-taking innovation induced by competition are seen to outweigh the costs incurred by the duplication of operations. New digital technologies can be tailored to match the demands of individual business users. The outcome of competition is a fragmentation of demand and supply, as new profitable markets in networks and services attract new competitors, who realise latent but unsatisfied demand, anticipate new market niches, and raise the size of the total telecommunications market.

The problem with the liberal view is that the market is idealised as the best form of organisation, with no explanation of the technical and economic constraints to competition and promotion of economic concentration in the telecommunications sector. What is required is a shift from this preoccupation with markets to an explanatory theory of telecommunications as a technological and economic system of production. This chapter is divided into two parts. The first part examines the ways in which the introduction of a cluster of new technologies, centred on the conversion of analogue to digital signals, has transformed the economics of telecommunications, and redefined the ways the system can be organised. New forms of institutional dynamism are required to expand and modernise the infrastructure. But there are technical and economic limits to competition. The hierarchical structure of local and long-distance monopolies has been reinforced by new levels of economy of scale and system. Such cost reductions are related to the volume of traffic carried and controlled by the infrastructure. However, single suppliers have not yet captured the economies of scope needed to prevent competition in the provision of customised value-added services serving market niches. The second part of the chapter examines the comparative performance of the three organisational paths of modernisation: national monopoly, private competition and decentralised cooperation. My argument is that the mix of cooperation and competition in Denmark and Finland provides an efficient alternative way of securing the advantages of centralised control by cooperative agreements, combined with the benefits of competition to improve efficiency and innovation in technologies and services.

1. Technology and economics of the digital infrastructure

Since all telecommunications services can be converted into streams of digital information a distinction should be made between: (i) the digital infrastructure or 'bearer service' for the transportation of traffic; and (ii) the provision of teleservices (voice, picture, data, mobile, etc.) and value-added services transported over the infrastructure, which are used by the customer.[1] Whereas a teleservice provides communication of voice, data or images between users who possess the required terminal equipment, a value-added service is tailored to the requirements of particular information systems and offered to users, individually or collectively, by a value-added services provider. The introduction of digital switching for telephony provided the basis for Integrated Services Digital Network (ISDN), offering transmission over 64 kilobits-per-second channels, capable of carrying most teleservices with the exception of moving images. The advantage of ISDN is that its signals can be transmitted to user premises over the existing analogue network designed for telephony.

Economies of scale

Economies of scale in digital transmission and switching systems, which derive from the intensive and extensive expansion of capacity to handle large volumes of traffic at low average costs, may eliminate or reduce opportunities for competition in local and long-distance telecommunications.

In the local component of the digital infrastructure, the traditional advantages of economies of scale and provision of local services by a single supplier have not been undermined by the alternative transmission technologies of optical fibre and mobile radio.

Installed for long-distance transmission during the 1980s, digital broadband optical fibre networks may gradually substitute for huge sunk capital in local analogue transmission networks using twisted pair technologies by the first decade of the twenty-first century. Although many high-volume corporate users of telecommunications have direct fibre transmission circuits to local exchanges, some form of shared access system may be required to divide the high fixed costs of optical transmission among a large number of smaller users.[2] Additional revenues from large potential markets in broadband entertainment services – namely cable television and high definition television – in addition to voice telephony will be necessary to extend 'fibre-to-the-home'.

Economies of scale in copper pair local transmission have not, however, prevented local competition from alternative mobile technologies. Most Western European countries have licensed private operators of analogue and digital mobile networks. Requiring small initial fixed capital investment, the provision of subscriber access to mobile radio communications is mainly a function of the variable costs of the usage of mobile capacity.[3] In 1992, for example, many of the early digital cellular mobile networks had quickly recouped their original investments.[4] Mobile services are, however, being integrated into the transmission, switching and signalling systems of local networks. Mobile subscribers can be tracked using the self-routing capability of asynchronous transfer mode (ATM) techniques for switching packets of information through the broadband optical network. Economic studies point to the cost-reducing advantages of integrated common local access for large volumes of traffic in voice, mobile and entertainment television services.[5] When mobile technologies are introduced to complement investments in optical fibre and copper wire technologies, economies of scale may be secured by operating large volumes of traffic over a single ISDN bearer network for local access: reaffirming the geographical monopoly of local networks.

In long-distance transmission, economies of scale which stem from improvements in the speed and capacity of transmission, have not prevented competition.[6] But the scope for competition is limited and long-distance transmission is likely to remain controlled by either a dominant member of a small oligopoly or a single monopoly.[7] During the 1980s, an annual reduction of about 70 per cent in cost of fibre optic wires accelerated investment in high-capacity fibre optics for long-distance transmission.[8] Modern digital telecommunication techniques combining optical fibre transmission, packet-switching and ATM switching used in broadband ISDN networks have substantially improved the utilisation of bandwidth capacity in long-distance networks.

Yet potential scale economies in transmission had to be accompanied by improvements in the scale and capacity of the digital exchange, permitting the switching of a greater number of calls for a given fixed capital investment.[9] Switching digitisation began with the substitution of a high-speed electronic computer for the electromechanical hardware controlling the crossbar switch. Inexpensive alterations in call set-up procedures could be made by changing software stored in the computer's memory, permitting greater flexibility and faster connections. The first digital switching system using a digital controller called stored programme control was a private branch exchange, the 101-ESS, introduced in 1963. The first stored programme controlled switch combined with an electronic time-division switching system, Western Electric's 4-ESS, was introduced in 1976. The main advantage of digital switching is that it removes the need for costly analogue to digital interfaces and conversions when connected to digital transmission.

In the few countries where provision of the infrastructure has been liberalised, long-distance networks are supplied by an oligopoly dominated by a single firm. In the United States, for example, while new long-distance competitors have experienced rapid growth rates in market share of 14 to 15 per cent per year, they have had less impact on the overall market share. In 1991, after fifteen years of competition, the long-distance telecommunications market in the United States was still dominated by AT&T with a market share of

68 per cent, followed by MCI and Sprint with market shares of 12 per cent and 8 per cent, respectively.[10] Despite the rapid growth of Mercury's optical fibre long-distance network, British Telecom's market share of long-distance transmission is not expected to fall much below 90 per cent during the 1990s.

When the communications services furnished by competing long-distance carriers are based on a comparison between the monopoly carrier's rates (not production costs) and the stand-alone costs of the rival system, lower prices do not necessarily stem from the efficiency of the competitor. Because a monopoly's rate structure purposely lowers rates to promote universal service by raising rates in profitable parts, this part of the system is always threatened by cream-skimming, as competing carriers build up duplicate facilities along profitable, high-volume routes, or bypass, as corporate traffic is diverted over private leased-lines rather than public networks.[11] Under short-run static conditions, the supply of cheaper competitive services, therefore, is no indication of the inefficiency of national monopolies. However, under long-run conditions of radical technological change, competing common carriers using new transmission technologies can operate long-distance services at lower costs than monopolies operating with older plant and equipment. If a single monopoly is unable to adapt its organisation and successfully introduce new digital technologies during a dynamic phase, competition in the long-distance component of telecommunications can be an alternative policy instrument for stimulating innovation and cost-reducing economies, while accepting the costs of duplication, cream-skimming and bypass.

Economies of scope

As distinguished from scale economies, which relate costs to the volume of traffic carried, economies of scope are the reductions in costs obtained by using the same plant and equipment to provide services differentiated by distance (local, long-distance and international services) and by variety (multiple teleservices and value-added services). In 1990 the growth in world value-added services demanded by corporate users was estimated at 22 per cent a year, compared with 4 per cent in local telephone services and 7 per cent in long-distance services.[12]

While it is more efficient to terminate local, long-distance and international calls over a single local subscriber loop, there is no need for all services to be supplied by a single firm. In justifying the state monopoly model, Phillips (1986:34), for example, wrongly assumes that the costs of furnishing national telecommunications services will rise if local and long-distance components are broken up. The demarcation between local access and long-distance networks using fewer high-capacity digital switches (which provides the basis for decentralised ownership and management), has not disappeared with more integrated approaches to network design and operation. In his empirical analysis of the post-divestiture period in the United States, Waverman (1989) finds no evidence to support the view that costs of providing local and long-distance services are lower (economies of scope) with monopoly service provision, compared with a decentralised system of multiple firm supply.[13]

Although many PTOs in Europe have retained a monopoly on the transmission infrastructure and provision of basic teleservices (telephony and telex), most industrialised countries have introduced open competition in the provision of value-added services. Using a range of cheap terminal equipment and leased-line circuits large companies have built digital networks and services tailored to their specific needs. As we have seen, in the 1970s, the voice, data and telex services communicated by corporations were carried over separate analogue networks, and in the 1980s, integrated digital networks substituted for discrete analogue networks. Voice, data and image services were carried on a single digital bit stream over private integrated digital networks, improving service differentiation and lowering the cost of individual services transmitted.[14] Service applications such as a network of designer workstations, requiring optical fibre transmission, are currently more suited to high-volume routes of traffic carried by private rather than public switched networks. Thus the costly conversion to digital technology was accomplished more quickly on a smaller scale within the sphere of private rather than public telecommunications. Operating with high capacity and flexible private automated branch exchanges (PABXs), private networks have been upgraded to switch digital voice, data and image services at low cost, before such services were available over the public network.

Attempts to divert corporate traffic back on to the public network depend on the extent to which national ISDN infrastructures exhibit economies of scale and scope.[15] Economies of scope in the provision of ISDN derive from the reductions in average costs associated with redesign of telephone networks to carry differentiated digital voice, data, facsimile and image services. In advanced industrialised countries, programmes of investment in ISDN have been undertaken in two phases. The first phase began in the 1980s when long-distance transmission bandwidth capacity was upgraded by installing optical fibre cable and digital switches, and using existing local analogue capacity to furnish a range of narrowband teleservices, excluding moving images and high-speed data transfer. In the second phase, which will be completed in the early twenty-first century, analogue equipment in local exchange systems will be substituted by digital transmission and switching, as entire networks are converted to broadband ISDN and capable of switching services currently supplied by broadcasting and cable television companies.

Designed to internalise all scope economies, the long-run viability of national ISDNs will be undermined unless large volumes of corporate user traffic are carried over the public network.[16] Public ISDNs are in competition with services offered by value-added service providers, such as IBM and GEIS, also seeking economies of scope by supplying differentiated services to many customers. If public ISDN infrastructures incorporate few service applications and fail to develop compatible terminal equipment, large business users may continue to rely on private PABX networks using proprietary interfaces which are often incompatible with ISDN technology. With large volumes of corporate traffic bypassing the public networks, the resulting smaller-scale public ISDN systems may be confined to the provision of facilities for the small and medium-sized sites of large companies, and smaller users unable to justify private digital networks.

In the mid-1980s, national monopolies like France Télécom and Deutsche Telekom planned to mitigate demands for specialised, private leased-line networks by initiating huge investments in nationwide ISDN infrastructures (combining narrowband and broadband capacity), to be completed by the early twenty-first century. Yet such large expenditures represent fixed capital which must be recovered over a turnover period of many years by operating large volumes of traffic. Utilising the huge bandwidth capacity of single mode fibre, growing traffic volumes and a range of teleservices can then be carried at low average costs per message. But large technological investments entail the risk that if demand is not forthcoming, the state or private investors will be saddled with huge unpaid fixed costs. There are obvious scale and scope advantages of combining telecommunications and cable television over the same ISDN networks at some point in the future. While it is likely that telephone terminals will eventually have the capability of sending a moving image to the user, the question is whether this will come about in ten years or fifty.[17] In the intervening years, without the inclusion of large business users, the operation of ISDNs at below capacity may lengthen the turnover time of fixed capital, increase costs and limit the range of services made available.

Economies of system

By contrast to economies of scale and scope which relate costs to the volume of traffic and services carried, economies of system are the reductions in costs which stem from centralised control over the ways in which traffic and services are transported through different parts of the transmission network.[18] The functions of control can be centralised in a single exchange or node (a point in the network where communications channels converge), or decentralised among public and private exchanges with no dominant single node. In the traditional operation of public switched telephone networks (PSTNs), a 'hierarchy of control' is represented in the shape of a pyramid. Under the supervision of a national or long-distance operator, centralised control of through traffic between local and long-distance networks is performed by a controlling computer at the apex of the pyramid. Regardless of their form of ownership, the local and trunk exchanges at lower levels of the pyramid are distribution points for communication to and from the centre. Figure 3 shows the structure and system of control in a narrowband ISDN network.

The progress towards ISDN has been facilitated by the adoption of systems for high-speed signalling and computerised network control. First, in the operation of analogue telephone networks, the control of the movement and charging of messages was carried along the same transmission circuit as the message. With the digitisation of switching and transmission, control has been removed from the message and transmitted along a separate high-speed common channel signalling system using a packet-switching network (SS 7) to improve the routing of traffic over the ISDN. Several hundred traffic circuits can be controlled by a single pair of signalling channels along a particular route, permitting faster call set-up times. Whereas an average three-minute call using the old analogue signalling system entailed a call set-up time of twenty

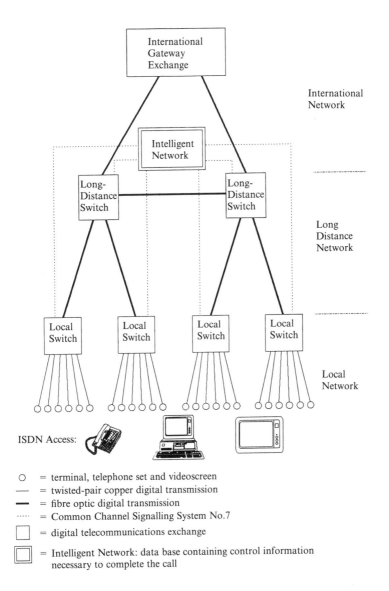

Figure 3: Public integrated services digital network

seconds, during which time the telephone conversation opened up a transmission circuit which could not be used for other calls, the digital signalling system has reduced call set-up times to only three to four seconds, without absorbing valuable local and trunk switching capacity.[19]

Second, ISDN digital access is complemented by the introduction of a service control architecture, the so-called 'intelligent network', which offers greater flexibility and control in the routing of calls to match the requirements of constantly changing information systems.[20] Software is centralised in a few data bases called Service Control Points, which are either separated from or adjacent to the switch. These data bases contain information about how calls should be charged and to which terminals messages should be transmitted. Rather than absorb transmission capacity, the high-speed signalling network is used to interrogate the digital exchange or computerised data base in the intelligent network for instructions about the routing of the call. Ordinary voice and data messages continue to be processed by the switch, while calls requiring special treatment are momentarily stored in the exchange, where the relevant data base is consulted for advice, before the call is directed to its destination.[21]

Utilising the vast reservoir of idle switching capacity in public exchanges (required to accommodate the load factor), system economies can be obtained through the provision of a number of low cost flexible services for routing traffic. The intelligent network offers new routing services for residential customers, including the freephone service and forwarding of a message to an alternative destination. Large corporate users are being offered specialised network management and control services, such as virtual private networks, using the capacity of the public switched telephone network. Corporate users are offered the choice of transferring network management to the operator, or controlling and managing their own virtual private network. In this way, the high fixed costs entailed in investing in the plant and equipment used in managing discrete corporate networks are transformed into the low variable costs of a centralised and shared service purchased from common carriers or value-added service providers.

With access to the intelligent network, a number of independent value-added service providers can offer customer-specific routing services. A distinction, however, must be made between the delivery of such services and operation of the intelligent network using facilities of the underlying bearer network. Network planning and call routing in the operation of the intelligent network require an integrated and standardised approach to number identification, billing and signalling. The market mechanism may be a hindrance rather than a help in the technically and organisationally complex task of managing large-scale intelligent networks. A number of multiple, often competing, interconnected networks and services have to be coordinated to prevent fraudulent operation and overcomplicated charging of services.[22] In this context, either a single integrated organisation or a cooperative arrangement between independent local and long-distance carriers, are the forms of organisation best equipped to operate intelligent network systems.

Diverging technological paths

After the divestiture of AT&T in 1984, Huber (1987) put forward the argument that digital technologies have undermined what I have termed the economies of system attributed to centrally controlled telephone networks.[23] Assuming a dramatic cheapening of switching relative to transmission costs, Huber argues that the old technical and economic logic of the hierarchical structure has been superseded by the concept of an open network system. When switching is cheap and transmission expensive, the most viable technological structure is a 'ring', not a pyramid (see figure 4).

The PBXs, computers and intelligent terminals directly communicate with adjacent nodes along a 'geodesic' – a path of

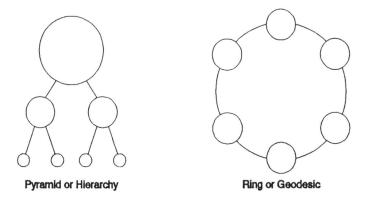

Pyramid or Hierarchy   **Ring or Geodesic**

Figure 4: Competing technological architectures

minimum length. Whereas transmission is kept to a minimum, computer controlled switches and intelligent terminals are dispersed throughout the network. There is no requirement for communication to take place to and from the centre. As networks become more intelligent and flexible, expanding markets in communication services can be realised by large-scale companies. To help the customers manage this increasingly complex and fragmented telecommunications environment, systems integrators operate least-cost routing, switching users around as capacity becomes available, and link up local, long-distance, mobile and value-added networks, to provide corporate users with one-stop access to a variety of services. Paradoxically, Huber argues that the decentralised network will promote economic concentration; with a small number of large, vertically integrated firms providing system integration to reassemble the pieces of the fragmented global network for large users.[24]

By contrast, Noam (1987 and 1992) draws liberal conclusions from the ways in which centrifugal technological change has redefined the possibilities for supplying networks and services. Hierarchical and centralised telephone infrastructures operated by monopolists are being superseded by a 'network of networks' and 'system of systems', in the shape of a mosaic of interconnected public and private sub-networks, operated under seamless and decentralised control. In his view, the growth in technological and operational alternatives, and corresponding increase in service applications tailored to customised needs, have undermined the economies of scale, scope and system attained by centralised telephone networks. Intelligence previously confined in centralised switches and stored programme control computers is increasingly embodied in computer terminals and sophisticated PABXs located in the periphery of private corporate networks, outside the hierarchical system.

Consequently the future of telecommunications may develop along one of two diverging technological paths: on the one hand, ISDN symbolises the technical, economic and social logic of hierarchical and centralised networks; on the other, the open network architecture (ONA) in the United States is a step towards the development of open telecommunications systems.[25] ONA was formulated by the FCC's Third Computer Inquiry to open up the switching component of the public network to competition. Public switching is disaggregated into separate modular functions which provide separate access, interconnection and competition in the provision of each of them. ONA permits private suppliers to use components of the switch, such as computerised data bases, to furnish intelligent network services, and resell new services. Following the pattern of development in computing, and to some extent driven by the commercial interests of the data processing industry, ONA replaces the hierarchical and centralised technological architecture with a distributed network structure.

I want to argue that such decentralising developments are being counteracted by the opposing tendency of centripetal technological change which is reinforcing the operational efficiency of the centralised and hierarchical bearer network. First, it is improbable that the centralised network will be displaced because intensive economies of scale secured through innovations in transmission capacity, such as packet-switching and fibre optic transmission, have reduced transmission costs at least as rapidly as the decline in switching costs.[26] Such evidence does not support the cost advantages of the decentralised network architecture put forward by Huber (1987). Consequently, rather than evolving towards 'a much less hierarchical, decentralised network model as Huber envisions (the geodesic network), intermediate layers of switching may instead be replaced by transmission', thus supporting a centralised architecture operating with fewer high-capacity exchanges (Flamm 1989: 60–61).

Second, the search for system economies by centralising network management and control may undermine Noam's (1987) preferred model of a market of networks under independent ownership and control. Using rapid out-of-band signalling, a centralised computer in the intelligent network controls the availability of capacity and services on selected transmission routes. The introduction of higher-capacity digital exchanges reduces the number of trunk exchanges in long-distance networks and permits a better utilisation of equipment in accommodating peak traffic loads.[27] System economies are so large with this form of centralised control that decisions about the routing and delivery of services over international telecommunications networks can be administered by foreign common carriers. Since about 50 per cent of international circuit capacity is idle at predictable times, such excess capacity can be utilised to furnish alternative routes carrying global traffic through a limited number of international telecommunications hubs.[28]

In summary, then, the need to sustain high levels of capacity utilisation by searching for economies of scale and system is reaffirming the monopolistic characteristics associated with the transportation and control of traffic carried over hierarchical telecommunications networks. An accompanying trend towards concentration in service provision depends, however, on the extent to which ISDN networks exhibit economies of scope. Currently, value-added network services, such as electronic data interchange, have been more rapidly supplied by competing firms serving specialised market segments, rather than by a single monopoly. Analogous to the early telephone history, the drive to obtain high levels of capacity utilisation does not weaken the argument for a cooperative structure of regional monopolies interconnected to long-distance carriers. Coordination of common facilities for local and long-distance communications, which mark the boundaries between components of the network, can be secured by the creation of cooperative institutions that can guarantee efficient through connections between independently-owned or controlled operations.[29]

2. Organisational forms: monopoly, competition and cooperation

In relation to the previous discussion of the technical and economic limits to competition in the telecommunications infrastructure, this section examines the comparative performance of three paths of modernisation.

State monopoly: the case of France

The leading European example of telecommunications modernisation in the hands of a state monopoly is France, which has shown a commitment to *grands projects*, based on large-scale investments designed to create and control new markets. The contemporary French telecommunications network grew out of a situation in the 1950s, when France had one of the most backward telephone networks in Europe. In response to public pressures for a solution to 'the crisis of the telephone', the network was rapidly expanded under the supervision of the PTT, the Direction Générale des Télécommunications (DGT), which ensured that equipment was purchased from domestically owned equipment suppliers.[30] Between 1975 and 1985, the number of main telephone lines grew from 7 million to 25 million.

In 1990, France had the most advanced digital telecommunications system in the world (see table 1). France Télécom's strategy of supplying network capacity in anticipation of demand, assumed a virtuous circle of self-generating growth: as the network increased in scale and capacity, a range of teleservices could be offered to a growing circle of subscribers, at lower prices, yielding substantial economies of scale and scope. France Télécom has constructed the world's largest packet-switched data network, Transpac, with 70,000 lines installed by 1990 and connections to fifty-eight countries; the leading videotext service, Minitel; and achieved the highest digitisation of transmission and switching capacity: the share of local lines connected to digital local exchanges and use of advanced SS 7 signalling system in the network was higher than any other country.

Table 1 Degree of digitisation in all telephone subscriber lines, 12 December 1990

Country	Degree of digitisation (%)
France	78.73
Norway	48.08
Sweden	40.38
Belgium	40.27
Iceland	39.72
Portugal	36.02
Italy	35.11
Finland	35.11

Source: Telecommunications Statistics, Ministry of Transport and Communications, Helsinki 1992

In 1978, senior management in DGT realised that by the early 1980s the backlog in telephone demand would soon be satisfied, and attempted to expand the DGT's telecommunications monopoly to include dominance over the new potential sources of growth in teleservices.[31] Approved by the government, the DGT launched its Télématique programme, which began with the development of a nationwide videotext service, consumer-oriented fax, followed in the 1980s with the development of a cable television system and ISDN infrastructure.

The most distinctive aspect of this supply-side strategy was the videotext programme. The decision to provide free of charge Minitel terminals that use the Teletel services, anticipated that the growth in traffic volumes would cover the fixed costs and raise capacity utilisation by achieving a better 'fill' of the Transpac public data network. By the late 1980s the service reached a mass market of users. By contrast, the public videotext services introduced by the Deutsche Bundespost – called Bildschirmtext – and British Telecom's Prestel service were less successful because users had to pay for terminals and terminals were difficult to operate. By 1991 the Minitel policy cost FFr10 billion (£1bn).[32] Yet with 5.6 million homes and offices connected to the videotext system it provided a mass market of residential subscribers able to utilise additional teleservices. The large subscriber population provided a critical mass for the rapid growth in service providers, offering electronic mail, electronic data interchange, travel reservations, train and airline schedules, financial services, etc.

By 1989, however, questions were raised about the commercial viability of France Télécom's strategy of supplying the market with a diversified range of teleservices. According to the Cour des Comptes, France's public financial watchdog, the total cost of videotext by the end of 1987 was about FFr8 billion, excluding high R&D costs.[33] Yet the DGT's revenues from the high usage of the system did not exceed FFr3 billion. Consequently, the high costs of providing terminals free of charge to promote system usage would not be recovered until 1995. However, a subsequent audit by Coopers and Lybrand – conducted on France Télécom's behalf – disagreed, pointing out that Minitel will have made FFr4.3 billion profit by the year 2000, if the extra traffic it generates is included.[34]

Although the original aim of Télétel was to supply universal information services to the public, by 1987 the French economic policy-makers wanted to extend the system to include corporate value-added services. Collaborative links between users, private equipment and information service providers, and France Télécom were instituted to generate innovative services over Transpac. France Télécom formed a horizontal grouping of independent subsidiaries under the holding company, Cogecom (one of Cogecom's main subsidiaries was Transpac), to provide new value-added services for corporate customers. For example, France Télécom and a few French banks formed a joint company to operate an electronic payment service. But corporate usage of the Télétel system remained largely domestic. The development of value-added services in France was constrained by high pricing of leased-lines, while France Télécom remained committed to preventing any competition from alternative suppliers.[35] By contrast, liberalisation in Britain resulted in the rapid growth of private value-added networks and services: 'As a result, business users from all over Europe had come to evaluate Britain as far more competitive in value-added services than France. Consequently, foreign multinationals were clearly favouring Britain rather than France as the main location for their European operations' (Humphreys 1990: 221).

Nevertheless, in 1988, France became the first country in the world to launch a commercially operated ISDN.[36] By comparison to other European PTOs, France Télécom introduced its basic rate (64 kilobits-per-second) and primary rate (2 million bits-per-second) services simultaneously. The new network, called Numeris, was created by converging the digitised public switching network with separate telex, public data and voice networks into a single high-capacity system. France was able to take the lead in this field because it had already developed the world's most extensive digital telephone switching network, with about 80 per cent of the long-distance network digitised by 1991. Thus ISDN technology could be incorporated into the existing network without having to invest in a separate system, as Germany and Britain have done. The ISDN service was available to business users and residential subscribers in the Paris and Brittany regions in 1988, and by 1990 was available on a nationwide basis and interconnected to other national networks. Although demand for ISDN services has not yet met early predictions of growth – an estimated 500,000 subscribers were expected to use the service by 1995 (this was the predicted installed base of subscribers needed to support a wide range of teleservices) – by the end of 1991 Numeris had 150,000 subscribers nationwide, six times more than in 1990.[37]

In 1990 France Télécom adopted a new strategic policy of responding to the specific demands of the large business users, while continuing to satisfy public service obligations. It introduced two intelligent network services in 1991 which were offered on a nationwide basis to mass subscribers: one data base specialised in the delivery of a freephone service and the other offered a smart card service allowing travellers to have a call made from any location charged to their own account. A third data base introduced in 1992 offered virtual private networks, designed to substitute cheaper and specialised public telecommunications services for the profitable segment of telecommunications traffic carried over private networks. Yet the development of intelligent network services has lagged behind the United States: estimates in 1989 suggested that revenues from such services earned by France Télécom were less than one-fifth of those earned by the Regional Bell Operating Companies.[38]

As France Télécom enters the 1990s, the pace of modernisation has been given an added impetus by competition from privatised foreign operators. But unlike its British and American rivals, France Télécom has still to make the transformation towards more commercial decision-making: it remains organised on functional, rather than customer-facing, lines, and control over the network is largely separate from the marketing side of operations. Although carriers like British Telecom and AT&T are not permitted to compete in the French market, they have offered multinational corporations advanced services in order to locate corporate telecommunications hubs outside France. By contrast to AT&T and BT, which have expanded internationally by acquisitions of foreign companies, France Télécom is seeking the internationalisation of its telecommunications services through cooperation with other PTOs, particularly with European operators.[39] France Télécom is committed to interconnecting Numeris with other national ISDNs, and has part ownership in an international data services network, called Infonet, jointly owned by eleven PTOs and MCI. Forming a joint venture with Deutsche Telekom, called Eunetcom, France Télécom will provide worldwide telecommunications services for international corporate customers, and intends to offer a one-stop-shopping service, utilising the worldwide Transpac data network, eventually linking any location throughout the world with custom-designed networks to keep pace with the global communications services offered by private competitors.

In summary, the ambitious state-led model of restructuring in France has a more mixed record than its enthusiastic advocates suggest. On the positive side, the French state's commitment to a supply-led strategy in search of economies of scale and system by expanding network capacity has created one of the world's most digital telecommunications infrastructures. Public service obligations for a nationwide ISDN providing access to residential subscribers, and small and large business users have not been jeopardised by more recent efforts to provide advanced telecommunications services for multinational corporate users. Indeed according to Jean-François Berry, head of the French telephone users' association, which represents 600 large corporations, French telecommunications users have some of the lowest telephone charges in the world (see table 2) and access to the most advanced services.[40]

Table 2 Average telephone costs per month, 1989 (all charges, FFr)

	Domestic	Business*
US – New York	145	1,584
France	156	1,681
Britain	219	2,540
W. Germany	225	2,236
Japan	356	3,544

* excluding VAT; US includes tax

Source: Logica, cited in *FT*, 7 December 1989

On the negative side, certain large capital investments in digital technologies and services have turned out to be not the most commercially successful. In particular, efforts to obtain economies of scope have not always been justified by the demand from customers for particular services. France Télécom's technology-push strategy has made disappointing attempts to replicate in other services the distinctive characteristics of the telephone network: 'ubiquity of presence, inter-operability, standardisation around a simple level of service. It seemed ill-suited to a period when the thrust of tele-communications technology was towards service and network diversification, reflecting the increasing differentiation of customer needs' (Ergas 1992: 11). Launched in 1992, France Télécom's cabling television programme was intended to be an embryonic broadband ISDN network of the future. Yet by March 1992, it had only secured an installed base of 870,000 subscribers; below the original goal of 5 million for that year, and well below the level required to recover initial costs.[41] Neither did the national monopoly anticipate the huge growth in the market for cellular mobile telephony. By 1991, cellular penetration in France was one quarter of the level in Britain, and less than 10 per cent of the levels achieved in Sweden and Norway.

Privatisation and competition: the case of Britain

Repeating the policy mistake made in the early telephone development of the 1880s and 1890s, Britain has been preoccupied with opening up the sphere of telecommunications to the market, and has taken no account of the technical limits to liberalisation imposed by economies of scale, scope and system. The failure to dismantle the national operator has produced the problem of private monopoly. By contrast to the long time horizons implied in the supply-side strategy adopted in France, investment in Britain has been dictated by short-term demand originating from a narrow set of large corporate users, and the need to achieve profitability by rapidly recouping fixed costs.

Infrastructural competition
The creation of Mercury, the new long-distance and international common carrier, has not weakened BT's dominance of national telecommunications. The decision to retain a dominant entity in the British telecommunications market meant that competition from Mercury had to be artificially maintained by adopting a version of the 'infant industry' policy: by preventing competition in telecommunications transmission before 1990, and by prohibiting the resale of private leased circuits until 1991.[42] Yet by 1993, while Mercury controlled 18 per cent of the international market, BT had only captured 7 per cent of the long-distance market.

Mercury was required to meet service obligations of a non-commercial character, by extending its service to major cities in peripheral Britain. But the infant national carrier was in no position to furnish a voice service uniform in price and quality throughout the country until a customer base was established. Competition from Mercury has focused on markets for private leased-line circuits. It created a full-scale long-distance switched service inaugurated in 1986 which has cream-skimmed BT's profitable business intercity traffic.[43] In the early 1980s, for example, only 300 large users of BT's private line and long-distance business accounted for one-third of BT's revenues and half of its profits. Hence Mercury's principal investment in a high-capacity optical fibre cable 'figure-of-eight' network between London, Bristol, Birmingham, Manchester and Leeds was designed to capture BT's profitable corporate traffic: particularly long-distance transmission between major business centres and financial users concentrated in the City of London. Mercury's network was confined to intercity routes of high-volume business traffic covering 60 per cent of the business user population and only 20 per cent of BT's traffic.

Utilising more advanced fibre optic technology, Mercury has lowered its operating costs, undercut tariffs based on cost-averaging over BT's larger system, and introduced new services quicker than

BT could replace plant and equipment. In 1986 Mercury set its prices for long-distance calls at 15 to 20 per cent below those of BT. By 1988, the net saving from using Mercury's network varied between 5 and 25 per cent of BT's bill. Compared with BT, Mercury's network offered substantial savings for users with large volumes of traffic originating from specific sites. In response to the new competition, BT accelerated the digitisation of the trunk network where Mercury had established a service, thus contributing to a duplication of plant concentrated along intercity routes, and forcing a quicker devaluation of BT's sunk capital in long-distance transmission. BT established kilostream and megastream (64 kbps and 2 mbps circuits) leased-lines for business users, and built a microwave overlay network in the centre of London.

In responding to common carrier competition BT has abused its monopoly position in two respects. First, in order to prevent the exercise of monopoly power BT was subjected to the RPI-3 formula for a period of five years. Under this formula BT was prohibited from raising inland tariffs by more than the Retail Price Index, minus 3 per cent. This formula applied to such a broad bundle of tariffs that there was still considerable scope for tariff rebalancing practices.[44] By as early as 1982, just prior to the establishment of Mercury's service, BT's large business users benefited from reductions of 35 per cent in trunk charges and 33 per cent in international communications. In the mid-1980s BT charged the lowest rates for private circuits and international communications in Europe. In May 1982, BT sharply reduced tariffs for long-distance calls: local charges were increased while rates charged for long-distance and private-line services were reduced.[45] In 1992 a study by the European Consumers Bureau showed that peak-rate local calls cost more in Britain than in any of the other fourteen European countries surveyed.[46]

Second, competition in long-distance and international network components has been undermined by the terms of interconnection between BT and Mercury. BT has overcharged Mercury for access to the local network. Without access to local exchange operations Mercury's long-distance switched service would be ineffective because it would only be able to furnish connections with a few subscribers. Oftel's task of policing this interconnect agreement has been rendered difficult by the fact that Mercury's system, which diverts traffic revenue from the public network, should bear the costs of operating a bypass network; namely the provision of peak capacity and erosion of the value of BT's universal service incurred by the growth in Mercury's market share.

Private networks and services
The rapid growth of corporate networks and value-added services using BT's and Mercury's leased-lines resulted in large volumes of traffic bypassing public voice and data networks. Private circuits are offered at lower costs than equivalent transmission on the public network. Yet private circuits continue to rely on interconnection with the public network for communication with the outside world and additional capacity when private networks are congested. However, the costs of private circuits do not cover the public network costs of network control, switching and additional peak load capacity. Moreover, reductions in the volume of traffic carried over the public network (against which sunk capital investments have been made), push up the average costs of operating a smaller public network for remaining residential and small users.

Bypass was, however, mitigated in Britain by the decision to restrict interconnections to the public network and other private networks, and prevent arbitrage resale of private leased line capacity until 1991. The Telecommunications Act of 1984 created the Branch Systems General Licence (BSGL) in order to prevent excessive growth in leased-line private networks by inhibiting the interconnection of privately provided circuits to public ones and other private networks, and, with a few exceptions, prohibiting the carriage of third party traffic. These restrictions on leased-lines also prevented the emergence of an independent sector of network management of voice and data services.[47] For example, network management companies like EDS and Hoskyns have been unable to reap economies of scale and scope by gathering together traffic from several customers. Cost economies in network management can only be secured where corporate networks extend to other countries. Between 1984 and 1987, BT responded to the increase in traffic carried over private networks by increasing charges for leased-lines, which reduced the demand for such circuits. Interconnection restrictions between public and private networks were relaxed in 1987 when the BSGL was revised. In June 1989, the Secretary of State for Industry announced that a new class of branch systems licence would be issued that would allow unrestricted routing of calls over leased circuits from one private network to another.

In Britain, the slow development of ISDN encouraged

corporations to build their own private integrated networks. By 1987, for example, Britain accounted for 25 per cent of the total number of private data networks in Western Europe. BT's plan to replace analogue exchanges with digital technologies by the early twenty-first century has been slower than many other PTOs. Whereas an embryonic ISDN service was available in France and Germany in 1989, the implementation of BT's version called Integrated Digital Access (IDA) had slipped by two years. In Japan, for example, under pressure from the government, NTT has brought forward its target for modernising its network by six years to 1995 and promised to introduce a range of new services.

BT compensated for its failure to accelerate investment in a nationwide ISDN infrastructure by concentrating on the provision of global services for large multinational business customers, such as digital leased-lines and the world's most advanced optical fibre network (called the Flexible Access Service) in the City of London, in competition with Mercury. Indeed, one of Oftel's responsibilities has been to encourage multinational corporations to locate information intensive activities in Britain. It also aimed to create a leading transatlantic hub in Britain which routes international business traffic through London. By the mid-1980s, calls between Britain and the United States accounted for nearly half of the $700 million transatlantic telecommunications market, and almost one-third of multinationals in Europe routed their traffic through London.[48] This strategy undermined the traditional policy of co-operation in transnational telecommunications with other European PTTs, and rendered BT more susceptible to the requirements of multinational customers.

In 1990, BT embarked on a process of internal reorganisation, called Operation Sovereign, to remove layers of bureaucracy, improve productivity, and make the company more customer-oriented. The company aimed to reduce the workforce from 210,200 at the beginning of 1992 to 120,000 by 1996. In opposition to the view that BT should be divided into separate subsidiaries of international, national and local networks, the Chairman of British Telecom, Iain Vaillance, argued that the 1990 reorganisation of BT to offer business customers global 'one-stop-shopping' services from a single provider was justified by centrifugal technological change: 'in a digital environment networks are best run in a seamless fashion; the old hierarchy of local, trunk and international exchanges is obsolescent'.[49]

Emulating AT&T's expansion into the provision of global telecommunications, BT aims to manage large private networks operated by multinational corporations and route corporate traffic through its national and international networks. In 1990, multinational corporate users accounted for 15 per cent of BT's customer base but 85 per cent of its revenue.[50] As part of this strategy of globalisation BT acquired Tymnet, an American data communications network. By the end of 1990, BT and IBM were negotiating a partnership to furnish global 'one-stop-shopping' services to handle voice and data communications for multinational corporate customers. Under this proposed agreement, BT would provide worldwide telecommunications management and IBM would supply the value-added services, such as EDI and electronic mail, carried over the network.

In 1991, following the recommendations of the Duopoly Review conducted by the Department of Trade and Industry, the government concluded that limited competition between BT and Mercury should be replaced by allowing more fixed-link competition.[51] Cable television companies were permitted to carry telephone and television services in the local loop and competing common carriers were allowed to establish rival long-distance services. In 1992, for example, British Rail Telecommunications (BRT) applied for a Public Telecommunications Operator licence to compete with BT and Mercury. BRT plans to use the Channel Tunnel to carry cables linking its British network to European customers. BT will be prevented from abusing its monopoly by being obliged to offer 'equal access' to customers over BT's local network. With equal access, users dial a code to use BT for long-distance calls, or another for Mercury and others for new competitors.

Disallowed on mainland Europe, the Duopoly Review has opened up possibilities for arbitrage: fully liberalised private networks are allowed to resell leased-line capacity at a rate above the rental charge but below the price of an equivalent volume of capacity on the public networks (primarily BT or Mercury). Since June 1991, companies with private digital backbone networks for in-house use can resell spare bandwidth capacity and services, including voice and a range of value-added services in competition with the duopoly. In 1993, for example, Reuters formed a joint venture with US Sprint to provide private-line resale services in Britain. Since September 1992, the British government has been considering the possibility of ending the duopoly held by BT and Mercury in international telephone traffic by sanctioning 'simple resale'. This policy would allow rival operators to lease international cable and satellite capacity in bulk from BT and Mercury and resell capacity to customers at lower rates.

In summary, this change in regulation marks a turning point in telecommunications organisation in Britain. It represents an attempt to usher in the world's most open telecommunications system, by encouraging the growth of a mixture of private leased-line networks with connections across the public ISDN where private dedicated circuits cannot be cost-justified.[52] But competition has neither eroded BT's monopoly position nor led to improvements in productivity and efficiency. BT still dominates with 92 per cent of the British telecommunications market. In comparison to a number of leading telecommunications carriers throughout the world BT is the least efficient carrier according to the standard industry measure of lines per employee (see table 3).

Table 3 Telephone company efficiency, 1991

PTOs	Lines per employee
SIP	256
Bell Atlantic	217
Pacific Telesis	216
Ameritech	215
NTT	204
US West	192
South Western Bell	181
Bell South	173
NYNEX	162
Telefonica	167
BT	112

Source: FT, 1 November 1991

The long-run feasibility of operating private leased-line digital networks and services depends on the economies of scale, scope and system secured by public ISDN networks: that is to say, on the difference between transmission and operating costs incurred by installing a private network using proprietary protocols and signalling, and the benefits of new public ISDN infrastructures, which conform to the International Telegraph and Telephone Consultative Committee (CCITT) standards. Since ISDN will eventually offer lower transmission costs, nation-wide connectivity over a single compatible end-to-end network, and a wider range of cheaper integrated voice, data, graphics, and videoconferencing services, private networks may eventually be displaced by an integrated and standardised public network.

Following widespread criticism that BT was making excessive profits, £3.07 billion in 1991 (more than the profits of General Motors, IBM, Ford, Siemens, Hitachi and Daimler Benz combined), in June 1992 Oftel told BT to reduce its prices by 7.5 per cent below the rate of inflation and invest profits in a way which benefits the British economy as a whole.[53] Oftel was forced to intervene in BT's detailed investment decisions, by requiring that, by 1997, BT should have made digital services universally available to 99 per cent of the population, and installed 3.53 million kilometres of optical fibres. Substituting for the failure of the market mechanism, the strong hand of regulatory intervention was thus required to initiate moves towards the creation of a nationwide broadband ISDN infrastructure.

Cooperation: the Nordic regional systems

There is a third path of modernisation which lies between national monopoly and private competition. In the period of analogue telecommunications, the possibility of a decentralised organisation was demonstrated by the independent telephone companies in the United States and regional monopolies in the Netherlands, Finland and Denmark. The creation of regional monopolies in the United States in 1984 represents a reversal of the traditional drive to scale and thus can be included under this decentralised model. Here I want to focus on Denmark and Finland, the two leading examples of the regional model. The performance of Denmark and Finland in handling the transition to digital telecommunications indicates the viability of this alternative.

The innovation strategy of the Nordic regional systems consists of a dynamic mixture of cooperation and competition. On the one hand, supply-led investments in digital technology and nationwide data and mobile services, plus joint R&D efforts in the deployment of new services, have been secured by cooperation between small-scale independently owned or managed regional and long-distance companies. On the other hand, internal managerial rivalry between the regional companies, combined with external competition from new carriers and service providers has been a stimulus to market-driven innovation and efficiency. Moreover, the absence of procurement policies based on 'national champions' traditionally found in other European countries such as France and Britain, has accelerated technological progress in these Nordic countries, by permitting the rapid introduction of price-competitive innovative digital equipment from a selection of suppliers.

Denmark

The dilemma for small countries, like Denmark and Finland, is that in concentrating on the modernisation of the domestic infra-structure, reductions in domestic prices and improvements in services may not be sufficient to prevent large corporate customers located in these countries from selecting foreign carriers or information service companies to furnish their global telecom-munications.[54] Indeed the principal rationale for consolidating Denmark's four regional monopolies and single trunk operator under a holding company, Tele Danmark, in 1991, was to prevent the problem of bypass in the international sphere. By 1992, a number of global carriers, including AT&T, BT, FT and US Sprint, offered global value-added services over private leased-line networks to corporate customers in Denmark. If large volumes of profitable corporate traffic and value-added services are diverted over the networks of global carriers, the Danish operators risk 'being reduced to mere suppliers of bulk communicating capacity to large private national and global carriers who control services, equipment and the customer base and have the global presence needed to service the international business community' (Østergaard 1992: 95). Consequent reductions in the volume of traffic would push up the average costs of operating a smaller domestic network, while reducing the range of services provided.

The policy of consolidation adapted the Danish telecommunica-tions sector to international competition by introducing the advantages of centralised strategic decision-making, and combined economies of scale, scope and system of all the domestic operators to provide global services for Danish corporate customers. The political agreement of 1989, which recommended consolidation, aimed to make Denmark a hub for northern European traffic, using fibre optic cable and radio connections to Eastern Europe and Canada.[55] While the traditional geographical structure of regionally managed operations has been retained to ensure continued flexibility and closeness to customers in local service provision, new subsidiary companies with functional structures have been established to provide a single point of contact for nationwide data and mobile services.[56] Telecom Denmark operates dedicated exchanges to provide nationwide telex, data, and mobile communications.[57]

By comparison to the financial risk entailed in France Télécom's supply-led strategy, Denmark's conversion to broadband ISDN is designed to meet current demand for cable television services. Regulations in Denmark do not prevent regional operators from carrying broadband entertainment services. Regional operators have a monopoly over the provision of cable television (Community Antenna Television, CATV, and Master Antenna Television, MATV). In 1985, Telecom Denmark, the international carrier and operator of the interregional network, established a hybrid system of CATV and MATV services, operating over fibre optic capacity installed in the interregional telephone network.[58] The high fixed costs entailed in this investment can be quickly recouped by the economies of scale and scope obtained by carrying large volumes of traffic in cable television channels. The expansion of fibre optic transmission in the high-volume triangle network between Århus, Kolding, Åbenraa, Odense and Copenhagen was completed in early 1990, and was being extended nationally in the areas of Copenhagen, Funen, South Jutland, and the Great Belt, and internationally by submarine fibre optic cable link with Germany. By 1992, 97 per cent of the municipalities in Denmark had at least one exchange connected to Denmark's fibre optic network.[59]

Between 1990 and 1991, the number of operating telephone installations connected to digital exchanges increased from 28 to 33.4 per cent. [60] Telecom Denmark is building up ISDN capacity based on digital switches supplied by Siemens and is upgrading the capacity of the interregional network.[61] In 1991, the four regional operators introduced an intelligent network which they have used to provide services tailored to the requirements of customers in their geographical areas. Telecom Denmark is introducing virtual private network services in cooperation with other Nordic countries based on the intelligent network to serve the needs of national and international corporate customers.

Finland
In contrast to the Danish path of consolidation, the restructuring of the Finnish regional system has turned towards strong domestic

competition between two groups, responding quickly to market demand for new services. On the one hand, there is a federation of forty-nine private local companies, the telco group, providing connections to 72 per cent of Finland's 2.5 million subscribers.[62] On the other hand, Telecom Finland, a public corporation with concessionary operating status rather than a government department, is mandated to provide long-distance and international traffic together with some local services in outlying rural areas.

The high standards of productivity and innovation in Finland stem from several factors: the possibility of direct comparison between the performance of operators; the involvement of user ownership in regional companies gives local subscribers the power to influence service quality and prices; and an open market to foreign and domestic suppliers (Ericsson, Siemens, Alcatel, and Nokia – the Finnish manufacturer) offers access to price-competitive and advanced digital technology and services tailored to the requirements of the Finnish networks.[63]

Prior to the Act of 1987, which liberalised value-added services and terminal equipment supply, there was no legislation preventing competitive initiatives in data communication services. The Helsinki Telephone Company (HTC) and thirty-seven other telco companies entered the market in 1985 by establishing a joint venture called Datatie Oy in competition with Telecom Finland's Datex leased-line services for business customers. Competition reduced prices by 50 per cent within six months, improved the range and quality of services, and increased total revenues and the size of the market.[64]

Both the telco group and Telecom Finland have furnished a range of data services. HTC, for example, has been involved in providing private data networks for corporations and developed Citynet, a Metropolitan Area Network (MAN) of fibre optic or copper pair transmission to connect computer facilities of large customers, mainly banks and corporate headquarters, in Helsinki. Telecom Finland responded by launching a similar MAN service, called Telegate, which interconnects local area networks (LANs) to leased or public switched lines offering a transmission capacity of up to 34 megabits-per-second. In 1993, Telecom Finland's fibre optic network used in Helsinki's MAN will be connected to a national broadband network operated by Yritysverkot, the state-controlled nationwide data services subsidiary, which has connections to five major cities in Finland. Unlike many other European PTOs, the telco group and

Telecom Finland may provide cable television services, and are permitted to supply broadband entertainment services over the fibre optic networks to achieve further economies of scale and scope.

In the market for digital mobile communications services, two operators – Telecom Finland and Radiolinja, a consortium led by HTC – were granted concessions to operate GSM networks. Following the rapid take-up of Telecom Finland's analogue Nordic Mobile Teleophone (NMT) network (with 250,000 subscribers Finland was ranked in the top three countries in the world in terms of mobile phone penetration), both GSM operators expect the market for digital mobile services to develop rapidly.[65]

Competition between the two groups has also driven innovation in the provision of duplicate intelligent network services. Telecom Finland is leading developments with an array of new services, ranging from freephone services for residential customers and electronic data interchange, to Fastel, a virtual private network service connecting corporate PABXs into single units of control. The telco group responded by forming a competing virtual private network product, called the Diana Service, brought into operation in May 1991. Using the intelligent network of the telco group, the Diana Service is operated over Datatie's long-distance network and offers to control corporate PABX networks with locations throughout the country.

In the provision of nationwide ISDN, the private and state operators have, however, recognised the continued importance of cooperation. The Finnish ISDN is a joint venture between HTC, Telecom Finland and Nokia, the domestic equipment manufacturer. A preliminary version of ISDN, called Diginet, offers a 64 kilobits-per-second service through the public exchange to the subscriber's terminal. Telecom Finland and the telco group are operating local exchanges, which are interconnected to carry ISDN services such as CAD/CAM connections, high-speed fax, and videoconferencing. While the state-owned trunk network was fully digital at the end of 1992, 46 per cent of the exchanges of Finland's local telephone companies were digitised.[66] At the beginning of 1992, there were ISDN lines on the networks of thirteen local telephone companies.

Intensified competition was the impetus behind the organisational restructuring of the two groups. On the one hand, since 1992 Telecom Finland has been restructured from a profit-centre organisation (which operated as ten subsidiaries to run local tele-phone companies), into a customer-oriented company serving market segments with centrally managed nationwide services. This shift towards a slimmer, more flexible company has been accompanied by efforts to match the high levels of productivity of the telco companies (with an average of 4.6 employees per 1,000 lines the telcos were almost twice as efficient as state local operations). Telecom Finland aimed to reduce its workforce from 10,000 to 6,000 employees, and by February 1993 it had already succeeded in reducing the number of employees to 7,000.[67]

On the other hand, the telco group has been reorganised to offer unified nationwide services. Rather than merging into a single company, it has created joint business plans, harmonised accounting methods, and centralised some aspects of strategic decision-making 'to combine the virtues of being small and close to the market and the economy of scale and integrity of service requiring larger size' (Karpakka 1992a: 11). In 1991 the private companies formed a business group called the TeleGroup of Finland. While HTC is responsible for marketing the group's nationwide services, twelve larger telco operators will coordinate the activities of smaller telcos in each of the twelve new numbering regions. Cooperation, mainly in the form of joint ventures between the telcos and large users, has increasingly been necessary where projects require large-scale and centralised R&D, and where economies of scale, scope and system can be obtained by the provision of nationwide services – such as account management for corporate networks – over a centrally managed network offering a single point of contact.[68]

From 1 January 1994, liberalisation will be extended to full infrastructural competition: the telco group can use the capacity of its long-distance data network to offer switched voice services; Telecom Finland will be allowed to compete in the local loop; and new long-distance operators, such as Telivo, a subsidiary of the national electricity company, can offer switched services.

Yet the benefits of efficiency and innovation must be weighed against the diseconomies of competition. First, there will be significant duplication of capacity as the telco group builds a long-distance network – offering voice, data and mobile communications, combined with intelligent network services – along the routes of Telecom Finland's existing network; and as Telecom Finland provides access to its cellular mobile and fibre optic networks which compete in the local areas of the telco group. Second, the shift away from a clear structural separation of cooperating local and long-distance networks to a national competitive duopoly may lead to problems of organisational complexity in controlling the system. Under the new multi-operator regime, local operators are obliged to offer equal access to the competing trunk operators. Consisting of regional, national trunk and international levels, a simplified numbering scheme for twelve regions has been introduced to accommodate the numerous interconnections between multiple networks. But the technical and regulatory complexity of policing competition under the new arrangement may incur diseconomies of system in terms of difficulties in charging, invoicing and guaranteeing adequate physical interconnections.[69] Moreover, while the telcos have traditionally provided centralised control in their local operation areas, the establishment of centralised control and operation of the embryonic national voice network 'is a real challenge to the fragmented telco network, since the benefits of large-scale operations are undeniable in this area'.[70]

In summary, then, Denmark and Finland are among the lowest-cost providers of business communications in Europe in terms of monthly telephone and data circuit costs, and have maintained low national rates for PSTN services. While connection charges are relatively high for data services, Denmark's rental and usage rates are some of the lowest in Europe. With a population of 5.16 million and 2.97 million subscribers, Denmark was fourth in world ranking of telephone density. Similarly, despite the large geographical size of the country, with 2.7 million subscribers and 53 connections per 100 inhabitants, Finland was ranked fifth in the world for telephone density. In 1989, Denmark was ranked third and Finland seventh in the OECD for business telephone charges (France was ranked fourteenth and Britain ninth).[71] Finland is among the top three operators in the number of mobile telephones per head of population.

A comparative study of capital and labour productivity concluded that the smallest European carriers have more efficient organisational structures than large networks: 'Whereas one would have expected BT to be benefiting from economies of scale and have lower unit costs, the Danish telecom system . . . proved to be more efficient than BT . . . These results suggest that it might have been beneficial for BT's productivity if the organisation had been split into separate regional companies, instead of introducing a second carrier' (Foreman-Peck and Manning: 65). While Denmark and Finland have achieved higher levels of productivity than BT, France

Télécom was, however, the most efficient according to the measure of the number of lines per employee: in 1987, for example, the ratio was 151.81 in France, 142.71 in Denmark, 113.05 in Finland, compared with only 99.23 in Britain. (Finland's relatively low figure – which represented the average for the two groups – reflected the low labour productivity of the P&T at this time).[72] A study by the European Commission also concluded that smaller European networks like Denmark are more efficient than larger networks like BT and Deutsche Telekom.[73] Setting BT's productivity at 100, table 4 shows that Denmark had more efficient local and long-distance operations than BT or the Bundespost in 1985.

Table 4 International comparison of telecommunications total factor productivity (with increasing returns to scale)

Output	Britain (1986)	FRG (1985)	Denmark (1985)
Local	100	132	240
Long-distance	100	105	251

Source: European Commission (1988)

Conclusion

This chapter began with a discussion of the ways in which the new economies of scale, scope and system of digital technologies have altered the possibilities for organising the telecommunications infrastructure. In the first section, I argued that there are technical and economic limits to competition in digital telecommunications. While competition in value-added services and terminal equipment has developed rapidly, there is little basis for competition in local exchange operations, and economies of scale in long-distance transmission may limit the number of suppliers in this market to an oligopoly dominated by a major operator. In the second section, I showed that the decentralised structure of the Nordic regional systems offers an efficient alternative path of modernisation to monopoly in France and competition in Britain. In the next chapter I want to consider what can be concluded both from the discussion of the three paths of modernisation in this chapter and from those chapters which preceded it.

Notes

1. House of Lords Select Committee on the European Communities, Session 1987–1988 6th Report (1987), p7, 'European Community Telecommunications Policy. With Evidence', 17 November 1987, HMSO, London.

2. One solution is to extend fibre transmission from an exchange to a distribution point and use copper pairs for the final extension to the subscriber. As the costs of optical technology decline relative to copper, the extension of 'fibre-to-the-home' may become possible. J.R. Stern and R. Wood (1989),'The longer term future of the local network', pp161–169 *British Telecom Technology Journal*, Vol. 7, No. 2.

3. J.C. Arnbak (1992), 'Telling the Future of Networks using Fairy Tales or Chaos Theory?', paper presented to the Institute for Information Studies, Witley Park, 28 September 1992.

4. P. Taylor (1992a), 'Cellular systems given new impetus', *Financial Times*, 8 September 1992.

5. Stern and Wood, p166, op. cit.

6. Satellite systems have not provided an alternative to terrestrial long-distance transmission because limitations of the radio spectrum make it difficult to use satellites for two-way communications with large numbers of individual subscribers. However, some large corporations, such as American Express and IBM, rent satellite channels to connect global sites in a private network.

7. See W.H. Melody, p96 (1986), 'Telecommunication – policy directions for the technology and information services', pp77–106 *Oxford Surveys in Information Technology*, Vol. 3., Oxford University Press, Oxford.

8. K. Flamm (1989), 'Technological Advance and Costs: Computers versus Communications', pp13–61 in *Changing the Rules: Technological Change, International Competition, and Regulation in Communications*, (eds) R.W. Crandall and K. Flamm, The Brookings Institution, Washington D.C.

9. A switch consists of a switching system and control function. A control function sets up connections; and the message is transmitted over lines feeding into the switching system. A digital exchange switches voice or data, encoded in a bit stream, through separate channels (space-division switching), or time slots on a single path shared among multiple channels (time-division switching).

10. North American Telecommunications Association (1991), *Telecommunications Market Review and Forecast*, Second edition, cited in J.N. Budwey (1991), 'North America's Communications Industry', pp224–233, *Telecommunications*, Vol. 25, No. 10.

11. Leased lines, charged at a flat monthly rate, used in corporate networks create opportunities for arbitrage; that is to say, reselling leased-line capacity at a rate exceeding the rental charge, but less than the cost of obtaining the equivalent volume of capacity on the public network. In such instances, PTOs lose revenues due to the growing volume of leased-line traffic bypassing the public network, and face higher average costs due to reductions in the volume of corporate traffic on the public

network. H. Ergas, p12 (1984), 'Annex: Regulation of Leased Line Utilisation', pp12–13 in *Changing Market Structures in Telecommunications*, eds H. Ergas and J. Okayama, Elsevier Science Publishers, North-Holland. Indeed, the 1987 EC Green Paper accepts the argument put forward by most European PTOs that they suffer substantial financial damage from arbitrage sales.

12. H.Dixon (1990), 'A clearer line to markets abroad'. *Financial Times*, 6 March 1990.
13. On the contrary, with the appropriate regulation to ensure equal access, independent geographical monopolies can provide local calls and terminate long-distance calls, and the trunk carrier can enter into bilateral monopoly negotiations with local operators to receive its share of long-distance revenues. L. Waverman, p81 (1989), 'U.S. Interexchange Competition', pp62–113, in *Changing the Rules: Technological Change, International Competition, and Regulation in Communications*, (eds) R.W. Crandall and K. Flamm, The Brookings Institution, Washington D.C.
14. See chapter 5.
15. A similar argument is put forward by P. Slaa (1988), 'A Dutch Perspective on ISDN', paper for the Communications Policy Research Conference, Windsor, UK, 22–24 June 1988.
16. B. Bauer (1988), 'Private Integrated Networks: A Trigger for Public Demand', pp41–47, *Telecommunications*, October 1988.
17. House of Lords Select Committee on the European Communities, p9 (1987), op. cit.
18. See chapter 2 on economies of system in analogue telephone networks.
19. F.A. Onians (1989), 'A View of the Intelligent Network', *Eurocomm 88, Proceedings of the International Congress on Business, Public and Home Communications* (ed.) T.M. Schuringa, North-Holland, Amsterdam.
20. The concept was developed by the laboratory of the regional Bell operating companies in the United States.
21. Excess capacity is built into the switching, signalling and data processing components of the intelligent network to handle additional traffic loads without delays. M. Pierce, F. Fromm and F. Fink (1988), 'Impact of the Intelligent Network on the Capacity of Network Elements', pp25–30, *IEEE Communications Magazine*, December 1988.
22. See chapter 2 on economies of system and organisational complexity.
23. This view of a decentralised architecture has been advocated by P.W. Huber (1987), 'The Geodesic Network', 1987 Report on Competition in the Telephone Industry, prepared for the Department of Justice in connection with the court's decision in *US* v. *Western Electric*, 552 F. Supp. 131, 194–5 (D.D.C. 1982).
24. Huber, p1.6, op. cit.
25. The concept of ONA must be distinguished from that of OSI associated with network standardisation such as ISDN. The less radical version of ONA being implemented by the European Commission is Open Network Provision (ONP), which aims to make public switching systems available to competitive suppliers of value-added services.

26. P. Temin, p347 (1987), *The Fall of the Bell System: A Study in Prices and Politics*, Cambridge University Press, Cambridge. Similarly in his econometric examination of post-divestiture telecommunications, Flamm (1989) finds not only that transmission equipment has become cheaper quicker than switches, transmission capacity has improved faster than switching. Flamm pp27, 32, op. cit.

27. D.M. Leakey (1988), 'The Future of the Public Telecommunication Network', *Telecommunications*, May 1988.

28. H. Small (1989), 'The Single Market: Opportunities and Threats for European Telcos', *Telecommunications*, May 1989.

29. Evans and Grossman make a similar argument to dismiss the claims of AT&T economists that the planning and operation of complex systems like telecommunications can be accomplished most efficiently by integrated firms which own local, long-distance, manufacturing and research facilities. However, their argument seeks to justify the role of the market mechanism in accomplishing the coordination of the telecommunications system. See D.S. Evans and S.J. Grossman (1983), 'Integration', chapter 5 in *Breaking Up Bell*, (ed.) D.S. Evans, North-Holland, New York.

30. The problems of promoting French national champions in equipment supply, by forcing foreign suppliers out of the market, and replacing them with domestic producers proved unviable given the market size. See H. Ergas (1992), 'France Télécom: Has the model worked?', Economics and Statistics Department, OECD, Paris.

31. P. Humphreys, p218 (1990), 'The Political Economy of Telecommunications in France: A Case Study in "Telematics"', pp198–227 in *The Political Economy of Communications* (eds) K. Dyson and P. Humphreys, Routledge, London.

32. H. Dixon (1989), 'France hooked on Minitel', *Financial Times*, 12 December 1989.

33. Humphreys, p220, op. cit.

34. W. Dawkins (1992), 'France Télécom enters the real world', *Financial Times*, 22 June 1992.

35. Ergas, p12 (1992), op. cit.

36. P. Betts (1988), 'France opens integrated telecom network', *Financial Times*, 30 November 1988.

37. Dawkins, op. cit.

38. Ergas (1992), op. cit.

39. S. McClelland (1991), 'France', *Telecommunications*, Vol. 25, No. 10.

40. W. Dawkins and H. Dixon (1989), 'The apron strings are being untied', *Financial Times*, 7 December 1989.

41. Dawkins, op. cit.

42. J. Vickers and G. Yarrow, p239 (1988), *Privatisation: An Economic Analysis*, MIT Press, Cambridge, Mass.

43. N. Garnham (1985), 'Telecommunications policy in the United Kingdom', pp7–29, *Media, Culture and Society*, Vol. 7.

44. pp15–16, ibid.

45. In 1983, for example, the price of an average three-minute local call in France was £0.05 in comparison with a rate of £0.086 in Britain,

whereas the rate charged for three-minute international calls was £3.72 in France compared with £1.62 in Britain.

46. J. Wolf (1992), 'UK's phone calls most expensive', *Guardian*, 13 January 1992.

47. M.E. Beesley and B. Laidlaw, p57 (1989), 'The Future of Telecommunications: An Assessment of the Role of Competition in UK Policy', No. 42, Research Monographs, The Institute of Economic Affairs.

48. R.R. Bruce, J.P. Cunard and M.D. Director, p454 (1986), *From Telecommunications to Electronic Services*, Butterworths, Washington D.C.

49. I. Vaillance, 'BT is not asking for privileges', letter, *Financial Times*, 28 June 1990.

50. C. Leadbeater (1990b), 'BT squares up to its international competition', *Financial Times*, 11 May 1990.

51. Conclusions informed by a previous report issued by the Department of Trade and Industry (1990), 'Competition and Choice: Telecommunications Policy for the 1990s: A Consultative Document', presented to parliament November 1990.

52. J. Harnett (1989), 'Era of private integrated networks', *Financial Times Survey: International Telecommunications*, 19 July 1989.

53. *Guardian* Leader Comment, 'BT and the busy life of Sir Bryan', 10 June 1992; and H. Dixon (1992a), 'BT told to cut prices or face monopolies probe', *Financial Times*, 10 June 1992.

54. In contrast to British Telecom, which has invested heavily in long-distance and international digital technologies in an attempt to become one of the world's main providers of global corporate communications, the small size of the Danish and Finnish operators has prevented them from embarking on comparable strategies of internationalisation. B.S. Østergaard, p95 (1992), 'Is Small Still Beautiful? An Analysis of the Structural Changes in Denmark Leading to the Creation of the Tele Danmark Holding Company', chapter 8 in *Telecommunication: New Signposts and Old Roads*, (eds) P. Slaa and F. Klaver, IOS Press, Amsterdam.

55. B.L. Petersen (1992), Counsellor, Tele Danmark, interview by A. Davies, 27 November 1992.

56. Competition was introduced in the provision of mobile services on 1 January 1991. Dansk Mobil Telefon received a licence to build an alternative public mobile communication network (GSM) in competition with Tele Danmark.

57. In 1990, Tele Danmark's mobile telephone services had a national coverage with 175,943 subscribers. Two nationwide public data transmission services were available to Danish users. In 1992, Datex, a circuit-switched data network for transmission rates up to 48 kilobits-per-second, had 17,389 subscribers; and Datapak, a packet-switched data network for transmission rates up to 64 kilobits-per-second, had 2,839 subscribers. *Tele Yearbook, Denmark 1991* (1992), statistical information on telecommunications services in Denmark compiled by the National Telecom Agency.

58. See chapter 7 on the division between regional and international operations established on 1 January 1987.
59. J.S. Anderson, Deputy Permanent Secretary, General Directorate of Posts and Telegraphs, interview by A. Davies, 26 November 1992.
60. *Tele Yearbook, Denmark 1991*, p42, op. cit.
61. J. Bright (1991), 'Denmark', *Telecommunications*, Vol. 25, No. 10.
62. The Local Telephone Companies in Finland Annual Report (1992), p6.
63. J. Karpakka (1992a), 'Telecommunications Liberalisation in Finland', mimeograph, The Association of Telephone Companies in Finland, 28 August 1992.
64. Annual Report op. cit. p5. (1992).
65. S. McClelland (1991), 'Finland', *Telecommunications*, Vol. 25, No. 10.
66. Telephone Statistics 1991 (1992), The Association of Telephone Companies in Finland.
67. J. Karpakka (1992b), Head of Department, Value Added Networks, Helsinki Telephone Company, interview by A. Davies, 30 November 1992.
68. The Telco Group formed a joint R&D company, called OMNITELE, responsible for developing new services such as GSM and data networks.
69. O. Mattila (1992), Telecommunications Administration Centre, interview by A. Davies, 1 December 1992.
70. World Bank Report, p61, op. cit.
71. OECD, Information Computer Communications Policy (1990), *Performance Indicators for Public Telecommunications Operators*, OECD, Paris.
72. OECD, op. cit.
73. European Commission (1988), 'Research on the "Cost of Non-Europe"' *Basic Findings Volume 1*, Commission of the European Communities, Luxembourg.

9 Conclusion

This book began with a discussion of the economy of the telephone infrastructure and the different ways in which that system could be organised. While private competition played a role in the early expansion of the telephone system, the economics of large-scale telecommunications systems dictated that phases of competition soon passed into cycles of concentration and centralisation. The system consisted of a hierarchy of local monopolies interlinked by a single long-distance operator. The efficiency of local monopolies was determined by the cheapness with which an exchange service could be furnished by a single supplier. A monopoly emerged in long-distance transmission because a single firm could operate and control large volumes of through traffic between local exchanges more cheaply than several suppliers.

During the transitional period of the first technological divide, the traditional telegraph monopolies experienced competition from a radical communications technology in the form of the telephone. In Europe, monopolistic telegraph interests attempted to conserve sunk capital in the telegraphs from the massive devaluation incurred by competition from the telephone. Eventually the state-owned postal and telegraph monopolies placed the new innovation under state control. In the United States, the use of the telegraph as the predominant means of electrical communication was superseded by a telephone system controlled and operated by a private monopoly.

Alfred Chandler (1977) argued that because of the technological and economic characteristics of the telegraphs and telephones, the most efficient form of organisation was a national monopoly. In his view, the only difference between monopolies in Europe and the United States was the difference between public or private ownership. A similar argument could be applied to the current wave of radical innovation in digital technologies and their impact on the structure of the modern telecommunications industry. The drive to sustain economies of scale, scope and system could result in the emergence of a new level of oligopolistic domination on a world scale, uniting information processing and telecommunications.

Contrary to this technologically deterministic view, I argued that it was the political decisions of countries in the industrialised world which determined the ways in which the monopoly structure of telecommunications infrastructure was organised. The institutional structure of the telephone system could be decomposed into smaller organisational parts. Similarly, the restructuring of telecommunications in the period of digital technologies indicates that this decentralised organisational form offers an alternative path of modernisation to monopoly and competition.

Yet the technological characteristics of the telephone infrastructure have been radically transformed by the introduction of digital technologies, and this has redefined the possibilities for organising the infrastructure. The telecommunications infrastructure is no longer primarily dedicated to the provision of a single service, voice telephony, offered at cross-subsidised prices to a national market. With the development of converged information processing and digital communications, there has been proliferation of new services, such as electronic mail, videoconferencing, call forwarding, electronic data interchange invoicing networks, etc.

Large monopolies have yet to secure economies of scope in the provision of differentiated value-added services for diverging market segments. On the contrary, value-added services are best supplied in a decentralised way by individual companies which can provide services tailored to the requirements of the information systems of particular users and industries. In response to the need to furnish a range of value-added services to match different customer needs, every country in the industrialised world has introduced policies of competition in the provision of terminal equipment and value-added services. Even in France – which has the most state-controlled national telecommunications system and where France Télécom followed a successful policy of permitting competition in the supply of information services over the Minitel system – service innovation has been most effectively stimulated by competition. Yet when France Télécom tried to control future market developments with its supply-side télématique strategy, the state monopoly failed to accommodate the range of corporate requirements for value-added or mobile services. Therefore, the most viable policy is to separate the task of retailing value-added services to customers, from the construction and operation of the transmission and switching infra-structure.

The combination of political and economic forces, which are currently shaping the future technological trajectory of the telecommunications infrastructure, suggest that the structure of the centralised and hierarchical network is unlikely to be superseded by a decentralised geodesic architecture. On the one hand, the develop-ment of a geodesic network depends on the politics of regulation: i.e. the opening up of the switching and transmission parts of the infrastructure to competition. In most European countries, the traditional postal–industrial complex has defended the centralised and hierarchical network by maintaining monopolistic control of the infrastructure. On the other hand, even in those countries where the operation of the infrastructure is opened up to competition, the search to raise capacity utilisation by obtaining the economies of scale and system (which stem from the operation of high volumes of traffic over the new digital telecommunications infrastructure) is reinforcing the hierarchical technological architecture.

Economies of scale and system which govern the development of telecommunications infrastructure indicate that private competition is an inefficient way of expanding and improving the capacity of the infrastructure. This view is corroborated by the experience of Britain where the policy of competition to promote the world's most open and decentralised telecommunications system has failed in two main respects.

First, competition in long-distance transmission has resulted in cream-skimming and bypass. Mercury has built a network to capture BT's profitable traffic between major business centres. Consequently duplicate digital plant and wires have been con-structed where the high-capacity digital transmission and switching could satisfy the entire market at lower costs than two suppliers. Competition in private leased-line operations has resulted in large volumes of traffic bypassing the public infrastructure and increasing the costs while reducing the range of services available to the public.

Second, the creation of a competing carrier has not eroded BT's dominant position in the market, nor acted as a stimulus to the dominant carrier's productivity. Thus 92 per cent of the British telecommunications infrastructure is dominated by a relatively inefficient private monopoly concerned with the pursuit of short-term profits. BT has a record of abusing its dominant position, particularly in the provision of poor interconnections to Mercury's network. Moreover, BT has been accused of using domestic revenues to cross-subsidise the development of its global communication services for multinational corporate customers. This problem can only be avoided as it was in the United States by separating regulated local services from highly competitive long-distance and international communications.

BT's investment strategies are governed by the need to recoup fixed costs quickly rather than to expand the capacity and services available over a nationwide network. In Britain, Oftel does not have the necessary political power to prevent BT from abusing its monopoly position. In Japan, by contrast, some improvements in the service provided by NTT were achieved after MPT threatened to divest the private monopoly of its local exchange operations. Subsequently, NTT accelerated the development of Integrated Network Services (Japan's ISDN) for residential and all sizes of business users. In June 1992, however, following widespread public criticism in the press, Oftel was forced to intervene where the market had failed by requiring that BT build a ubiquitous digital broadband infrastructure to serve the requirements of British society as a whole. The separation of BT's local business and long-distance business, with contracts between the two that are transparent to BT's competitors, was the recommended possible solution suggested by Sir Bryan Carsberg, Director General of Oftel, which he believed was required to prevent BT from raising prices of monopoly services and to improve interconnection with competitors.[1]

Despite the problems of layers of bureaucracy, poor innovation and low productivity associated with state monopoly PTOs, the performance of France Télécom demonstrates that the vertically and horizontally integrated structure of local, long-distance, international transmission, combined with manufacturing, research and development, can be a highly efficient path of modernisation. The capacity of nationwide systems can be planned from a single point of control, incurring no duplication of plant but risking a low uptake of services. Consequently, increases in the volume of traffic carried over the network depend on efforts to promote system utilisation and service innovation. With the success of the Minitel system, France has shown that services can be developed rapidly within the state monopoly structure. This is achieved by opening service provision to private companies, or public and private joint ventures. But this supply-side strategy entails the risk that huge fixed costs tied up in infrastructural projects will not be recovered unless the monopoly is able to capture the majority share of new and unknown future markets in information services.

The most appropriate organisational solution is to place the local and long-distance components of national telecommunications infrastructures under decentralised ownership or management. Unified ownership of local and long-distance operations is not a condition for the realisation of economies of scale, scope and system in digital networks. On the contrary, through traffic can be furnished by single or multiple carriers with equal access to local networks. A decentralised model of this kind emulates the most efficient aspects of organisational structures recently introduced in the United States, and more importantly, operated throughout the twentieth century in Denmark and Finland. It creates the basis for cooperation in the development of the digital ISDN infrastructure, and competition and dynamic innovation in the provision of competitive services.

This view is substantiated by the high productivity and service innovation attained by the Nordic regional systems. In Finland and Denmark, the decentralised, cooperative structure of regional monopolies interworked by a single state-owned long-distance monopoly is an organisational relic of early telephone history. Coordinated by a cooperative institutional framework and subject to licence agreements, regional monopolies were obliged to furnish standardised interconnections. As we saw in the cases of Finland and Denmark, a comparison between the performance of regional operators combined with closer contact with customers provided a powerful incentive to innovate and adapt to local needs. In the United States, a partial version of this policy has been implemented by breaking up AT&T's monopoly, and creating highly efficient regional monopolies, which have successfully converted to digital transmission while maintaining high levels of efficiency.

Indeed arguments to break up private monopolies along the lines of AT&T's divestiture or some version of the Danish and Finnish regional structure have gained support in Japan and to a lesser extent in Britain.[2] A recent OECD study measuring PTO performance found no evidence to support the scale and scope economic logic underpinning traditional public monopoly arrangements. It concluded that such large-scale monopolies should be dismantled to form service specific or regional entities.[3]

It is one of the ironies of history that just as the regional model of telecommunications is being held up as a possible solution in

THE SECOND DIVIDE: DIGITAL TELECOMMUNICATIONS

other industrialised countries, the Nordic countries where the model survived the first technological divide have introduced different measures to restructure their own systems. Nevertheless, the diverging solutions adopted by Denmark and Finland represent contrasting ways of introducing the organisational dynamism required to expand and modernise the system, while retaining the essential features of the regional model.

Denmark, on the one hand, has introduced perhaps the most rational organisational changes in Europe to cope with the conversion to digital technology and introduction of new competition. Under a new holding company, independently managed regional monopolies provide local and long-distance services, newly formed subsidiaries furnish a single point of contact for competitive nationwide mobile and data services, and a single operator provides international connections and global services for Danish corporate customers in competition with foreign carriers. Finland, on the other hand, has introduced the most radical changes in Europe by allowing full competition in local and long-distance data, mobile and voice services. Since competition is between a group of local operating companies and a state-owned company, the market resembles a duopoly rather than open competition. In contrast to Denmark where the infrastructural competition has so far been disallowed, the new regulation in Finland accepts the liberal view held in Britain that the costs of duplication (two parallel long-distance networks and the increasing complexity of interconnection) outweigh the benefits to innovation and efficiency induced by competition. Yet in contrast to Britain where there was an incumbent national monopoly when the second common carrier was created, the problem of the abuse of monopoly power in Finland may be avoided because competition there is balanced between two equally powerful and long-established groups.

Finally, I want to point out that the future development of national telecommunications infrastructures will be influenced by the restructuring of global information and communications systems. Traditionally, national PTTs cooperated in a highly profitable cartel which coordinated transnational communications and determined the prices of transmission between particular countries. With the progressive deregulation of national and world markets in telecommunications, this earlier pattern of cooperation has been weakened. International telecommunications transmission has shifted from a monopolistic to an open, competitive structure. National carriers recognise that the finance required to expand domestic telecommunications increasingly depends on profits from international calls. Large volumes of traffic in international corporate communications which bypass national telephone networks threaten to increase the costs of operating smaller national ISDN infrastructures.

Two different types of supplier are lining up to supply global telecommunications services for widely dispersed multinational corporations. First, private and public common carriers have embarked on strategic alliances and foreign acquisitions to provide worldwide telecommunications digital capacity to cater for the growing trend towards outsourcing among large corporations – passing over management of their global telecommunications and data networks to a third party on a fee-paying basis. Liberalisation and privatisation gave international carriers like AT&T, BT and KDD an incentive to expand into other national markets. In 1989, for example, AT&T purchased Istel, the British information services provider, to combine AT&T's basic transmission facilities with Istel's experience in value-added services to offer network management and other services to companies in Europe. In 1991, BT established a subsidiary called Synchordia in the United States to operate an international network offering voice, data and video services to multinational companies in direct competition with companies like AT&T, MCI and France Télécom. In 1992, BT announced plans to invest $1 billion (£500 million) over the next ten years in a project called Cyclone, which will be responsible for the operation of a global network operating four high-capacity digital exchanges in New York, Frankfurt, London and Sydney, connected to a further twenty-eight switching centres at major business locations worldwide.[4]

Second, information service providers and computer companies like IBM, General Electric Information Services (GEIS) and Electronic Data Systems (EDS), intend to form alliances with telephone carriers to provide global communications services for corporate users. The market for serving the global communications needs of corporations is estimated to be worth $40–50 billion a year.[5] Despite an annual growth rate of 10–15 per cent a year, the potential of the market in international telephone traffic to be served by a wide range of suppliers is already being superseded by a trend towards consolidation as many national companies find it increasingly difficult to fund the R&D necessary to offer innovative global services.[6] According to BT's own predictions, by the end of the 1990s there may be as few as two American telecommunications groups operating internationally, two groups in the Pacific rim, and two in Europe.[7]

Following the lead taken by private carriers, state-owned operators which had previously concentrated on modernising national networks were forced to enter the race to supply this, the most profitable segment of telecommunications. State operators have entered into alliances and joint ventures to provide global telecommunications. In an innovative attempt to compete with the large global players, Swedish Telecom, Swiss Telecom and PTT-Telecom of the Netherlands have merged their relatively small international operations into a joint company called Unisource, with contracts to deliver its services in many countries. Unisource aims to match the economies of scale, scope and system in the provision of global telecommunications services, such as international virtual private networks, attained by companies like AT&T and BT.

This globalisation process does not, however, invalidate the argument for decentralisation of national telecommunications. On the contrary, it reinforces it. In order to compete effectively in world telecommunications, there is a danger that integrated local, long-distance and international carriers will underdevelop national systems while raising domestic monopoly prices to finance international acquisitions and expansion. The most effective way of preventing such abuses of monopoly power is to physically separate regulated domestic services from highly competitive international operations: permitting either combined long-distance and international businesses, like AT&T, or purely international operations, such as KDD in Japan, to offer global services.

The European Commission has the task of coordinating the organisation of the national infrastructures controlled by the twelve member states to create a pan-European digital information highway. Whereas competitive interregional fibre optic networks have already been established in the United States and Japan, in Europe a transnational broadband fibre optic network has yet to develop beyond bilateral agreements, limited in capacity and quality. The recent emphasis on competition law in EC regulatory policy after 1987 may have contributed towards the lack of coordinated planning which has retarded the development of a pan-European infrastructure.[8]

Since the EC Green Paper on the liberalisation of terminal equipment and telecommunications services in 1987, there has been a 1989 EC directive opening up value-added services to competition, and a directive on open network provision, setting out criteria permitting non-discriminatory access to leased-lines. These liberalising measures are steps towards the creation of price-competitive telecommunications services throughout the European Community – the single market network ideal of the 1987 Green Paper. Yet a free market in European service provision is unlikely to flourish indefinitely under the newly-liberalised European regulatory regime. The ensuing contest between global carriers like British Telecom and AT&T, who seek to be the leading providers of value-added services for multinational corporations, is reinforcing a tendency towards oligopolistic control of the European market. The growing domination of the transnational telecommunications market by privately-owned global carriers threatens to undermine national policies aimed at promoting democratic control of national and pan-European infrastructures and services. There is, therefore, a need for transnational cooperation between European operators – along the lines pursued by Sweden, the Netherlands and Switzerland – to strengthen the role of European national operators in the market for global telecommunication services.

Notes

1. *Telecommunications* (June 1992), 'Carsberg Alludes to BT's future', p8.
2. In Britain the case for the break up of BT into regional monopolies is made by N. Garnham (1990), 'Telecommunications in the UK: A Policy for the 1990s', *Fabian Society*, October 1990.
3. Confidential OECD report cited by D. Gilhooly (1990), 'OECD Measures PTT Performance', *CommunicationsWeek International*, 12 February 1990.
4. H. Dixon (1992b), 'BT to spend $1bn on global telecommunications network', *Financial Times*, 19 August 1992.
5. Iain Vaillance (chairman of BT), 'Engaged tone all around the world', *Financial Times*, 22 October 1991.
6. P. Taylor (1992b), 'Radical changes in the global marketplace', *Financial Times Survey*, 15 October 1992.
7. Iain Vaillance (chairman of BT), cited in C. Leadbeater (1990a), 'British Telecom tries to focus on the customer', *Financial Times*, 3 March 1990.
8. D. Gilhooly (1991), 'Shaping Telecoms Towards 1992', *CommunicationsWeek International*, 30 September–7 October 1991.

Bibliography

Andersen J.A. (1992), 'New Regulatory Challenges Following the Restructuring of the Telecommunications Sector in Denmark', *Communications Policy Research, '92.*

Anderson, J.S. (1992), Deputy Permanent Secretary of Posts and Telegraphs, interview by A. Davies, 26 November 1992.

Antonelli, C. (1987), 'The Emergence of the Network Firm', in *New Information Technology and Industrial Change: the Italian Case* (ed) C. Antonelli, Kluwer Academic Publishers, Dordrecht.

Antonelli, C. and H. Ergas, (n.d.), 'Computer Communications, The Costs of Coordination and Multinational Enterprise', mimeograph.

Arnbak, J.C. (1988), 'Telematics – aims and characteristics of a new technology'. Contribution to the international symposium, 'Telematics – Transportation and Spatial Development', 14–15 April 1988, The Netherlands Congress Centre, The Hague.

Arnbak, J.C. (1992), 'Telling the Future of Networks: using Fairy Tales or Chaos Theory?', paper presented to the Institute for Information Studies, Witley Park, 28 September 1992.

Aronson, S.H. (1977), 'Bell's Electrical Toy: What's the Use? The Sociology of Early Telephone Usage', in I. de Sola Pool, *The Social Impact of the Telephone*, MIT Press, Cambridge, Mass.

Association of Telephone Companies in Finland (1991), 'The Finnish Way, The Platform for Success: Private Enterprise in Public Telecommunications'.

Baldwin, F.G.C. (1938), *The History of The Telephone in the United Kingdom*, Chapman & Hall, London.

Bar, F. (1989a), 'Bank of America', OECD/BRIE telecom user group project.

Bar, F. (1989b), 'General Motors', OECD/BRIE telecom user-group project.

Bar, F. and M. Borrus (1987), 'From Public Access to Private Connections: Network Policy and National Advantage', paper presented to Fifteenth Telecommunications Policy Research Conference, Airlie House, Va., 27–30 September 1987.

Bauer, B. (1988), 'Private Integrated Networks: A Trigger for Public Demand', pp41–47, *Telecommunications*, October 1988.

Beesley, M.E. (1981), *Liberalisation of the Use of the British Telecommunications Network: Report to the Secretary of State*, HMSO, London.

Beesley, M.E. and B. Laidlaw (1989), p57 in 'The Future of Telecommunications: An Assessment of the Role of Competition in UK Policy', No. 42, Research Monographs, The Institute of Economic Affairs.

Bell, D. (1976), *The Coming of Post-Industrial Society: A Venture in Social Forecasting*, Basic Books, New York.

Beniger, J.R. (1986), *The Control Revolution: Technological and Economic Origins of the Information Society*, Harvard University Press, Cambridge, Mass.

Berle, A.A. and G.C. Means (1935), *The Modern Corporation and Private Property*, Macmillan, New York.

Betts, P. (1988), 'France opens integrated telecom network', *Financial Times*, 30 November 1988.

Bird, J. (1988), 'Interest grows in empty banks', *Sunday Times*, 20 November 1988.

Blackledge, P. (1989), interview by A. Davies, GPT, September 1989, Coventry.

Blair, J.M. (1972), *Economic Concentration: Structure, Behaviour and Public Policy*, Harcourt Brace Jovanovich, New York.

Briggs, P. (1989), interview by A. Davies, GEC, August 1989, Coventry.

Bright, J. (1991), 'Denmark', *Telecommunications*, Vol. 25, No. 10, October 1991.

Brock, G.W. (1981), *The Telecommunications Industry: The Dynamics of Market Structure*, Harvard University Press, Cambridge, Mass.

Brooks, J. (1975), *Telephone: The First Hundred Years*, Harper and Row, New York.

Bruce, R.R., J.P. Cunard and M.D. Director (1986), *From Telecommunications to Electronic Services*, Butterworths, Washington D.C.

Budwey, J.N. (1991), 'North America's Communications Industry', pp224–233, *Telecommunications*, Vol. 25, No. 10.

Cane, A. (1988), 'Countdown to user-friendly banking', *Financial Times*, 11 November 1988.

Chandler, A.D. (1962), *Strategy and Structure: Chapters in the History of the Industrial Enterprise*, MIT Press, Cambridge, Mass.

Chandler, A.D. (1977), *The Visible Hand: The Managerial Revolution in American Business*, Belknap Press, Harvard University Press, Cambridge, Mass.

Chandler, A.D. (1990), *Scale and Scope: The Dynamics of Industrial Capitalism*, Belknap Press, Cambridge, Mass.

Clapham, J.H. (1938), *An Economic History of Modern Britain*, Cambridge University Press, Cambridge.

Commission of the European Communities (1987), 'Towards a Dynamic European Economy', Green Paper on the Development of the Common Market for Telecommunications Services and Equipment, COM (87), 290, final, Brussels, 30 June 1987.

Communications Act of 1934, 73rd Congress, 2nd Session, S. 3285, ch. 652, 48 Stat. 1064, 1934.

Communications Week International (18 June 1990), 'Ford Expands Network'.

Coon, H. (1939), *American Tel & Tel: The Story of a Great Monopoly*, Longman, Green, New York.

Dang Nguyen, G. (1985), 'Telecommunications: A Challenge to the Old Order', in *Europe and the New Technologies*, (ed.) M. Sharp, Frances Pinter, London.

Danish Ministry of Communications (1986), 'The Issue of Installation and Operation of Certain Telecommunications Services Act', Minister of Communications, No. 270, 22 May 1986.

Danish Ministry of Communications (1990a), 'Political Agreement on the Telecommunications Structure', 22 June 1990, and 'Press Release', 23 June 1990, The Minister of Communications.

Danish Ministry of Communications (1990b), 'Act to Regulate Certain Aspects of the Telecommunications Sector', p6, Minister of Communications, Draft Proposal, 17 September 1990.

David, P.A. (1992), 'Heroes, Herds and Hysteresis in Technological History: Thomas Edison and the "Battle of the Systems" Reconsidered', pp129–180, *Industrial and Corporate Change*, Vol. 1, No. 1.

Dawkins, W. (1992), 'France Télécom enters the real world', *Financial Times*, 22 June 1992.

Dawkins, W. and H. Dixon (1989), 'The apron strings are being untied', *Financial Times*, 7 December 1989.

Department of Trade and Industry (1990), 'Competition and Choice: Telecommunications Policy for the 1990s: A Consultative Document', presented to parliament November 1990.

Derthick, M. and P.J. Quirk (1985), *The Politics of Deregulation*, The Brookings Institution, Washington D.C.

Dik, W. (1990), 'Royal PTT Netherlands: Strategy for the Future', pp10–13 in *1992: Single Market Communications Review*, (ed.) H. Chaloner, Vol. 2, Issue 3.

Dixon, H. (1989), 'France hooked on Minitel', *Financial Times*, 12 December 1989.

Dixon, H. (1990), 'A clearer line to markets abroad', *Financial Times*, 6 March 1990.

Dixon, H. (1992a), 'BT told to cut prices or face monopolies probe', *Financial Times*, 10 June 1992.

Dixon, H. (1992b), 'BT to spend $1bn on global telecommunications network', *Financial Times*, 19 August 1992.

Dixon, W. (1992), 'Ford's Strategic Multinational Network', pp80–84, *Telecommunications*, 1992.

Done, K. (1989), 'Gearing up for the race of the 1990s', *Financial Times*, 25 January 1989.

Done, K. (1992), 'From design studio to new car showroom', *Financial Times*, 11 May 1992.

Douglas, E.P. (1971), *The Coming of Age of American Business: Three Centuries of Enterprise, 1600–1900*, University of North Carolina Press, Chapel Hill.

DuBoff, R.B. (1983), 'The Telegraph and the Structure of Markets in the United States, 1845–1890', pp253–277, *Research in Economic History*, Vol. 8.

Dunne, N. (1993), 'Department gets enhanced role and a bigger budget', *Financial Times*, 19 February 1993.

Durkin, A. (1988), interview by A. Davies, N. Garnham and K. Morgan, GEC, April 1988, Coventry.

Ergas, H. (1984), 'Annex: Regulation of Leased Line Utilisation', pp12–13 in *Changing Market Structures in Telecommunications* (ed.) H. Ergas and J. Okayama, Elsevier Science Publishers, North-Holland.

Ergas, H. (1992), 'France Télécom: Has the Model Worked?', Economics and Statistics Department, OECD, Paris.

European Commission (1988), 'Research on the "Cost of Non-Europe"', *Basic Findings Volume 1*, Commission of the European Communities, Luxembourg.

Evagora, A. (1992a), 'Finland Creates Telecoms Duopoly', *Communications Week International*, 5 October 1992.

Evagora, A. (1992b), 'Telecom Finland Cited', *Communications Week International*, 23 November 1992.

Evans, D.S. and S.J. Grossman (1983), 'Integration', chapter 5 in *Breaking Up Bell* (ed.) D.S. Evans, North-Holland, New York.

Fike, W.H. (1992), 'Ford's fully-integrated operations across the EC', letter, *Financial Times*, 5 March 1992.

Fisher, M. (1989), interview by A. Davies, Courtaulds Textiles Division, September 1989, London.

Flamm, K. (1989), 'Technological Advance and Costs: Computers versus Communications', pp13–61 in *Changing the Rules: Technological Change, International Competition, and Regulation in Communications* (eds) R.W. Crandall and K. Flamm, The Brookings Institution, Washington D.C.

Foreman-Peck, J. and D. Manning (1988), 'How Well is BT Performing? An International Comparison of Telecommunications Total Factor Productivity', pp54–67, *Fiscal Studies*, Vol. 9, No. 3.

Freeburn, D. (1988 & 1989), interviews by A. Davies, Ford of Europe, May 1988 & January 1989, Brentwood.

Freeman, C. and C. Perez (1988), 'Structural Crises of Adjustment, Business Cycles and Investment Behaviour', pp38–66, in *Technical Change and Economic Theory*, (eds) G. Dosi, C. Freeman, R. Nelson, G. Silverberg and L. Soete, Pinter Publishers, London.

Gabel, R. (1969), 'The Early Competitive Era in Telephone Communication, 1893–1920', *Law and Contemporary Problems*, Vol. 34.

Garnett, G.W. (1985), *The Telephone Enterprise: The Evolution of the Bell System's Horizontal Structure, 1876-1909*, Johns Hopkins University Press, Baltimore.

Garnham, N. (1985), 'Telecommunications Policy in the United Kingdom', pp7–29, *Media, Culture and Society*, Vol. 7.

Garnham, N. (1987), 'Integrated Services Digital Network (ISDN) Research. A Background Paper', paper prepared for Programme for Information and Communication Technologies meeting 27 May 1987.

Garnham, N. (1990), 'Telecommunications in the UK: A Policy for the 1990s', *Fabian Society*, October 1990.

Gilhooly, D. (1987), 'The Politics of Switching', *Telecommunications*, 1987.

Gilhooly, D. (1990), 'OECD Measures PTT Performance', *Communications Week International*, 12 February 1990.

Gilhooly, D. (1991), 'Shaping Telecoms Toward 1992', *Communications-Week International*, 30 September–7 October 1991.

Gill, F. (1922), 'Inaugural Address', *The Institution of Electrical Engineers*, IEE Journal, Vol. 61, No. 313.

Gilroy, A.A. (1984), 'The American Telephone and Telegraph Company Divestiture: Background, Provisions, and Restructuring', Report No. 84–58 E, Congressional Research Service, 11 April 1984.

Gold, B. 'Changing Perspectives on Size, Scale and Returns: An Interpretive Survey', pp5–33, *Journal of Economic Literature*, Vol. 14.

Goodhart, D. and H. Dixon (1989), 'Fortress Rhine lowers the drawbridge', *Financial Times*, 30 June 1989.

Guardian Leader Comment, 10 June 1992. 'BT and the busy life of Sir Bryan'.

Halme, S.J. (1992), University of Technology, Helsinki, interview by A. Davies, 30 November 1992.

Hansard (1892), speech by Dr Cameron.

Hansard (1905a), speech of John Burns, Telephone Agreement.

Hansard (1905b), speech of Austen Chamberlain, Telephone Agreement.

Hansard (1982), 'The Future of Telecommunications in Britain', p1, presented to parliament by the Secretary of State for Industry, July 1982.

Harnett, J. (1989), 'Era of private integrated networks', *Financial Times Survey: International Telecommunications*, 19 July 1989.

Hayes, D. (1991), 'The ISDN Crosses New Borders', *CommunicationsWeek International*, 10 June 1991.

Heikkinen, P. (1992), Technical Director, The Association of Telephone Companies in Finland, interview by A. Davies, 30 November 1992.

Henck, F.W. and B. Strassburg (1988), *A Slippery Slope: The Long Road to the Breakup of the Bell System*, Greenwood Press, New York.

Herring, J.M. and G.C. Cross (1936), *Telecommunications: Economics and Regulation*, McGraw-Hill, New York.

Hills, J. (1986), *Deregulating Telecoms: Competition and Control in the United States, Japan and Britain*, Frances Pinter, London.

Holcombe, A.N. (1906) 'The Telephone in Great Britain', pp96–135, *Quarterly Journal of Economics*, November.

Holcombe, A.N. (1911) *Public Ownership of the Telephones on the Continent of Europe*, London, Houghton and Mifflin.

Van Hoogstraten, P. (1992) PTT-Telecom, interview by A. Davies, 4 September 1992.

Horowitz, R.B. (1989), *The Irony of Regulatory Reform: The Deregulation of American Telecommunications*, Oxford University Press, Oxford.

Huber, P.W. (1987), 'The Geodesic Network', 1987 Report on Competition in the Telephone Industry, prepared for the Department of Justice in connection with the court's decision in *US* v. *Western Electric*, 552 F. Supp. 131, 194–5 (D.D.C 1982).

Hughes, T.P. (1980) 'The Order of the Technological World', *History of Technology*, Fifth Annual Volume (eds) A. Rupert Hall and N. Smith, Mansell Publishing, London.

Hughes, T.P. (1983), *Networks of Power: Electrification in Western Society, 1880–1930*, Johns Hopkins University Press, Baltimore.

Hughes, T.P. (1987), 'The Evolution of Large Technological Systems', pp51–82 in *The Social Construction of Technological Systems: New*

Directions in the Sociology and History of Technology (eds) W.E. Bijker, T.P. Hughes and T.J. Pinch, MIT Press, Cambridge, Mass.

Humphreys, P. (1990), 'The Political Economy of Telecommunications in France: A Case Study of "Telematics"', pp198–227 in *The Political Economy of Communications* (eds) K. Dyson and P. Humphreys, Routledge, London.

Kingston Communications, 'The History and Development of Kingston Communications (Hull) PLC, 1904 to Present Day', Kingston Communications, circa 1990.

Jeppesen, S.E., K.B. Poulsen and F. Schneider (1987), 'The Status and Future Development of the Danish Telecommunications Sector', paper prepared for the FAST/COM 3-project: The Spectrum of Possible Future Market Configurations for Telecommunications.

Johnson, L.L. (1978), 'Boundaries to Monopoly and Regulation in Modern Telecommunications', pp127–155 in *Communications for Tomorrow: Policy Perspectives for the 1980s* (ed.) G.O. Robinson, Praeger Publishers, New York.

de Jonquieres, G. (1985), 'Deregulation, Japanese-style', *Financial Times*, 29 March 1985.

Josephson, M. (1934), *The Robber Barons: The Great American Capitalists*, Harcourt, Brace and Co., New York.

Joskow, P.L. and R. Schmalensee (1983), *Markets for Power: An Analysis of Electric Utility Deregulation*, MIT Press, Cambridge, Mass.

Kahn, A.E. (1983), 'The Passing of the Public Utility Concept: A Reprise', chapter 1 in *Telecommunications Regulation Today and Tomorrow* (ed.) E.M. Noam, Harcourt Brace Jovanovich, New York.

Karpakka, J. (1992a), 'Telecommunications Liberalisation in Finland', mimeograph of The Association of Telephone Companies in Finland, 28 August 1992.

Karpakka, J. (1992b), Head of Department, Value Added Networks, Helsinki Telephone Company, interview by A. Davies, 30 November 1992.

Karpakka, J. (1992c), Head of Department, Value Added Networks, Helsinki Telephone Company, interview by A. Davies, 3 February 1993.

Katz, M.L. and C. Shapiro (1985), 'Network Externalities, Competition and Compatibility', pp424–440, *American Economic Review*, Vol. 75, No. 3.

Kehoe, L. (1992), 'Driving down a superhighway', *Financial Times*, 19 November 1992.

Kieve, J. (1973), *The Electrical Telegraph: A Social and Economic History*, David and Charles, Newton Abbot.

Kosonen, M. (1992), 'Liberalisation of Telecommunication in Finland', 7th Conference European Communications Policy Research, Sorø Storko, Denmark, 21–23 October 1992.

Laws, M. (1990), 'Private Nets are Turning to Third Parties', *CommunicationsWeek International*, 1 October 1990.

Leadbeater, C. (1990a), 'British Telecom tries to focus on the customer', *Financial Times*, 3 March 1990.

Leadbeater, C. (1990b), 'BT squares up to its international competition', *Financial Times*, 11 May 1990.

Leadbeater, C. and K. Done (1989), 'Ford eager to acquire "major enterprise"', *Financial Times*, 1 May 1989.

Leakey, D.M. (1988), 'The Future of the Public Telecommunication Network', *Telecommunications*, May 1988.

Lindegaard, J. (1992), Managing Director, KTAS, interview by A. Davies, 3 December 1992.

Littlechild, S.C. (1979), *Elements of Telecommunications Economics*, IEE, Peregrinus, London.

Lusa, J. (1987), 'Private Networks Proliferate Following Divestiture', *Communications Systems Worldwide*, November 1987.

Mandel, E. (1975), *Late Capitalism*, Verso, London.

Marsh, P. (1987), 'GEC to link subsidiaries in computer network', and 'Meeting of the minds on GEC's glasnost', *Financial Times*, 14 August 1987.

Marx, K. (1973), *Grundrisse: Foundations of the Critique of Political Economy*, Penguin, Harmondsworth.

Marx, K. (1976), *Capital: Volume One*, Penguin, Harmondsworth.

Mattila, O. (1992), Telecommunications Administration Centre, interview by A. Davies, 1 December 1992.

McClelland, S. (1991), 'Finland', *Telecommunications*, Vol. 25, No. 10.

McClelland, S. (1991), 'France', *Telecommunications*, Vol. 25, No. 10.

McKendrick, G. (1985), 'The Impact of New Trends in Telecommunications Services on Users', *Second Special Session on Telecommunications Policy*, OECD, 18–20 November 1985.

McKendrick, G. (1989), Executive Director INTUG, interview by A. Davies, 16 August 1989.

McLean, S. (1988), interview by A. Davies and K. Morgan, Barclays Bank, May 1988, Knutsford.

McNulty, M. (1988 & 1989), interviews by A. Davies, Courtaulds, April 1988 & January 1989, Coventry.

Melody, W.H. (1986), 'Telecommunication – policy directions for the technology and information services', pp77–106 *Oxford Surveys in Information Technology*, Vol. 3, Oxford University Press, Oxford.

Melody, W.H. (1989), 'Efficiency and Social Policy in Telecommunications: Lessons from the U.S. Experience', pp657–688, *Journal of Economic Issues*, Vol. XXIII, No. 3.

Morgan, K. (1987), 'Breaching the Monopoly: Telecommunications and the State in Britain', University of Sussex, *Working Paper Series on Government–Industry Relations*, No. 7.

Mueller, M. (1989), 'The Switchboard Problem: Scale, Signalling, and Organisation in Manual Telephone Switching, 1877–1897', pp534–560, *Technology and Culture*, Vol. 30, No. 3.

Mulgan, G.J. (1991), *Communications and Control*, Polity Press, Cambridge.

Murray, E. (1927), *The Post Office*, Putnam's Sons, London.

Murray, R. (1975), 'The Internationalisation of Capital and the Nation State', pp107–134 in *International Firms and Modern Imperialism* (ed.) H. Radice, Penguin, Harmondsworth.

National Telecom Agency (1992), *Tele Yearbook, Denmark 1991*, Statistical information on Telecommunications Services in Denmark compiled by the National Telecom Agency.

Noam, E.M. (1987), 'The Public Telecommunications Network: A Concept in Transition', pp30–47, *Journal of Communication*, Winter, 1987.

Noam, E.M. (1992), 'Rise of the "System of Systems"', *Communications-Week International*, 19 October 1992.

Nora, S. and A. Minc (1980) (French edn 1978), *The Computerisation of Society: A Report to the President of France*, MIT Press, Cambridge, Mass.

OECD, Information Computer Communications Policy (1990), *Performance Indicators for Public Telecommunications Operators*, OECD, Paris.

Onians, F.A. (1989), 'A View of the Intelligent Network', *Eurocomm 88, Proceedings of the International Congress on Business, Public and Home Communications* (ed.) T.M. Schuringa, North-Holland, Amsterdam.

Østergaard, B.S. (1992), 'Is Small Still Beautiful? An Analysis of the Structural Changes in Denmark Leading to the Creation of the Tele Danmark Holding Company', chapter 8 in *Telecommunication: New Signposts and Old Roads* (eds) P. Slaa and F. Klaver, IOS Press, Amsterdam.

Panzar, J.C. and R.D. Willig (1982), 'Economies of Scope', pp268–272, *American Economic Review*, Vol. 71, No. 2.

Parkes, C. (1992a), 'German telecoms earmarked for sale', *Financial Times*, 7 February 1992.

Parkes, C. (1992b), 'Eye-catching but with little for sale', *Financial Times*, 11 August 1992.

Perez, C. (1985), 'Microelectronics, Long Waves and World Structural Change: New Perspectives for Developing Countries', pp441–463, *World Development*, Vol. 13.

Petersen, B.L. (1992), Tele Danmark, interview by A. Davies, 27 November 1992.

Phillips, A. (1986), 'Development in Telecommunications: The Competitive Approach in the United States and the PTT Approach of the Deutsche Bundespost in the European Environment', *A Report to the Deutsche Bundespost*.

Pierce, M., F. Fromm and F. Fink (1988), 'Impact of the Intelligent Network on the Capacity of the Network Elements', pp25–30, *IEE Communications Magazine*, December 1988.

Piore, M.J. and C.F. Sabel (1984), *The Second Industrial Divide: Possibilities for Prosperity*, Basic Books, New York.

Poe, R. (1991), 'Banks don't Count on Outsourcing', *CommunicationsWeek International*, 13 May 1991.

Porter, G. (1973) *The Rise of Big Business, 1860–1910*, Harvard University, AHM Publishing Corporation.

Porter, M.E. and V.E. Millar, (1985), 'How information gives you competitive advantage', *Harvard Business Review*, August 1985.

Poulantzas, N. (1978) *State, Power, Socialism*, Verso, London.

Raun, L. (1989), 'Holland's telecoms agency rings in the New Year changes', *Financial Times*, 30 December 1989.

Rawsthorn, A. (1988), 'A system to cut out inefficiency', *Financial Times*, 18 November 1988.

Rawstorne, P. (1988), 'Profits in the files', *Financial Times*, 8 March 1988.

Report of the Post Office Review Committee (1977), Chairman Mr C.F. Carter, presented to parliament by the Secretary of State for Industry, July.

Reynolds, N. (1989), interview by A. Davies, Courtaulds, January 1989, Coventry.

Richardson, G.B. (1972), 'The Organisation of Industry', pp883–896, *Economic Journal*, September 1972.

Robertson, J.H. (1947) *The Story of the Telephone: A History of the Telecommunications Industry of Britain*, Pitman and Sons, London.

Rosenberg, N. (1976), *Perspectives on Technology*, Cambridge University Press, Cambridge.

Rosenberg, N. (1992), 'Economic Experiments', pp181–203, *Industrial and Corporate Change*, Vol. 1, No. 1.

Sabel, C. and J. Zeitlin (1985), 'Historical Alternatives to Mass Production: Politics, Markets and Technology in Nineteenth-Century Industrialisation', pp133–176, *Past and Present*, No. 108.

Sauvant, K.P. (1986), *International Transactions in Services: The Politics of Transborder Data Flows*, Westview Press, Boulder.

Schenker, J.L. (1991), 'Searching for a Single Solution', *Communications-Week International*, 13 May 1991.

Schiller, D. (1982a), 'Business Users and the Telecommunications Network', pp84–96, *Journal of Communication*, Autumn 1982.

Schiller, D. (1982b), *Telematics and Government*, Ablex Publishing Corporation, Norwood.

Schiller, D. and R.-L. Fregoso (1991), 'A private view of the digital world', pp195–208, *Telecommunications Policy*, June 1991.

Schkolknik, F. (1992), Managing Director, KTAS, interview by A. Davies, 26 November 1992.

Schmidt, S.K. (1991), 'Taking the Long Road to Liberalisation', pp209–222, *Telecommunications Policy*, June 1991.

Schumpeter, J.A. (1939), *Business Cycles: A Theoretical, Historical and Statistical Analysis of the Capitalist Process*, abridged version (1964) R. Fels, Porcupine Press, Philadelphia.

Schumpeter, J.A. (1943), *Capitalism, Socialism and Democracy*, George Allen and Unwin, London.

Slaa, P. (1988), 'A Dutch Perspective on ISDN', paper for the Communications Policy Research Conference, Windsor, UK, 22–24 June 1988.

Small, H. (1989), 'The Single Market: Opportunities and Threats for European Telcos', *Telecommunications*, May 1989.

Smith, G.D. (1985), *The Anatomy of Business Enterprise: Bell, Western Electric, and the Origins of the American Telephone Industry*, Johns Hopkins University Press, Baltimore.

Stern, J.R. and R. Wood (1989), 'The longer term future of the local network', pp161–169, *British Telecom Technology Journal*, Vol. 7, No. 2.

Sweeney, J. (1988 & 1989), interviews by A. Davies, Barclays Bank, May 1988 & January 1989, Knutsford.

Taylor, P. (1992a), 'Cellular systems given new impetus', *Financial Times*, 8 September 1992.

Taylor, P. (1992b), 'Radical changes in the global marketplace', *Financial Times Survey*, 15 October 1992.

Telco Annual Report (1992), The Local Telephone Companies in Finland.

Telecommunications (June 1992), p8, 'Carsberg Alludes to BT's future'.

Temin, P. (1987), *The Fall of the Bell System: A Study in Prices and Politics*, Cambridge University Press, Cambridge.

Thomas, F. (1988), 'The Politics of Growth: The German Telephone System' in *The Development of Large Technical Systems* (eds) R. Mayntz and T.P. Hughes, Campus Verlag, Frankfurt am Main.

Thompson, R.L. (1947) *Wiring a Continent: The History of the Telegraph Industry in the United States 1832–1866*, Princeton University Press, Princeton.

Trebing, H.M. (1969) 'Common Carrier Regulation – The Silent Crisis', pp299–329 in *Communications: Part 1, Law and Contemporary Problems*, Vol. 34.

Unger, R. (1987), *False Necessity*, Cambridge University Press, Cambridge.

Ungerer, H. (1987), p86, Oral evidence, 23 July 1987, Select Committee on the European Communities, *European Community Telecommunications Policy*, with evidence, HMSO, London.

Vaillance, I. (1990), 'BT is not asking for privileges', letter, *Financial Times*, 28 June 1990.

Vaillance, I. (1991), 'Engaged tone all around the world', *Financial Times*, 22 October 1991.

Vickers, J. and G. Yarrow (1988), *Privatization: An Economic Analysis*, MIT Press, Cambridge, Mass.

Virtanen, T. (1992), Assistant Director, Telecom Finland, interview by A. Davies, 1 December 1992.

Wagstyl, S. (1989), 'NTT under fire as critics seek to ring the changes', *Financial Times*, 10 October 1989.

Waverman, L. (1989), 'U.S. Interexchange Competition', pp62–113 in *Changing the Rules: Technological Change, International Competition, and Regulation in Communications* (eds) R.W. Crandall and K. Flamm, The Brookings Institution, Washington D.C.

Webb, H.L. (1910), *The Development of the Telephone in Europe*, Electrical Press, London.

Weber, M. (1948, reprinted 1991), *From Max Weber: Essays in Sociology* (eds) H.H. Gerth and C. Wright Mills, Routledge, London.

Weber, M. (1964), *The Theory of Social and Economic Organisation*, The Free Press, New York.

Wieland, B. (1989), 'From good connections to public access: telecommunications use and telecommunications policy in West Germany', report to final seminar on Information networks and business strategies, OECD, Paris 19–20 October 1989.

Wolf, J. (1992), 'UK's phone calls most expensive', *Guardian*, 13 January 1992.

World Bank Report (1992), 'The Study of Alternative Solutions for the
  Provision of Telecommunications Services in Developing Countries: Case
  Study based on Regulatory and Organisational Structures in Finland',
  November 1992, prepared by Telecon. Ltd for Finnish International
  Development Agency, Ministry of Transport and Communications of
  Finland, and The World Bank.

Index

American Telegraph and Telephone
  (AT&T), 9, 33–49, 156–165,
  206–207, 247–249
  formation, 56–61
  leased services, 97–98, 139–140
Analogue technology, 2, 20–29,
  105–106, 109–111
Association of Telephone
  Companies (Finland), 190
Austria, 61, 64–65, 66

Bar, F. and M. Borrus, 141
Barclays Bank, 119–122
Barre government, 154
Belgium, 66
Bell, Alexander Graham, 34
Bell, D., 50n
Bell Labs, 163
Bell System see AT&T
Beniger, J.R., 91, 96
Blair, J.M., 102
Britain
  Beesley Report, 167
  British Telecommunications Act
    1981, 148, 168
  British Telecommunications Act
    1984, 169
  digital telecommunications,
    221–228
  liberalisation and privatisation,
    148, 149, 165–170, 243–244
  nationalisation, 71–72
  telegraph, 62–65
  telephone, municipal, 73–74
  telephone national, 67-72, 81
British Telecom (BT), 139, 168–170,
  173, 206–207, 222–228,
  243–244
Bureaucracy, 8, 12, 44, 92, 225
Bypass, 11, 161, 177n, 224

Cable and Wireless, 167
Carter Report 1977, 166
Chandler, A.D., 19, 29–31, 33,
  43–44, 49, 49n, 50n, 91, 93–94,
  114n, 143n, 242
Chirac government, 155
Clinton Administration, 1
Comparative political economy, 8
Competition, 5, 10, 32-33, 203
  international, 246
  ruinous, 22, 36
Computer, 100–103,105–108, 111
Cooke, E. and C. Wheatstone, 62
Cooperation, 7, 32–33, 180–182,
  189–192, 199, 228, 233, 246
Corporate information systems,
  102–104,
  electronics industry, 135–138
  motor vehicle industry, 128–134
  retail banking, 118–122
  textiles and clothing, 122–128
Corporate users 10, 99–100,
  106–109, 147, 152, 155, 159–160,
  166–167, 170, 182–183, 193,
  220
Corporatism, 184, 188, 189
Cost structure, 21–22, 24, 36–37,
  205, 208–209, 243
Courtaulds, 123–128
Craft system, 7–8
Cream-skimming, 152, 162, 176n,
  222

Data processing, 95, 100–102, 108
David, P.A., 51n
Decentralisation, 8, 9–10, 13, 32–33,
  40, 44, 49, 67, 150, 174, 188,
  228, 245
  decentralised alternative, 72–80
  Nordic regional systems, 179–200

Denmark, 75–76, 179–189, 199–200, 229–230, 245–246
The Concordat 1950,181
Political Agreement, 185–188
Social Democratic party, 184–185
Telecommunications Act 1986, 184
Telecommunications Act 1990, 186
Deregulation
Finland, 196–199
United States, 158–162
Digital technology, 2, 20, 105–106, 204–216
DuBoff, R.B., 93

Economics *see* economies of scale, scope and system concentration, 6, 11, 33–34, 243
Economies of scale, 6, 13, 19, 29, 45, 63, 72, 139, 158
analogue technologies, 23–26
capacity utilisation, 24–26, 38
digital technologies, 205–207
extensive, 24
intensive, 24–26
Economies of scope, 39, 48, 139
analogue technologies, 27–29
digital technologies, 210–215
Economies of system, 39, 48, 139
analogue technologies, 27–29
digital technologies, 210–215
Edison, 64
Electric power, 19, 32
Electric Telegraph Company (Britain), 62
Electronic alliance, 147, 152, 153–154, 157, 160, 161, 165, 179
Equipment supply, 150–151
Ergas, H., 221, 236–237n
Erie Telegraph and Telephone Company (United States), 46
Eunetcom, 220
European Commission (EC), 149, 183, 186, 197, 248–249

European Free Trade Association (EFTA), 197
Exchange, 20, 23, 36, 97–98, 206

Federal Communications Commission (FCC), 60
Federal Department of Justice, 47, 58
Fibre optics, 111, 205–206, 209
Finance, 42, 45, 46, 47, 209, 221, 244
Finland, 76–78, 189–200, 245–246
Communist Party, 192
Telecommunications Act 1987, 194
Telecommunications Act 1990, 197
Fixed capital, 6, 11, 19, 21–23, 31, 38, 41, 109–111, 149-150, 205–207, 209, 221
Flamm, K., 215
Flexible production, 3, 4, 7–8, 89, 103–104, 117, 123, 129
Forbes, W., 35
Ford Motor Company, 92, 94, 129–134
France, 63, 65, 66–67, 153–156, 216–221, 244
Telecommunications Law 1987, 155
France Télécom, 140, 156, 216–221, 244
Freeman, C. and C. Perez, 15n

Geodesic network, 213–214
Germany, 61, 63, 73, 151–153
Telecommunications Act 1927, 65
Telecommunications Law 1989, 155
Telegraph Law, 1892, 65
Globalisation, 12, 246–249

Helsinki Telephone Company (HTC), 190, 192–193, 196, 231–233
Huber, P.W., 213–214, 215
Hughes, T.P., 51n
Humphreys, P., 154, 219

Hungary, 61, 66

IBM, 100, 111, 139–140, 160, 163, 168, 170, 226
Independent telephone companies (United States), 41, 44–48
Infonet, 220
Information, 4, 11, 89, 90–92, 94, 95
Infrastructure, 11, 19
    analogue, 20–33
    communications and transport, 3, 29
    digital, 204–216
    mass production, 1–2, 91
Institutional change, 5–7, 106–109
Italy, 61, 65, 73
Integrated Services Digital Network (ISDN), 110–111, 204, 208–210, 214, 219, 225, 227–228, 232
Integration, 30
    horizontal, 38
    vertical, 39
    vertical and horizontal, 163–164, 244
Intelligent network, 212, 215, 219, 232
Interests,
    innovating (new), 5–6, 10, 13, *see* electronic alliance
    traditional (established), 5–6, 10, 13, 147, 161, *see* postal-industrial complex
International telecommunications, 4, 12, 99–100, 111–113, 140, 246–249
    hubs, 215, 220, 225, 229
Interstate Commerce Commission (ICC), 58

Japan, 170–173
    Business Communications Law 1982, 170
    Nippon Denshin Denwa Kabushiki Kaisha Law 1985, 171

Kahn, A. 203

Katz, M.L. and C. Shapiro, 49–50n
Kingsbury Committment, 47–48, 58, 158, 161
Kohl government, 153

Labour process, 30, 32
    Taylorism, 43–44
Liberal view, 12, 200, 203
Liberalisation, 10, 13–14, 109, 148–149, 166–168, 170, 183, 192–196, 206
Local telecommunications technology, 23, 27, 36, 205–206
Long-distance telecommunications technology, 24–25, 27–28, 37–40, 45–46, 47, 97, 205–206

Management, 32, 42–43
    centralised, 40, 42, 64, 94
    decentralised, 40, 44, 49, 94, 96, 150
    management competition, 190, 228
    management style, 32, 182
    managerial hierarchy, 30, 92
Mandel, E., 15n, 113n
Marx, K., 3, 49n, 114n, 142n
    general conditions of production, 98
    particular conditions of production, 117
    turnover time of fixed capital, 21
Mass production, 1–2, 3, 7, 89, 90–100, 103
Mercury, 167–168, 222–224, 226–227, 243
Methodological individualism, 141
Microwave Communications Incorporated (MCI), 159
Military, 12, 59–60, 62, 63, 64, 83n, 163, 169
Ministry of International Trade and Industry (MITI), 170–171
Ministry of Posts and Telecommunications (MPT), 170–173
Minitel, 154, 217–218, 242
Mobile telecommunications technology, 205–206

Monopoly, 9–10, 13, 32, *see*
    national monopolies
  hierarchy of, 9, 20
  monopoly question, 57
  power, 5–6, 58
Morgan, J.P., 42, 43, 46
Morse, C.W., 47, 62
Multidivisional corporation,
    94–95
Municipal telphones, 58, 70–71,
    73–74, 78–79
Murray, R., 15n

Nation state, 12, 13, 31, 55
  neo-liberal 166–167
  socialist, 154–155
National Association of
    Independent Telephone
    Exchanges (United States), 46
National monopoly
  public ownership in Europe,
    61–72, 148–156
  state regulation in the United
    States, 56–61
Nationalisation, 59, 71–72
Natural duopoly, 37
Natural monopoly, 9, 13, 19, 48,
    203
Netherlands, 78–79, 150
Network externalities, 49n
Network management and control,
    27, 210–212
New deal, 60
Noam, E.M., 175n, 214–215
Nora-Minc Report, 154
Nordic countries, 74–78, 228–235,
    245–246
Norway, 64, 75
NTT, 170–173, 225, 244

Office of Telecommunications
    (Oftel), 169–170, 173, 223, 225,
    228
Open Network Architecture (ONA),
    214–215, 237n
Open Network Provision (OPN),
    149, 237n, 249
Open Systems Integration (OSI),
    111, 115–116n, 237n

Organisational complexity, 27, 213,
    234
Organisational form, 7, 14, 32, 33,
    43–44, 179, 199, 216
Outsourcing, 139

Panzar, J.C. and R.D. Willig,
    50n
Patents, 34, 37–40
Perez, C., 103
Phillips, A., 208
Physical conditions of production,
    3–4, 90–91, 102–103
Piore, M.J. and C.F. Sabel, 6–7,
    15n, 51n
Politics, 6–7, 10, 11–12, 31, 55,
    141–142, 147, 173, 179, 199
  power, 57
  war of position, 157
Porter, G., 96
Porter, M.E. and V.E. Millar, 90
Postal, 8, 9, 26, 35, 61–62
Postal-industrial complex, 148, 153,
    155–156, 165, 169, 179, 243
Postal, Telegraphs and Telephones
    (PTT), 72
Postalisation, 59, 60, 62–64
Poulantzas, N., 81n
Private networks, 96–98, 111–113,
    118–138
Privatisation, 150, 153, 165–173,
    186, 197
PTT-Telecom, 150, 248
Public Telecommunications
    Operators (PTO), 150

Railways, 8, 19, 28, 29, 35, 43, 58,
    60, 96–97
Reagan Administration, 163–164
Regional Bell Operating Companies
    (RBOC), 164, 220
Regional systems, 75–78, 179–200
Regulation, 57–61, 158
Research and Development (R&D),
    40, 164, 233, 247
Richardson, G.B., 57n
Roosevelt Administration, 60
Rosenberg, N., 7, 113n
Russia, 61, 63, 76, 189

Sabel, C. and J. Zeitlin, 81n
Satellite technology, 112, 115n
Schiller, D., 175n
Schülter government, 184
Schumpeter, J.A., 15n
    creative destruction, 5
    monopoly power, 5–6
Scudamore Report, 62
Sherman anti-trust, 47, 57, 163
Standardisation, see economies of
    system
State monopoly, 61–72, 148–156
State regulation, 56–61,158
Switzerland, 61, 64, 65
Systems Network Architecture
    (SNA), 111

Taylor, F.W., 43–44
Technoloy, 31–32
    innovation and competition, 5
    radical technological change, 2,
        15n, 31, 90
    technological determination, 30
    technological divide, 6-10, 19, 147
    technological paths, 213–215, 243
    technological progress, 7, 30–32
    technological revolution, 2–4, 89,
        104–106, 141
Tele Danmark, 186, 188, 229–230
Telecom Finland, 197, 231–233
Telecommunications
    analogue to digital, 2
    expansion of mass production,
        99–100
    system of production, 8, 20, 203
    space and time, 1–2, 91
    territorial non-coincidence, 12
    turnover time of capital, 93–94
Telegraphs, 1–2, 6, 8–9, 34, 56,
        62–64, 93, 96–98
Telekom (Deutsche), 152–153, 220
Telematics, 154, 217
Telephone technology, 8–9, 20–21,
        34, 97–98

Telephone, Telegraph and Cable
    Company (TTTC) (United
    States), 46, 47
Television, 205, 209, 230
Terminal, 20, 108
Thatcher government, 167
Trade Unions, see postal-industrial
    complex
Transmission, 20, 107–108

Unger, R., 51n
Unisource, 199, 248, 249
United States, 33–49, 56–61,
        156–165
    above 890 decision, 158
    Carterphone, 159–160
    Communications Act 1934, 60,
        158
    Computer Inquiry (First, Second
        and Third), 160
    Computer Inquiry (Third), 214
    Consent Decree, 163
    Divesiture (United States),
        162–165
    Hush-a-phone, 159
    Mann-Elkins Act 1910, 58
    Modification of Final Judgement,
        164
    Specialised Common Carrier,
        159
Universal service, 11–12, 158, 161,
        174, 188, 198, 207, 220, 228

Vail, Theodore, 35, 37, 42–43, 47, 59
Value-added services, 108–109,
        139–140, 168, 203, 208, 242

Waverman, L., 208
Weber, M., 8, 51n
Western Electric Company (United
    States), 35, 43, 157, 163
Western Union, 33–37, 47, 97

Xerox, 163